AMERICA'S
TRADE
CRISIS

CONGRESSMAN DON BONKER

AMERICA'S TRADE CRISIS

The Making of the
U.S. Trade Deficit

Houghton Mifflin Company
Boston · 1988

For information about permission to reproduce selections from
this book, write to Permissions, Houghton Mifflin Company,
2 Park Street, Boston, Massachusetts 02108.

Library of Congress Cataloging-in-Publication Data

Bonker, Don, date.
America's trade crisis : the making of the U.S. trade deficit /
Don Bonker.
p. cm.
Bibliography: p.
Includes index.
ISBN 0-395-47039-0
1. Balance of trade—United States. 2. United States—Commerce.
I. Title.
HF3031.B63 1988   88-9645
382.1′7′0973—dc19   CIP

Printed in the United States of America

S 10 9 8 7 6 5 4 3 2 1

*To my wife, Carolyn,
and my children, Dawn Elyse and Jonathan*

ACKNOWLEDGMENTS

Writing a book while serving in the U.S. Congress is no easy task, and it was accomplished only by extensive travel between the two Washingtons. Logging over 200,000 miles' air travel in eighteen months, I did not lack for time to research and write!

The completion of the book, however, would not have been possible without the considerable staff support I received, particularly from Carole Grunberg, staff director of the Foreign Affairs Committee's Subcommittee on International Economic Policy and Trade, and Sue Eckert, Megan Bowman, Lars Bang-Jensen, Ashley Bystrom, Donna LaTorre, Ted Bristol, Rick Holtzapple, Jim Peyser, Mike Luis, and Scott Jackson.

Two individuals deserve special thanks for their long hours and moral support throughout this project. Mark Murray and Linda Suter were indispensable in refining and preparing the manuscript.

I'm indebted to several of the nation's leading trade specialists—Pat Choate, director of policy analysis for TRW, and Fred Bergsten, director of the Institute for International Economics—for their encouragement and valuable counsel. I was also assisted by Kent Hughes, Ellen Levinson, and Dale Hathaway. My special thanks to the Library of Congress, especially

Glennon Harrison and Patricia Wertman, and to the Competitiveness Caucus for their assistance.

I want to acknowledge Rafe Sagalyn, my agent, for his guidance through the maze of the publishing world. The editors and staff of Houghton Mifflin have been extraordinarily helpful and patient. My special thanks to Austin Olney for his early support, Mike Janeway for his guidance and substantive input, Gerry Morse for her impeccable job of manuscript editing, and Sarah Flynn for her ability to enforce deadlines graciously.

Finally, as any author knows, a project of this magnitude comes at a sacrifice to family. To my wife, Carolyn, who gave me inspiration and support, and my young children, Dawn Elyse and Jonathan, who displayed patience and understanding throughout, go my heartfelt thanks and appreciation. The book is really a testimony to their love and encouragement.

CONTENTS

ONE

===

Prologue

WHEN I BEGAN writing this book late in 1986, the United States was suffering from the loss of its once dominant position in the world economy and fear of its new status as a debtor nation. Underscoring those haunting new facts of life in America were the grim monthly reports of the U.S. trade deficit.

One year later, as I was finishing the manuscript, the nation's sorry trade performance finally sent stock and bond markets reeling. Wall Street's sensitivity to U.S. trade figures wreaked havoc on our credit markets and unleashed a wave of panic and financial distress around the world.

The August 1987 trade figures, only a bit worse than expected, ignited the spectacular sell-off in the markets, but the ingredients of combustion had been there for some time. The trade data only intensified fears about a tumbling dollar and higher interest rates. That led to the possibility of either more foreign investments in U.S. dollars and Treasury bills or rapid inflation, which would drive foreign investors out of the market. The confusion alone was destabilizing.

There were other contributing factors. That week the United States and West Germany were engaged in a bitter quarrel over interest rates, the Congress and President Ronald Reagan were fighting over how best to reduce budget deficits, and the United States was on the brink of all-out war in the Persian Gulf. It was also becoming painfully evident that U.S. borrowing and consumption had run its course. The Third World debt burden was worsening. And the volatility of the dollar showed no signs of easing.

In a sense, the cause did not matter. Panics are driven by fear, and thus what happened during the week of 19 October 1987 had dramatically altered the world financial and trading system, perhaps for decades.

When Ronald Reagan came to office in 1981, the United States enjoyed a stable, if not favorable, trade position. The United States was then the world's largest creditor nation. But when the Reagan administration leaves office, its legacies will be a structural trade deficit and a foreign debt that clearly imperils the nation's economic well-being.

During most of the 1980s, the United States has been on an economic joy ride, consuming and borrowing as if there were no tomorrow.

Whether one blames Reaganomics, a debt-ridden consuming public, or Wall Street herd psychology, the 1987 crash was a shocking warning that, economically, the United States is living on borrowed time and that even fifty-eight years after the "Great Crash" of 1929, with all the safeguards installed since then, the whole economic system could fall apart.

It is time for the nation's political leadership to develop clearly stated policies for tackling the trade problem. As students of history know, it has traditionally been the Democratic Party that has embraced a policy of free trade for the United States and the Republican Party that has erected protectionist barriers to keep out foreign goods. This historical distinction has blurred in recent years, and in 1987 both parties were factionalized and adrift over trade. If our two major parties do not take steps to define their identities on the trade issue, there will be no coherence or consistency to the process of setting national policy. Individual senators and members of Congress will be left to their whims and to an array of narrow special-interest pressures when trade issues come to a vote.

As a U.S. congressman, I have listened to top government officials, business leaders, and noted economists analyze and debate economic and trade issues. As chairman of a key House of Representatives subcommittee on International Economic Policy and Trade and head of the bipartisan House Export Task Force, I have delved further into these issues. As chairman of the Speaker of the House's Trade Task Force and the Democratic National Committee's trade group, I have worked to shape new policies to improve America's competitiveness at home and abroad. By organizing trade conferences and workshops and working closely with trade specialists and business leaders, I have come to appreciate obstacles that frustrate exporters as well as what it takes to compete in foreign markets.

I have also organized and led trade missions to a number of foreign countries and brought foreign delegations to the United States to talk about wood products, housing, telecommunications, agriculture, and high technology. By working with government and business leaders, I have come to realize both the challenge and the opportunities of competing in international markets.

As a congressman from a state heavily dependent on two-way trade, I have dealt with the issue close at hand. Trade is vital to Washington State. Sixty percent of all Boeing airplanes, 90 percent of eastern Washington wheat, 50 percent of our timber and lumber products, and half of our high technology products are sold in overseas markets. Its proximity to the Pacific Rim countries of Asia makes Washington State a natural port of entry for much of the cargo that moves across the Pacific Ocean. Protectionist action that targets Asian countries could trigger retaliation that would severely hurt West Coast states, especially those with major port facilities.

But trade has a flip side in the Pacific Northwest. Timber and lumber producers, traditionally the economic backbone of the region, have been crippled by unfair trade practices—subsidized Canadian imports, discriminatory tariffs in Japan and other nations, countries that buy our logs for their sawmills but refuse to purchase our finished lumber. My position opposing log exports helped me win election to Congress in 1974. I have seen both sides of the trade picture.

Each year, more of our economic fate rests in the hands of other countries. By 1990 we Americans may be adjusting to painful austerity programs and a lower standard of living amid depressed world prices and a climate of political havoc in all countries. These problems have been ignored for so long that they are nearly out of hand. Now we face a second danger—the search for a quick fix, regardless of the consequences. As discontent sweeps across the country and public pressure builds on Congress to do *something* to protect U.S. jobs, the political reaction could translate into shortsighted solutions that overlook the true root causes of the problem. Such reaction would threaten our economic future and undermine the world trading system that we've worked to establish over the past fifty years.

Certainly, the United States must demand that other nations play by the rules in the international marketplace. But we also need better overseas marketing strategies and long-term planning, education, and training to improve U.S. competitiveness. I am convinced that export promotion, rather than restrictions on imports, is the best route to lowering the U.S. trade deficit.

Only if Americans are well informed and knowledgeable will the public pressure exerted on Congress to deal with our trade crisis reflect more than the demands of special interests. But trade policies have rarely been the subject of dinner table discussions in America. The general public in many other nations, however, often follows new trade policy developments in Washington closely. Congressman Ed Jenkins, Democrat, of Georgia, sponsor of protectionist textile legislation in the 1987 congressional session, is as well known in Hong Kong as in his home district. The 1987 free-trade talks between Canada and the United States were front-page news in Canada but largely ignored by the U.S. population.

Decisions made by the Reagan administration and its successor will chart the course for the world economy for decades to come. The first step is to arouse the American public and its leaders to the enormity of the task ahead and the urgent need for creative and responsible action to preserve the world trading system and create a healthy economy for our nation's future.

=====

TWO

Trade Crisis in America

AT 1:35 P.M. on Monday, 15 September 1986, three squat
tugboats eased the Korean ship *Japan Apollo* away from Terminal 18 of the Port of Seattle. Working with one tug fore and two
tugs aft, the pilots pulled and nudged the freighter past Harbor
Island's towering orange cranes and rows of stacked containers.
After a slow, sweeping turn, the *Apollo* pulled away from her
three escorts and steamed westward into hazy sunlight, beginning an eleven-day voyage to the Far East.

In many ways, the *Japan Apollo* illustrates America's international trade position in the 1980s. An examination of the
ship's cargo shows the central role that trade plays in our
nation's economy—the benefits trade brings to some and the
ominous problems it creates for others.

Two days previously, the *Apollo* had docked at Terminal 18
with her six hundred ocean freight containers packed wall to
wall with videocassette recorders, televisions, motorcycles, auto
parts, dolls, toys, and other manufactured goods from the factories of Taiwan, Korea, and Japan.

As the *Apollo* began her westward haul, she was still carrying
six hundred containers, but the outbound cargo consisted of

animal hides, wood chips, and other low-value commodities plus some raw materials.

Steaming into Seattle, the *Apollo* carried $65 million in foreign imports destined for sale to American consumers. But she departed with only $11 million in U.S. exports—one-sixth the amount imported.

This lopsided trade balance is typical of ships in and out of Seattle. In 1987, the Port of Seattle handled $22 billion in foreign imports compared to roughly $4.5 billion in exports, a 5-to-1 ratio. Nationwide figures are not much better. In 1987, foreign imports totaled $424 billion compared to U.S. exports of $253 billion. The resulting trade deficit represents a shortfall of $700 for every man, woman, and child in the United States.[1]

Looking around downtown Seattle, it's easy to discern the significance of import trade. The ships, cranes, cargoes, buildings, and trucks of the port dominate nearly any view of Puget Sound. Over eleven hundred men and women work for the Port Authority, and this doesn't even begin to take into account thousands of longshore workers, stevedores, or freight handlers. Well over 100,000 jobs in King County depend on the port.

A myriad of imported consumer goods moves across the docks destined for markets in the United States and Canada: $2 billion in apparel, $1.5 billion in audio equipment, $1 billion in telecommunications equipment, and $840 billion in cars and trucks.[2]

You can't escape the brawny, fast-paced, chaotic nature of international trade as you drive through the sprawling docks. Semis race back and forth from ships to nearby container storage yards, ignoring the prominent speed limit signs.

Oblivious to the constant stream of eighteen-wheel traffic just outside his window, Lee MacGregor, Terminal 18 manager for Stevedoring Services of America, sits in the nerve center of the entire operation. In a single day, MacGregor's office may clear over one thousand containers and $100 million of merchandise. MacGregor sums up the imbalance between exports and imports in a single sentence. "What we get coming inbound is finished products, while outgoing you've got your raw materials —hides, waste paper, and junk like that."

Imports keep the port busy and spread economic benefits to the immediate area, but the ominous disparity in export trade points out the dramatic changes that have shaped our domestic and international economy in the 1980s. Where once "the world traveled on America's wheels," even American corporations are touting the qualities of Japanese workmanship. Chrysler promotes its small, Mitsubishi-made import, saying, "Colt is all the Japanese you need to know."

Three hundred thousand men and women — nearly one third of the entire auto industry — lost their jobs during the 1980–1982 recession. Sprawling complexes like Chrysler's Clairpointe plant and Ford's Michigan casting center shut their gates, leaving multimillion-dollar facilities idle and thousands of lifelong employees uncertain of their future.

Despite the overall economic recovery, employment is still down by 150,000 jobs from 1979, and industry analysts predict more wrenching changes in the years ahead. American production capacity will exceed demand by roughly 1.5 million units by 1992, which can only mean more shutdowns, more layoffs, and more community dislocations. In mid 1987, General Motors announced plans to shut down as many as five facilities and to lay off more than 35,000 workers.

Many of the auto industry's woes can be traced to international forces. Thirty years ago, American workers built two thirds of all the cars and trucks worldwide. Today, that figure has dropped to only 25 percent. While Japanese auto production has jumped by 50 percent in the last ten years, American output has declined.

When new plants do come on line, they are mainly foreign owned, like the Michigan Mazda plant or a second Honda facility in Ohio. These new plants are good news for American workers, but they raise serious questions about the future of the American auto industry.[3]

From the factory line to the farm, America is reeling from shifting international trade flows and national economic policies. Farm foreclosure sales have reached their highest levels since the Great Depression. Nationwide, over 220,000 farmers have gone under since 1980.[4]

Phil Hoffman, a grain elevator and farm supply operator in northeast Missouri, has seen the impact of the farm crisis on friends and neighbors. "A couple of guys I went to school with had a real hard time. One guy bought some land at the wrong time, got too much in debt, and just couldn't make it. He still farms with his dad, but he's basically a hired hand. That's pretty tough to take for a guy who's thirty-eight or thirty-nine with a wife and a couple of kids. Now he's got to start all over again."

Over two thousand Missouri farmers have filed for bankruptcy since 1981, and the number is increasing every year. While some of these farmers are seeking court protection to reorganize and get back on their feet, the majority are liquidating farms that may have been in the family for generations.[5]

Hoffman points to drought, bad crops, and soaring interest rates as factors behind the area's farm crisis, but he notes the importance of international markets. "It goes clear back to the Nixon embargo. Our government cut off soybean exports, so the Japanese had to look elsewhere. They made all these investments in Brazil and Argentina. Now they're major competitors."

America's traditionally stable resource- and manufacturing-based economy is fast becoming a victim of changing economic times. Once robust communities are fighting for their lives against powerful forces of decline. To many unemployed workers, the problem is trade. Loggers and lumber mill workers all across the country waged a bitter fight against subsidized Canadian lumber, which had seized a significant portion of the U.S. housing market.

The situation is not much better when it comes to exports. Japan, a major consumer of wood products, maintains high tariffs on lumber, plywood, and other finished products, but no duty on unprocessed logs. China, another growing market, buys only raw logs, except for a token number of finished wood products. Lumber workers don't need a degree in economics to understand what's happening in their industry. When logging trucks bypass mills to load ships bound for Japan or China, the result is closed plants, lost jobs, and hard times for their families.

Similar trade problems threaten nearly every major U.S. industry. Commodity producers—agriculture, copper, steel, aluminum, petroleum—now must struggle to compete in foreign or even domestic markets.

America's trade crisis is no longer an abstract concept; it's an immediate and painful reality. In September 1986, 138,000 men and women lost their jobs in the manufacturing sector. So did 22,000 farmers and agricultural workers. A major economic realignment of worldwide proportions is coming at the expense of the United States.[6]

Beyond foreign cars, textiles, and shoes, the import invasion is bringing tough questions about the "American way." The United States emerged from World War II as the world's major political and economic power. We came up an easy winner in every category of the economic Olympics—half the world's production, most of the world's hard currency reserves, and a greatly expanded industrial base. High rates of investment and war-driven research gave America an inexhaustible supply of new technology.

Our huge postwar aid programs—the Marshall Plan in Europe and the rebuilding of Japan—laid the groundwork for economic resurgence in those countries. U.S. foreign aid fostered economic growth in Third World nations. As a result, nations we helped rebuild are now formidable competitors.

In the past, America was the engine that drove economic activity in other nations. Reports on America's coffee-drinking habits could mean boom or bust for Brazilian coffee ranchers. In the late 1980s, it is a different story. Highly competitive Brazilian commuter aircraft are displacing U.S. planes in the world market.

Increasingly, the world economy drives the American economy. Bankers carefully monitor the latest renegotiation of less developed countries' (LDCs) debts to anticipate how new agreements might affect financial and trade markets. High-technology companies, trying to hold on to their share of international markets, nervously eye foreign developments. Iowa farmers watch vital foreign markets evaporate in the wake of world surplus.

Foreign economic events touch the lives of all Americans —consumers, workers, bankers, businesspeople, educators, and government officials. Only the service industries appear to be protected from the forces that threaten so many sectors of the economy. But how long can banks, insurance companies, lawyers, and stock brokers thrive while major industries are in decline?

U.S. economic dominance has been eroding for years. Despite our impressive human and natural resources, our well-trained and productive work force, and our high standard of living, the gap began closing in the 1970s. In some industries, notably consumer electronics and machine tools, economic leadership passed to Europe, Japan, and the newly industrialized countries. America's technological lead has been narrowed in most fields and eliminated in many. Once we boasted 70 percent of the world's technology manufacturing; by 1986, we had posted a shocking $2 billion trade deficit in technology products.[7]

Despite our declining industrial base, economic dislocations, and other ominous economic trends, the White House proudly displayed a different view of the economy: 11 million new jobs and month after month of economic growth. Ignoring the warning signs, President Reagan liked to boast that America had pulled the rest of the world out of the world recession of 1981–1982 and that our economy was the envy of other nations.

The country was going through a fundamental transition not unlike the industrial revolution of the late nineteenth century. For many sections of the nation, it was a painful adjustment with demographic, political, and even psychological effects.

While the indicators gave mixed signals and the nation's economists argued over what had become of an elusive economic rebound, some indisputable facts emerged. First, the staggering trade deficit was responsible for our stalled domestic economy. The relentless tide of imports all but eliminated the demand for many domestically produced goods, causing significantly slower growth in sector after sector of the U.S. economy.

America was not only losing its dominance in world markets, it could barely compete against imports at home. For the first time, top government officials and leading economists blamed trade deficits for the anemic growth rate in the domestic economy. Paul Volcker, chairman of the Federal Reserve Board through most of the Reagan years, said the trade imbalance was unsustainable and warned that if it wasn't corrected, the trade deficit would drive the United States into a recession.[8]

The evidence was widespread and shocking—plant closures, job displacements, lost investments, wage and benefit reductions, were reported daily. Many companies were accepting lower profits, some were losing money, and others were watching their market share plummet.

On 18 September 1986, Treasury Secretary James A. Baker III warned that the U.S. trade deficit could not be allowed to continue indefinitely and, if unchecked, would undermine the global trading system.

Trade tensions began to appear on all fronts. Disputes jeopardized free trade talks between Canada and the United States, whose two-way trade totals more than $150 billion. The situation was no better across the Atlantic as U.S. and European negotiators argued bitterly over steel and agricultural subsidies.

The severe debt problems of South American nations had sharply reduced U.S. sales. In the booming Pacific arena, high trade imbalances and unfair trade practices made Japan, Korea, Taiwan, and other countries convenient targets for retaliation.

As the *Japan Apollo* was steaming out of Seattle on 15 September, trade and financial officials from ninety nations were gathering for critical negotiations at Punta del Este, Uruguay. Technically, the meeting was to set an agenda for full negotiation of a new General Agreement on Trade and Tariffs (GATT) beginning in June 1987 in Geneva. Many observers felt that the future of the entire international trading system was hanging on the outcome of the talks at Punta del Este.

Never before had the world's trading nations met in such an atmosphere of tension and trade hostilities. U.S. Trade Representative Clayton Yeutter announced that our delegation would walk out of the talks if our demands were not made a part of the Geneva agenda. Other nations, particularly those with developing economies and agricultural producers, had their own agendas. And nearly every nation represented at Punta del Este had an ax to grind with Japan, which maintained a sizable trade surplus worldwide.

Throughout the week, negotiators made little or no progress. On the last day, the U.S. team said that it was packing up to go home. Time was running out and nothing had been resolved. Anxious negotiators pressed on through the final day and long into the night. Finally, an eleventh-hour agreement requiring fancy diplomacy and some ambiguous language was reached.

The Reagan administration could point to a victory, but it was only buying time; the real issues would take years to settle. Meanwhile, the U.S. economy would continue to suffer and pressure would build for Congress to take action.

On Capitol Hill that 15 September, the Senate Finance Committee was considering action on a major trade bill designed to reduce the U.S. trade deficit and to promote U.S. exports. Three hundred trade bills, many of them protectionist, were on the congressional docket. A comprehensive bill passed the House in May 1986 by an enormous margin, but it drew a fire storm of criticism from the White House and nearly every major U.S. newspaper. The House sponsors tried to defend the legislation as necessary and fair, but the President and editorial writers hammered away, calling the bill protectionist, destructionist, and worse.

So, on 15 September, Senate Finance Committee members were feeling the heat. Each senator knew the political risks of taking tough action, but their constituents were suffering from import competition and calling for relief. At the same time, the administration was striking a tougher position. In just one week, President Reagan threatened retaliation against Brazil for its computer industry promotion policies, slammed the European Community (EC) for U.S. export losses in Spain and Portugal, imposed steep new restrictions on machine tool imports, and slapped a 35 percent tariff on cedar roofing and siding imports from Canada.

To foreign leaders, the rhetorical noises on Capitol Hill and the get-tough policy in the White House were nothing to take lightly. Canada's Prime Minister Brian Mulroney angrily denounced the President's action on cedar roofing and siding and immediately slapped tariffs on a whole range of U.S. products crossing into Canada. When President Reagan announced that he would subsidize grain sales to the Soviet Union, Australia reacted bitterly by threatening to reexamine its security and strategic pacts with the United States.

From the Port of Seattle to trade negotiations in Uruguay to the halls of Congress, the United States and its trading partners teetered on the edge of worldwide economic turmoil on 15 September 1986. One year later, on 19 October 1987, a stunned world anxiously watched a stock market crash that nearly toppled the world trading system. It was sparked by a routine Department of Commerce report on the U.S. trade position, which had actually shown a slight improvement for the previous month. Nonetheless, it was enough to jolt international confidence in the U.S. economy and highlight the perilous state of the world financial and trading system.

Ironically, just as an increase in trade and investments was bringing nations closer to a truly international economy, domestic pressures and global frictions were drawing the world trading system toward economic brinkmanship.

THREE

How America Is Losing
the Trade War

IN SEVEN SHORT YEARS, from 1980 to 1987, America went from a relatively comfortable trade position to a humiliating $160 billion deficit. If this had been a seven-year trade war, the United States would have lost battles against every country, leaving our once mighty economy in a perilous condition.

America's defeats on the economic battlefields of Europe were significant, but our heaviest losses shifted from the Atlantic to the Pacific theater, where Asian imports battered our Western frontier. To the north, the United States was in retreat from Canada's preemptive attacks on our domestic economy. The news was not much better on the southern border, where conventional U.S. economic strikes were no longer hitting their targets in debt-ridden Latin American countries.

Even more worrisome was the absence of any overall U.S. strategy to deal with the crisis. Throughout most of the early 1980s, the United States did not realize it was in a trade war, let alone that it was losing badly and retreating in virtually every major sector of the economy.

The list of casualties was frightening. One of America's principal sources of economic strength had been its farm belt. In 1981, U.S. farmers posted a 25 billion trade surplus.[1] But after six years of constant pounding by European agricultural producers, our farmers were clinging to a mere $3.4 billion surplus, and they even suffered unprecedented deficits for three consecutive months in 1986.[2] U.S. agricultural producers had been accelerating production for what they had thought was an expanding global market. This sudden reversal left them with huge surpluses, depressed prices, and widespread suffering throughout America's heartland.

Even America's new secret weapon of the 1960s, high technology, was no match for the superior products and lower costs of our trade adversaries. The United States had once held 70 percent of the world market for advanced technology and our research facilities were second to none. But in just five years, from 1981 to 1986, our high-tech surpluses fell from $27 billion to a $2 billion deficit.[3] Even more disturbing, America was becoming perilously dependent on foreign technology and components to meet its own domestic and military needs.

Instead of pressing an offensive position, America in the 1980s has turned defensive. At times, our trade policy has merely attempted to protect domestic industry against foreign invaders. The early 1980s saw America become a debtor nation for the first time in postwar history. Massive overseas borrowing financed our trade and budget deficits and held interest rates low enough for moderate economic growth, but it also made our economy dangerously addicted to foreign capital. After several years of record-breaking borrowing, the United States became the world's largest debtor nation, far surpassing Argentina, Brazil, and other struggling economies. Without continued enormous infusions of foreign capital, our economy would suffer convulsive shocks—bank and business failures, millions of lost jobs, and near economic chaos.

Could we have avoided the sharp trade reverses that took place in the 1980s? Were external forces responsible, or was the

United States simply asleep at the switch? What were the factors that brought the world's largest economy to near submission?

The Making of the U.S. Trade Deficit

Buoyed by a popular new President and confident of our dominant position in the global economy, Americans in 1980 were unaware of the emerging macroeconomic forces that would imperil our domestic economy. Our leaders were not only asleep at the switch; they threw many of the switches that put our country on a collision course with economic destruction.

The so-called Reagan revolution, enacted by a cowed Congress, was a highly stimulative economic program of massive tax reductions and heavy military spending that drove the budget deficit upward. Beyond its domestic implications, these policies had enormous effects worldwide. Once implemented, they heavily influenced capital flows among nations and eventually altered trading patterns between the United States and the rest of the world.

STRONG DOLLAR, WEAK ECONOMY

While congressional debate tended to focus on Japan's enormous trade surpluses and unfair trade practices, most economists agreed that the primary cause of the ballooning U.S. trade deficit was the overvalued U.S. dollar. Some laid as much as 80 percent of the blame for our trade crisis on this single factor.

During the first half of the 1980s, the value of the dollar rose by over 50 percent when measured against the currencies of our trading partners.[4] The strong dollar served as a 50 percent tax on exports and a 50 percent subsidy for imports.

While raw material costs, wages, productivity, and other factors play a major role in determining the value of a product, exchange rates control the price of the product in a given export market. To understand the impact of exchange rates on trade flows, imagine that in order to purchase U.S. exports, foreign importers must first buy U.S. dollars with their local currency.

In 1981, it cost 200 yen to buy one American dollar; in 1985, it cost 260 yen. This means that an item that cost $5.00 U.S. would have cost 1000 yen in 1981 and 1300 yen in 1985, an increase of 30 percent.

In Germany, the same $5.00 item would have cost 8.75 deutsche marks (DM) in 1981 but 16.75 DM in 1985, a staggering 90 percent increase. It's easy to see why U.S. exports plummeted as foreign buyers turned away from costly U.S. goods and toward domestic products.

On the other side of the equation, shifting exchange rates made foreign imports extremely attractive to U.S. consumers. In 1981, a small hand-held radio might have cost 1000 yen or $5.00. By 1985, that same 1000 yen radio cost only $3.85. A German-made telephone switching board valued at 35 DM would have cost $20 in 1981, but only $10.45 in 1985. Clearly, exchange rate fluctuations can dictate the success or failure of many U.S. companies.

Ideally, exchange rates reflect the true value of the goods traded, but in the 1980s, exchange rates were driven by a mounting frenzy of investment, speculation, and government intervention. Fast-moving capital markets prompted investors to search the world over for the highest return on their money.

During the early 1980s, excessive federal borrowing drove U.S. interest rates upward. Republicans and Democrats blamed each other for the federal budget deficit. Democrats pointed to Ronald Reagan's excessive 1981 tax cut and the largest peacetime military build-up in our nation's history. Ronald Reagan blamed the deficit on "forty years of Democratic spending."[5]

Regardless of who was to blame, simple supply and demand meant that borrowing overseas to finance the federal deficit drove up the value of the U.S. dollar relative to other world currencies. The soaring U.S. dollar attracted over $400 billion in foreign investments from Tokyo, Frankfurt, and other exchange centers.

In some respects, our trade deficits and our economic future lay not so much in the hands of policymakers, entrepreneurs, or factory workers, but at the feet of international monetary traders. Often more concerned with short-term fluctuations than the underlying strength and stability of national economies, these investors and speculators buy and sell staggering sums of currency. For 1986, total worldwide trade totaled $2.15 trillion; that amount changes hands every eleven days on the New York, London, and Tokyo exchanges.[6]

These enormous currency flows had a devastating impact on America's trade competitiveness. Foreign firms were able to gain footholds in the lucrative U.S. market and undercut U.S. firms in third-country markets. On the defensive, American companies began to move some or all of their production to countries that offered lower labor costs and exchange rate benefits.

While the overvalued dollar was causing massive layoffs in the United States, crippling our manufacturing base at home and eroding our market share abroad, the U.S. government blindly ignored the problem for years. If anything, the Reagan administration cited the strong dollar as global evidence that its supply-side fiscal policies were working. In his February 1985 *Economic Report* to Congress, President Reagan boasted: "Investors around the world have bid up the dollar as they have become increasingly confident in our economy. That confidence is an asset and not a liability."[7]

Under the President's free-market philosophy, the dollar's value was strictly a function of supply and demand worldwide and so, by definition, correct.

The architects of this view, led by Treasury Secretary Donald Regan and his assistant for monetary affairs, Beryl Sprinkel, routinely dismissed criticism of the overvalued dollar. Such official views of the strong dollar sent the wrong message to international speculators, for they signaled that the U.S. government would do nothing to correct currency imbalances.

Only in early 1985, after speculation drove the dollar to intolerable levels, did the Reagan White House belatedly reverse course. Beginning in July 1985, administration officials began "talking down" the dollar through a series of public and private statements intended to signal financial analysts that the party was over. Washington had finally seen the peril in the inflated dollar and would no longer ignore exchange rate distortions.

By mid 1985, the administration's subtle efforts had succeeded in halting the dollar's upward spiral, but its near-record strength continued to cripple U.S. traders and add to our foreign debt. Stronger medicine was necessary to bring the dollar back down. On September 22, U.S. Secretary of the Treasury James Baker met with the finance ministers of England, Japan, West Germany, and France.

The "Group of Five," as these countries were known, met in complete secrecy over an entire weekend at New York's Plaza Hotel while currency markets stood at a standstill. Their final communiqué stressed a collective commitment to stabilize world currency markets, even through central bank intervention in currency markets if necessary.

The Plaza accord had a stunning effect on financial markets. The mere suggestion of intervention produced the desired result. As fearful investors large and small sold off their U.S. currency, the dollar's descent became a self-fulfilling prophecy. One bank official described the currency realignment as "blind panic." The dollar quickly fell a record 5 percent in a single day against the German mark; within ten days it had dropped to a four-and-one-half-year low against the yen.

The new strategy was widely hailed by economists and the business community. *Washington Post* business columnist Hobart Rowen noted, "The Reagan Administration once again is adjusting its ideology to harsh domestic political realities

... [and] has been forced to join others who have counseled for some time that an active effort needs to be made to bring the dollar down ... Reagan and Baker should get credit for facing up to the real world."[8]

Others wondered why it had taken the administration so long to recognize the deindustrialization of America at the hands of the overvalued dollar, but all agreed that the late action was better than none.

By January 1987, the dollar had fallen roughly 40 percent against the currencies of our trading partners, although the exact change varied widely from nation to nation. Despite this rapid currency realignment, the U.S. trade position did not improve.

Month after month, administration officials and economists attempted to rationalize our continuing trade woes in the face of a rapidly falling dollar. One popular explanation was the so-called J-curve, which held that the falling dollar would worsen the nation's trade balance temporarily before bringing long-term improvement. Under this theory, a given volume of imports will cost more as the dollar falls, driving the trade deficit even deeper. Similarly, a given volume of U.S. exports will cost less, again hurting our balance of trade. This effect would only be temporary; then the falling dollar would naturally curb imports and boost U.S. exports. As the months marched by, however, America's trade deficit persistently climbed upward, to the disappointment of economists and traders alike.

Lost in the perception of a rapidly falling dollar was the fact that the dollar had not fallen uniformly against all currencies. After the administration's policy shift in February 1985, it fell sharply against a few currencies, held steady against others, and even rose relative to some. The dollar increased sharply vis-à-vis the currencies of Canada, Mexico, Hong Kong, Korea, and Brazil in 1985. Indeed, against the currencies of our top seven trading partners, representing 75 percent of the trade deficit, the dollar rose by 11 percent. The dollar's decline was noticeable only against the monetary units of Japan and European countries, which were not about to give up easily.

Many European and Japanese companies fought to counter the falling dollar by absorbing lower profits to maintain their market share in the United States. Despite the nearly 50 percent appreciation of the yen in 1985–1986, for example, Japanese automakers raised their prices only 15 percent. Toyota's U.S. profits dropped by 66 percent in 1986; Honda's fell 44 percent; Nissan posted the first-ever operating loss for a Japanese auto firm since the postwar recovery.

A falling dollar held out hope to U.S. exporters and policymakers, but it also carried some risks. How far could the dollar fall without destabilizing international currency markets? Could we halt the dollar's decline at a given point or would panic selling take over? At home, a devalued dollar would contribute to inflation by making imported products more expensive. Every 10 percent drop in the dollar's value produces an 11 percent jump in the cost of foreign goods. Worse yet, the falling dollar discouraged foreign investment in the United States, which was badly needed to finance federal budget deficits and hold down interest rates.

Analyst Stephen Marris of the Institute for International Economics worried that "devaluation of the dollar without the other two parts of the package—budget cuts by the U.S. and stimulus in Germany and Japan—is a recipe for disaster." The October 1987 stock market crash, precipitated by U.S. trade deficit figures and concern over Germany's refusal to adopt growth-oriented policies, bears out this warning. The 1980s left traders and economists alike perplexed and uncertain over future exchange rates and how currency values would affect international trade. Only time would tell whether a more competitive dollar and multilateral steps to stabilize exchange rates would shore up the shaky world financial system.

CRACKS IN THE WESTERN ALLIANCE

The United States and its Western allies were at odds over monetary and economic issues throughout the 1980s, but relations became more intense in late 1987 when the stock market crash and subsequent plunge of the dollar terrorized investors and traders alike.

Through the eight years of the Reagan administration, the U.S. government's economic policies accelerated consumption at home. By contrast, our trading partners in Europe and Japan pursued policies to restrain domestic consumption, increase exports, and maintain employment. The U.S. federal budget deficit emerged as the single most significant stimulative force in our nation's economy, doubling from 2.6 percent to 5.3 percent of gross national product (GNP) between 1981 and 1986. Meanwhile, Japan was lowering its deficit from 5.9 percent to 4.8 percent, and Germany curbed its deficit from 2.1 percent to 0.7 percent of GNP.[9]

Not surprisingly, the U.S. economy grew by an average annual rate of 4.2 percent from 1982 to 1985, while West Germany sputtered along at a 2.4 percent GNP growth rate. German industrial producers had to find markets elsewhere. What better place than the United States? Exports shot up 6.4 percent in 1984–1985, giving Germany a comfortable $25 billion trade surplus worldwide, $12 billion with the United States alone.[10]

Other industrial nations were, in effect, getting a free ride. U.S. overconsumption of imported goods kept foreign factories humming, but our own manufacturing base continued to weaken. U.S. production was up a meager 2.2 percent in 1985, while spending for goods and services increased 3.5 percent. This gap between production and consumption translates into an additional $50 billion in foreign imports.

Americans are so dependent upon foreign goods that in 1986 every one percent of growth in U.S. GNP was accompanied by a $9.5 billion increase in imports.[11] By contrast, every one percent of economic growth of our major trading partners raised U.S. exports by $4.5 billion—less than half as much. It was bad enough that the strong dollar had made U.S. products overpriced for most of the 1980s. Foreign markets were simply not growing enough to provide strong demand for our goods.

When improved exchange rates failed to bring down the trade deficit, the Reagan administration became frustrated and began to pin the blame on the slow economic growth in our principal trading partners.

Speaking before the U.S. Chamber of Commerce in 1986, Treasury Secretary Baker said the United States would pressure Japan and West Germany "to boost their economies to help cut the higher American trade deficit."[12] The administration called for other Western nations to follow the United States' lead by cutting taxes to stimulate growth, expanding their domestic markets, and creating more demand for American products.

America's trading partners were not impressed. Except for occasional lip service, Germany and Japan continued to resist stimulative measures for fear of worsening their own budget deficits or touching off a round of inflation.

LDC DEBT FORCES ECONOMIC RETREAT

The strong dollar and the contrasting growth policies of the United States and our Western allies were not the only forces driving up the U.S. trade deficit in the 1980s. The enormous debt burden in less developed countries also posed serious trade and financial problems.

The LDC debt crisis dates back to 1973, when the Organization of Petroleum Exporting Countries (OPEC) quadrupled world oil prices, generating enormous windfall profits. Oil-exporting countries pumped their huge surpluses into the world's financial centers. To meet the interest obligations on these accounts, bankers searched frantically for new ways to lend money.

Third World countries, desperate for capital to boost their own economic development, were only too willing to oblige the banks. It was like offering a bankrupt firm a new, unlimited line of credit. Many developing countries were being seriously hurt by skyrocketing oil prices, so a great deal of their borrowing went to pay for oil, not just for development. Even some of the oil-producing nations, such as Mexico and the poorer OPEC members, borrowed extensively against anticipated bonanza revenues from their oil.

In the short run, the arrangement was convenient for all parties involved. OPEC countries got maximum return on their petrodollars. The major banks made loans in record volumes and their books forecast strong returns. Developing countries got easy cash to prop up their economies. U.S. exporters were also benefiting, since much of the money loaned to the LDCs was used to purchase American goods and services. During the mid to late 1970s, exports to developing nations contributed to a favorable U.S. trade balance.

With no central reporting of the enormous transactions involving dozens of banks and developing nations, no one had any idea that the system was becoming so overextended. When the fragile house of cards came tumbling down in 1982, it shook the foundations of the international economic system.

On 13 August 1982, Mexico announced that it was suspending payments on its external obligations. International bankers reacted in near panic, fearing that other major debtors would follow suit, causing irreparable damage to the financial system. Mexico's situation was serious—runaway inflation of 99 percent in 1982, plummeting oil prices, and a heavy $86.1 billion foreign debt. With a relatively strong economy and substantial oil reserves, however, Mexico appeared better off than many other debtor nations.

Over the next five years, a number of other developing nations would default, or threaten to default, on their loan repayments, creating an ongoing crisis for Western banks and multilateral organizations like the International Monetary Fund (IMF) and crippling America's export potential. Recognizing their new leverage, a number of LDCs threatened the big banks with default in order to reschedule their payments or write off some of their debt. On more than one occasion, the U.S. government had to step in with loans and aid to prop up one of these countries and protect the banks from ruinous financial shocks.

The forces driving the eventual collapse are obvious in hindsight, and there is ample blame to go around. Developing nations simply borrowed too much. The international banks were willing accomplices, making huge loans with no realistic assessment of the developing world's ability to repay. When it came time to service these loans, the debtor countries found themselves in a difficult bind. Energy costs skyrocketed in the 1970s, draining their foreign exchange. Many of the projects undertaken by the LDCs had contributed to their overall infrastructure but done nothing to generate funds to repay the original loans.

It wasn't just the cost of oil that drained the foreign exchange of the developing countries. In October 1979, the U.S. government clamped down hard on monetary policy to fight inflation. This policy sent interest rates soaring, which in turn dramatically increased debt service on overseas loans. Given their perilous economic situation, the nations of Latin America and other debt-burdened regions had little choice but to export more and import less. In many cases, the IMF made reductions in imports and aggressive export programs a precondition for additional loans. Such a policy would generate more foreign exchange to repay the banks, but it was devastating to U.S. trade interests.

U.S. exports to seven of the largest debtor countries—Brazil, Mexico, Argentina, Venezuela, the Philippines, Chile, and Nigeria—declined from $34 billion in 1981 to $18.5 billion in 1983, accounting for more than one-half the total decline in U.S. exports during the period.[13] One study of a hundred industries showed that over 80 percent suffered export declines from the 1980 level. Exports of steel and motor vehicles dropped by 50 percent, machinery equipment was down 38 percent, construction materials declined by 80 percent, and agricultural equipment suffered an incredible 86 percent drop. U.S. exports to developing nations have yet to recover. In 1986, exports to debtor countries were still running about 20 percent below 1980 levels.

The sharp reversal of U.S. trade flows with debtor nations jeopardized America's industrial base and millions of plant jobs. Stuart Tucker of the Overseas Development Council detailed the employment losses in testimony to a House committee.

> In 1984, the United States had 500,000 fewer jobs due to the decline of exports to the Third World since 1980. Additionally, another 800,000 jobs have been lost which would have been created if the growth trend of the 1970s had continued after 1980. Thus, nearly 1.4 million U.S. jobs have been lost due to the recent recession in the Third World. This represents nearly 8.4 percent of official U.S. unemployment in 1985.[14]

While U.S. exporters were rapidly losing markets in the Third World, developing nations were accelerating their exports to America, from nearly $15 billion in 1981 to $125 billion in 1986. The U.S. trade balance with Latin America swung from a surplus of $1.1 billion to a deficit of $16 billion, a change concentrated mostly in manufacturing.[15]

Between 1980 and 1984, for example, Brazil expanded textile and apparel exports, which pounded the already beleaguered U.S. industry and intensified the pressure for import relief in states like North Carolina and South Carolina. Argentina has claimed 80 percent of the world soybean market lost by U.S. growers.

Again, the LDCs were not using their export earnings to purchase U.S. goods and services; instead, they were repaying their obligations to Western banks. Argentina needed 50 cents out of every dollar of export earnings for debt service.[16]

The LDC debt crisis pitted Western banks against U.S. workers and exporters. If the banks were paid up-front, it would be at the expense of U.S. exporters and domestic industries already under siege by foreign imports. If LDCs were allowed to use their foreign exchange to purchase U.S. goods, the banks would be forced to reschedule or even write off their loans.

This policy dilemma is reflected in the two major proposals to deal with LDC debt, plans offered by Treasury Secretary Baker and New Jersey Democratic Senator Bill Bradley. The Baker plan favors the commercial banks, calling for additional loans by both private and multilateral development banks. The Bradley plan calls for substantial write-offs of both interest and principal by the big banks, as well as increased foreign aid to stimulate economic growth and ease the need for severe austerity measures or aggressive trade initiatives by the LDCs.

The Battlefronts of Fair Trade

While the Reagan administration was stumbling over its fiscal and monetary policies, Congress was preoccupied with another factor behind our trade woes — unfair trade practices by foreign nations. Exchange rates or growth differentials mean very little to a congressman's unemployed or worried workers back home. If a community's mills are shut down and hundreds of constituents are laid off, it's easier to make a scapegoat of foreign imports. By 1985, many members of Congress were beating the same drum: not only our jobs and our economy, but our cultural traditions of fairness and competition were being exploited by others.

Clearly, many nations discriminate against U.S. exports and

provide lavish subsidies to boost their products into our market. Blaming our entire trade deficit on unfair foreign practices, however, does not square with the economic reality. While unfair trade practices capture the headlines, most economists believe they account for no more than 10 percent of the U.S. merchandise trade deficit.[17] Wholesale elimination of foreign trade-distorting practices would improve America's overall trade balance only modestly, particularly since many of the worst offenders are LDCs whose debt problems prevent them from importing any more from the United States.

Incredibly, our government had no systematic inventory of the foreign unfair trade practices until 1984, when Congress demanded an annual report from the administration. The idea was to prod the Executive Branch to document both the existing and potential barriers affecting goods, services, and investments and to facilitate negotiations to reduce or eliminate such barriers. The 1986 report details the discriminatory policies of forty nations and two regional trading bodies, covering 78 percent of all 1985 U.S. exports.[18]

What is "unfair trade"? Distortions in the world trading system can take many forms. Predatory exporting practices like dumping, subsidies, targeting, or counterfeiting give foreign companies a competitive edge in the United States and in third-country markets. Tariffs, quotas, nitpicking customs regulations, licenses, and other import restrictions prevent American products from competing in foreign markets. The administration's report defined unfair trade practices as "government laws, regulations, policies or practices intended either to protect domestic producers from foreign competition or artificially stimulate exports of particular domestic products."[19]

To be honest, no country, including the United States, is entirely pure when it comes to protecting domestic interests. In the world of trade, fairness is often in the eyes of the beholder. As Sir Roy Denman, the European Community's ambassador to the United States, wryly notes, "What one does oneself is fair trade, and what the other fellow does is unfair."[20]

Throughout the 1980s, it became obvious that many nations were playing fast and loose with international trade laws. U.S. exporters faced a maze of tariffs, quotas, and Byzantine regulations designed to keep their products out of foreign markets. Closer to home, subsidized imports displaced domestic manufacturers, throwing thousands out of work. U.S. firms won contracts overseas, only to see a competitor steal the deal with the help of a subsidized government loan package.

In the past, the procedures enacted by Congress to deal with unfair trade practices have done a good job of protecting U.S. businesses and U.S. consumers alike, but the Reagan administration has balked at enforcing these laws. President Reagan's reluctance to use his authority to counteract unfair foreign imports has prompted Congress to draft trade bills designed to force the President's hand on unfair trade practices.

The more prominent examples of unfair trade include the following:

Price Leadership

We're Number 1
40% below Intel and AMD
15%–20% below other Japanese suppliers

Win With the 10% Rule
Find AMD and Intel sockets . . .
Quote 10% below their price . . .
If they requote,
Go 10% again . . .
Don't quit till you *win!*

25% Disti Profit Margin
Guaranteed

Hitachi Eproms

Import Dumping

This memo, sent to U.S. distributors of Hitachi semiconductors in February 1985, is a classic illustration of dumping—generally, the practice of exporting at a loss in order to drive other producers out of the marketplace or to maintain domestic employment.[21]

As the memo makes clear, Hitachi was instructing its distributors to cut prices to whatever level necessary to gain market share, while guaranteeing them a 25 percent profit margin. As one representative of the U.S. industry testified before a Senate subcommittee, "It is clear to us that in our industry international trade lawlessness is the order of the day."[22]

In the early 1980s, Japan aggressively targeted the world semiconductor market, driving prices downward in an effort to capture U.S. market share. Even when semiconductor prices fell below production costs, the Japanese companies absorbed the losses. Japan's enormous semiconductor firms were much better equipped for a battle of attrition than their small U.S. counterparts. As a result, by mid decade, Japanese firms had captured about 90 percent of the U.S. market for certain chips.

In response to Japanese dumping, U.S. semiconductor companies filed three separate complaints with the Commerce Department. Commerce confirmed the industry's accusations and negotiated a far-reaching agreement requiring Japan to stop dumping in the U.S. market, dismantle import barriers that blocked U.S. sales in Japan, and stop dumping chips into other markets in order to displace U.S. manufacturers.

In April 1987, less than eight months after the semiconductor pact was reached, it was clear that Japan had failed to abide by the agreement. Citing evidence of continued dumping in other markets and continued barriers to the Japanese market, President Reagan slapped a $300 million tariff on certain Japanese televisions, computers, and other electronic products. In recent months, as Japan has taken steps to eliminate market barriers and third-country dumping, the President has gradually lifted these sanctions.

The Japanese semiconductor battle is only one example of dumping. Other cases range across the whole spectrum of American industry, from basic chemicals to the most sophisticated high technology.

Congress recognized the dumping problem as far back as 1916, when it passed a law providing a civil course of action for private damages against parties who dumped foreign merchandise in the United States. Five years later, Congress passed the Antidumping Act of 1921, which authorized investigations of alleged dumping practices and the imposition of antidumping duties. Worldwide, most governments have condemned dumping and instituted laws to penalize imports sold below fair market value.

Subsidy

In May 1986, a coalition of U.S. sawmills filed a petition with the U.S. government, accusing the Canadian government of unfairly assisting its lumber manufacturers and demanding retaliatory action. Pointing to the rapid increase in Canadian lumber imports, which had captured over one third of the entire U.S. market, the American lumber industry accused Canada of selling government-owned timber to its firms at unfairly low prices. Under the U.S. government's competitive bidding system, a given tree might cost $1500, depending on species and quality; under Canada's noncompetitive allocation system, an identical tree might sell for only $150.[23]

After five months of expensive legal efforts on both sides, the U.S. Department of Commerce ruled that Canada's timber pricing system did, in fact, confer an unfair advantage of roughly 15 percent on Canadian lumber imports. As a result, the department imposed an offsetting 15 percent import fee on all lumber from north of the border. Several months later, U.S.

and Canadian negotiators agreed on a settlement under which Canada would assess a 15 percent exit tax on all lumber shipments bound for the United States; Canada also pledged to revise its timber pricing system to eliminate any unfair advantage for its sawmills.

The Canadian timber case is a classic example of a subsidy that distorts normal trade flows. An illegal subsidy exists whenever a foreign government offers payments or other economic benefits that reduce an exporting firm's production costs or prices. Laws to impose countervailing duties to penalize foreign subsidies are the oldest U.S. procedures against unfair trade, dating back to 1897.

Subsidies are often hard to determine because governments, as a matter of course, provide many services that contribute to a country's general competitiveness—education, physical infrastructure, research, and so forth. Depending on the specific case, these types of assistance are generally considered an acceptable form of economic development.

When governments provide more direct assistance to specific exporting industries, however, they often cross the threshold into unfair subsidies. These can range from direct cash grants and tax breaks to reductions in utility or transportation rates.

Although many of these practices are considered unfair by international standards, the determination of what constitutes an unfair subsidy has become considerably more difficult in recent years. The variety and sophistication of subsidies has grown much faster than the body of international law governing them.

Targeting

Many foreign governments have begun to participate actively in the promotion of certain industries. This practice, known as "targeting," involves the identification of new and promising sectors, then taking whatever action is necessary to ensure their success.

Foreign government targeting has threatened a number of U.S. industries. Our private firms simply cannot compete with a foreign firm that has the unlimited resources of its government behind it.

Patents, Prices, Labels, and Trademarks

In addition to dumping, subsidy, and targeting, a number of sundry practices are considered unfair by U.S. law, including patent infringement, price fixing, false labeling, and trademark infringement. Long before 1980, when the United States had a favorable trade balance, Congress recognized these problems and provided a statutory framework for dealing with them. U.S. trade law provides relief when the activities of foreign governments, firms, or U.S. importers have been responsible for injury to a domestic industry.

In certain cases, our trade law allows temporary import relief even when no unfair foreign practices are alleged. When a rapid surge of imports captures a major share of the U.S. market and threatens the existence of domestic manufacturers, a U.S. industry can petition for temporary relief in the form of tariffs, quotas, or a negotiated restraint agreement. In theory, this provision is designed to give the U.S. industry a brief "breathing space" in which to modernize and become more competitive. After a short time, the import restrictions are lifted, and the U.S. industry must compete head to head with the foreign imports.

Predatory Export Financing

Fuji Electric Co. of Japan and other companies were in the final stages of assembling bids to build generators for the proposed $36 million Mae Moh power plant in Thailand. General Electric considered itself the leading candidate: Thai officials had called

GE's equipment technically the best. But on May 21, only 10 hours before the deadline for bids, Japan's export-financing agency offered the Thais subsidized loans and an $8 million grant to help them pay for the project. Not surprisingly, this financing package overcame GE's technical superiority. The Fuji consortium won the contract.[24]

GE's loss of the Mae Moh power plant contract illustrates another growing problem in international commerce. Increasingly, foreign governments are winning big-ticket contracts for their firms through the use of "mixed credits" — official export-promotion loans combined with foreign aid grants or other bargain-rate credits that make even an inferior bid irresistible to developing nations.

The *Wall Street Journal* noted that the use of mixed credits amounts to an "undeclared trade war" that is intensifying at a time when the United States and our major trading partners "already are in danger of falling into a traditional trade war."[25]

Mixed credits — also known as tied-aid or blended credits — have received less public attention than other unfair trade practices, but they have plagued U.S. companies competing overseas. In earlier times, international sales were financed by the purchaser, either through his own funds or borrowing. After World War I, the amount of individual sales began to rise rapidly, and exporters began to provide credit to purchasers by borrowing themselves. In time, commercial banks were reluctant to extend credit solely on the basis of the supplier's signature, which gave rise to the current system of government export credit guarantees.

In the late 1950s, the French began "sweetening" the export-financing pot to help their exporters by offering a type of foreign aid to developing countries that were having trouble financing their imports. French exporters began to rely on mixed credits as a means of beating their foreign competitors in strategic markets. In the 1970s, competition intensified and other nations followed suit.

Increasingly, sales on large-scale contracts are decided not on the quality of the goods but on the financing terms offered by the exporter and his government. Mixed-credit offers have grown from $212 million in 1975 to $2.1 billion in 1980 to $6.5 billion in 1984. Using the rule of thumb that each $1 billion of U.S. exports generates 25,000 jobs, a conservative estimate would be that over 500,000 American jobs have been lost to predatory foreign financing since 1980.[26]

As one frustrated executive, Jack Pierce, vice president of the Boeing Company, said, "The entire world is turning into the O.K. Corral. You've got barter, countertrade, private and multicurrency deals, government, government export credits — everything but the kitchen sink."[27]

The United States was not prepared to deal with this latest assault against free trade. Our government never initiated a mixed-credit offering and rarely did anything to protect our firms when other countries made lucrative offers. The lack of government financing prompted some firms to shift jobs and production overseas, where competitive mixed-credit support was available.

Until 1983, the closest the United States came to government-sponsored financing was the Export-Import Bank (Eximbank). Created in 1934 "to aid in financing and to facilitate exports and imports and the exchange of commodities," the bank was to support trade opportunities only when private banks were unable to provide financing. Ironically, the Eximbank was originally established to foster trade relations with the Soviet Union, and its first loan of $3.8 million financed the sale of U.S. silver bullion to Cuba, there to be minted into Cuban pesos.

As the trade deficit zoomed upward in the 1980s, U.S. exporters turned to the Eximbank to counter subsidized foreign financing. But the Reagan administration, seeking to terminate the bank, had greatly reduced its funding capacity.

Finally, Congress came to the rescue by setting up a mixed-credit program in 1983. The new program carried no additional funding but authorized the Eximbank to use existing bank funds and foreign aid to counter foreign mixed-credit offerings. The business community hailed the congressional action, but the Reagan administration refused to implement the mixed-credit program for more than two years.

The administration reflected the view of many U.S. policy-makers in its desire to negotiate an end to the practice of mixed credits, which not only distort trade flows but divert foreign-aid funds from the most truly needy nations. Foreign aid becomes an economic weapon, not a development tool. Unfortunately, as long as the United States was unwilling to fight back with mixed credits of our own, what incentive would France and other nations have to come to the bargaining table?

The President finally woke up to the problem of predatory foreign financing in late 1985, calling for a $300 million "war chest" to match financing by other nations, but the amount was meager compared to what other countries were doing.

As Norman Tebbit, former British secretary of State for Trade and Industry, has noted, the soft-loan race is going in the same direction as the strategic arms race: "We need multilateral disarmament in credit facilities, just as we need multilateral disarmament for defense."

Tariffs

Victor K. Kiam, president of Remington Products, outlined some of his company's problems before a House subcommittee.

> In Venezuela, where we have had access, we started to build a business. We invested in advertising. We exported. . . . Then the door was shut. So not only did we lose the continuing sales of our product in Venezuela, we lost our investment in advertising

which occurred over three years, and now we are out of business, and all the money we invested in the advertising is completely lost to us.[28]

When U.S. firms try to export their products, they often face a formidable array of barriers to those markets. The story of Remington's efforts to crack the Venezuelan market is indicative of the obstacles that exist worldwide. Remington shavers encountered stiff tariffs and customs taxes in Venezuela. Then a combination of foreign exchange and price manipulations by the government made imports uncompetitive against domestically produced goods. Remington also faced a complex import licensing system, followed by difficulty in obtaining foreign currency it needed for importing. Finally, as if these restrictions weren't enough, Venezuela does not allow the use of foreign-produced advertising. Mr. Kiam's familiar television commercials had to be produced in Venezuela.

Historically, tariffs or import fees have been the most common barrier to foreign merchandise. Often instituted simply to raise revenue, tariffs are also used to increase the price of imported goods to protect domestic industries.

Since 1947, negotiators have reduced tariffs to an average of less than 10 percent among industrialized countries. In contrast, many developing nations retain very high tariffs to protect domestic industries, although they often export to developed nations at lower rates.

A growing problem is the proliferation of exclusionary tariff arrangements between countries or regional areas. If two or more nations collude to offer each other reduced tariffs, other nations are frozen out from those markets and the open global trading system is undermined. Regional trading arrangements such as those of the European Community are extremely injurious to the United States and other non-European nations, but they are legal under international trade law.

Quotas

Another pervasive import barrier is the quota, ranging from a total ban on imports to quantitative restrictions on certain products. While quotas are generally illegal under international trade law, there are exceptions. A particularly frustrating case for American exporters is Japan's use of quotas on agricultural products. Japan's rice growers are not only protected from imports; they also receive subsidies. Even wheat imports are controlled to keep prices high and quantities restricted so that consumers do not switch from rice to wheat products.

The Japanese government also protects its beef industry through quotas that ensure that imported beef is not sold at a price lower than the local product. Japanese consumers pay a heavy penalty for these quotas—beef prices in Japan are four to six times the world market average. Small wonder that over-all food costs in Tokyo are 70 percent higher than in New York City and more than double those in Los Angeles.

OTHER NON-TARIFF BARRIERS

In addition to tariffs and quotas, nations employ a myriad of subtler, less tangible barriers to keep imports out and protect domestic interests. Non-tariff barriers include complex licensing requirements, currency restrictions, countertrade requirements, "buy-domestic" government procurement policies, service and investment restrictions, and a variety of fees.

Non-tariff barriers obscure exporters' understanding of how a country's import system works. All too often, these barriers go hand in hand with discrimination, corruption, and substantial financial risk to the potential importer.

While the gradual reduction in tariff rates worldwide in the last half century has helped to promote a more open global economy, the sharp rise in non-tariff barriers has worked in the opposite direction. Non-tariff barriers are particularly common in nations with heavy international debt burdens. By frustrating foreign exporters with a variety of barriers, debtor nations help to generate a positive balance of trade and foreign exchange to meet their debt obligations.

While debt-saddled countries can perhaps be excused for non-tariff barriers designed to restrict nonessential imports, these tactics are inexcusable among countries that are racking up sizable trade surpluses. Korea and Taiwan have made protectionist tariff and non-tariff barriers a cornerstone of their national economic development strategies. They have maintained high trade barriers long after their industries have become internationally competitive.

Fighting with One Hand Behind Our Back

Our government's traditional role of ensuring competition has protected domestic consumers, but at times has made it more difficult for U.S. firms to compete overseas. Few if any Americans would advocate rolling back our worker safety regulations, environmental standards, or antitrust laws, but it's important to recognize that most foreign firms operate under much more lax standards. In addition, our government has taken on a number of foreign policy and strategic responsibilities since World War II, many of which run counter to the needs of U.S. exporters.

Successive administrations have attempted to isolate Soviet-bloc nations economically, thus denying their markets to U.S. exporters. Obviously, we must carefully guard against letting sensitive U.S. technology fall into Soviet hands, but our government has imposed excessive restrictions on nonsensitive exports to our allies and the Soviets alike, which have hurt the United States where we are most competitive.

While the United States is preoccupied with foreign and strategic matters, other Western nations devote their resources to competing in the world economy. When the United States punishes a recalcitrant nation by employing economic sanctions, the Japanese and French step in and pick up where U.S. businesses left off. The cumulative cost of these policies may be as high as $25 billion a year in lost markets.[29]

Not only do our efforts to use trade as a foreign policy tool benefit foreign firms at the expense of U.S. firms, they are rarely effective without the full support and participation of our trade partners. When the Soviet Union invaded Afghanistan, President Jimmy Carter miscalculated the Russians' dependence on U.S. wheat and imposed an embargo on grain shipments. Unfortunately, the Soviets were able to meet their grain needs through new contracts with Argentina and Canada, and the grain embargo ended up hurting U.S. farmers more than the Soviet Union.

Candidate Ronald Reagan campaigned against Carter on the grain embargo issue. But as President, he also tried to use trade sanctions as a foreign policy lever by restricting sales of gas pipeline equipment when the Soviets imposed martial law in Poland. The results were painfully similar: the Soviets turned to foreign suppliers who were only too willing to exploit the U.S. government action once again. U.S. contracts were terminated, ordered equipment sat at storage facilities, and exporters absorbed millions of dollars in losses so that the U.S. government could show it was getting tough with the Russians.

The willingness to use trade embargoes to score foreign policy points is not limited to the Executive Branch. Numerous bills have been introduced in Congress to apply sanctions for foreign policy or human rights causes. Political liberals favor trade restrictions on right-wing governments like South Africa and Chile. Conservatives do not want any trade with Marxist countries. Both Democrats and Republicans readily support President Reagan's use of trade sanctions on terrorist countries.

The United States maintains sweeping economic sanctions against Cuba, Poland, Libya, Nicaragua, South Africa, and Syria and less extensive restrictions for the Soviet Union and Communist bloc and terrorism-supporting countries. The American people probably agree with many of these embargoes. Taken together, however, they have caused significant disruptions in U.S. trade and denied businesses access to a number of foreign markets.

Writing in the *Washington Post* on 17 November 1986, Frank E. Samuel Jr. said, "In some ways the crippling trade deficit is an inside job. To be sure, high tariffs, subsidies, dumping and other trade practices by foreign nations have all had their hand in it. But they couldn't have pulled it off without an accomplice: our own export controls."[30]

In the 1960s and 1970s, the one sector in which America enjoyed a substantial competitive lead was high technology. The United States led the world in high-tech research and production and held a dominant position in the world market. As more traditional industries deteriorated during this time, there was a robust confidence that the electronics industry would guarantee America's economic standing in the future. Since 1978, these industries have created over one million new jobs, making electronics firms, employing 2.5 million men and women, the largest manufacturing sector in the country.[31] Who would have predicted in 1980 that our $26 billion trade surplus in high-tech goods would turn to a $2 billion deficit in 1986?[32]

The malaise of American technology is more than an economic and trade problem; it has serious national security implications. With the decline of certain U.S. high-tech sectors, our nation is becoming increasingly dependent on foreign sources. The Pentagon's alarming reliance on foreign-made semiconductors, for example, could spread into other high-tech sectors, eroding our nation's military capability.

Our government's excessive restrictions on technology exports have been a major factor in the alarming decline of our country's competitive position. The President's Commission on

Industrial Competitiveness estimates that we are losing $7.6 billion per year in overseas business because of export controls on electronic products.[33] These missed export opportunities add up to 200,000 lost jobs.[34]

The law that governs the U.S. export control program, the Export Administration Act, imposes national security export restrictions on "dual use" technology—commercial goods that could have military application. While safeguards are needed to prevent militarily important Western technology from falling into the hands of the Soviet Union and its Warsaw Pact allies, our government's export control efforts have become a nightmare. The list of restricted articles has ballooned to over 200,000 items, many of them outdated or nonsensitive. The export control process has become so complicated that only technical experts can understand it.

What angers U.S. companies most is being denied a license to export a product, only to discover that the identical product is sold worldwide by foreign companies.

Obtaining an export license is fraught with mysterious delays and uncertainties. It often takes four weeks or more to get a license to export nonsensitive goods to one of our closest allies! License applications involving nonallied nations can take four to six months or more. It is not uncommon for U.S. companies to lose contracts because a prospective buyer knows about our Byzantine export licensing system and opts to buy from another nation.

In 1985, fewer than one percent of 121,000 export applications were denied by the U.S. government, yet every single one had to be thoroughly scrutinized. The General Accounting Office reported that one half of the 60,783 export licenses issued in 1981 could have been eliminated and handled in a less burdensome way, for these license applications involved products that were not "militarily significant."[35]

As Fred Bucy, former president of Texas Instruments and head of a Defense Science Board task force, noted, "We are squandering valuable resources trying to control all types of technology when we must concentrate on the technology which can give our adversaries a revolutionary leap in military capabilities."

In response to our sagging high-tech trade balance and numerous licensing "horror stories," Congress has attempted to reform our export control system. Several House bills have attempted to focus controls on truly critical technology while easing restrictions on nonsensitive goods. Unfortunately, the Department of Defense has blocked many of the most important reforms, branding one bill the "Khadafy-Gorbachev Relief Act of 1986."[36]

Only time will tell whether our nation will focus export controls on truly sensitive items, allowing less critical goods to compete in world markets. As Congress and the administration continue to debate the issue, however, our high-tech firms are losing their competitive grip on world markets.

Just as our trade competitors often maintain far less stringent environmental or worker safety standards, no other nation attempts to maintain such a high standard of international business practice as the United States. In the early 1970s, a series of scandals—one of which brought down a Japanese prime minister—led to intense scrutiny of U.S. businesses abroad, specifically the use of illicit payments to foreign government officials to secure overseas contracts.

After a series of highly publicized hearings in 1976, Congress enacted the Foreign Corrupt Practices Act (FCPA) to set a new ethical standard for U.S. firms overseas, despite the fact that bribery and other questionable practices are often tolerated, even encouraged, by other governments. While the effort to set standards of conduct for U.S. businesses operating abroad is laudable, the law places U.S. firms at a disadvantage in many markets, since our competitors are bound by no such standards.

In addition, the FCPA's ambiguities and paperwork have

confused and overburdened stateside firms. Under the law, U.S. executives can be prosecuted whether or not they were aware of the actions of their foreign agents so long as they had "reason to know" about bribes or other misconduct.

The Foreign Corrupt Practices Act has been on the books for a decade, yet there have been no successful prosecutions. Instead, confusion over the law and the fear of penalties have had a chilling effect on U.S. exporters, especially small and medium-size firms that simply do not have the resources to comply with the law's complex accounting and reporting procedures.

The Carter administration, recognizing that our self-imposed restraints were hurting U.S. exporters, attempted to get other countries to adopt similar standards. Our negotiators raised the issue before the Organization for Economic Cooperation and Development (OECD) in Paris, but it was not considered seriously. A congressional staff delegation visiting the OECD in 1984, urging support for an international code of business conduct, was rebuffed by the U.S. personnel there. "If you're promoting this idea," the ambassador said, "I have to ask, What have you been smoking?"[37]

Given the abuses that led to enactment of overseas business standards, the challenge for U.S. policymakers is not to overturn the law, but to remove the ambiguities and paperwork burden that have made the law onerous. More important, we must continue our efforts to persuade our trade competitors to adopt similar ethical standards.

Clearly, a myriad of factors contributed to our spiraling trade deficit in the 1980s. Some, like self-imposed unnecessary export restrictions, are completely within our ability to control. Others, like the federal budget deficit, will require difficult sacrifices and a national consensus before any solutions are possible. Still others, like foreign unfair trade barriers or other nations' willingness to adopt ethical standards for international business, will test the skills of our international negotiators.

One truth emerges again and again from the examination of our nation's trade decline over the past seven years: the rules of the game have changed forever. The United States is no longer an island unto itself, no longer the dominant force in the world economy. International economic forces and domestic policies have conspired to challenge our nation's international preeminence, to rob our nation of millions of jobs, and to make the United States the largest debtor nation in history.

In the future, every foreign or domestic policy must be considered not only on its own merits, but on its potential impact on U.S. trade, economic growth, and employment.

FOUR

The Politics of Trade

AS OUR NATION'S trade deficit pounded America's industrial and agricultural heartland in the 1980s, political leaders scrambled to stake out positions. Unfortunately, neither political party offered guidance to its elected officials on how to deal with specific trade issues. To further confuse matters, both parties seemed to be drifting in directions that were contrary to where they stood historically.

Indeed, for over a century the single issue that most distinguished the two political parties had been foreign trade. Traditionally, the Republicans have erected protectionist barriers and the Democrats have dismantled them in favor of less restrictive trade. Writing about this turnabout in a 1985 *Washington Post* article, Michael Barone notes,

> The Democratic Party from the time of Andrew Jackson tended to favor low tariffs and was hostile to trade barriers. The Republican Party from the time of Abraham Lincoln favored high tariffs and protection for American producers. Smoot-Hawley was passed by a Republican Congress in 1930; the architects of the low tariff free trade policies after World War II were Democrats such as Cordell Hull and Dean Acheson.[1]

The shift in Republican thinking came twenty-five years after they muscled through Congress the most protective law in the nation's history, the Smoot-Hawley Act in 1930. Democrats, for their part, carried the free-trade banner until the 1950s, when import-sensitive areas of the country began feeling the pressure of international competition. This surprising turnaround reveals a great deal about how economic trends and political forces can dramatically reshape the parties' stands on a fundamental issue.

With no direction from their platforms, leaders in both political parties in the early 1980s began calling for tougher trade policies in response to plant closures, lost jobs, and constituent discontent in their districts. Rising public alarm over jobs lost to foreign imports fueled the fire within Congress to adopt restrictive trade legislation. House Speaker Thomas P. ("Tip") O'Neill Jr. summed up the American public's frustration over the Reagan administration's trade policies: "They don't like the attitude of the President of the United States . . . They're upset because the President doesn't give a damn."[2]

Even Republican Senate Majority Leader Robert Dole, on a visit to Tokyo, warned of the "highly charged atmosphere" on Capitol Hill and of renewed efforts "to gain early political advantage on the trade issue."[3]

Given President Reagan's recurring free-trade theme and the Democrats' close affiliation with organized labor, which generally favors increased import controls, the Democrats were cast as protectionists. While it may have been convenient to put Democrats and Republicans on opposite sides of the trade issue, these efforts to label or stereotype the parties did not wash. If anything, free traders and protectionists alike could be found in both camps.

As trade climbed to the top of the nation's political agenda, both parties were stumbling around to establish and hone their respective positions. With their historical traditions forgotten or ignored and no philosophical basis to guide them, it is un-

likely that either political party will be in a position to articulate
a unified trade policy in the future.

Democrats: The Road from Free Trade

The party of Jefferson, Wilson, and Roosevelt laid the foundation for free and open trade among nations. Over the past
century, the Democrats have prided themselves on their international views and their vigilant efforts to resist protective tariffs. From 1928 to 1944, Democratic Party platforms repeatedly
assailed unilateral protective tariffs and called for reciprocal
tariff agreements between the United States and other nations.
The Democrats fully intended to distance their open-trading
position from the Republican-sponsored Smoot-Hawley Tariff
Act, which brought so much economic grief to the nation in the
1930s.

In the presidential campaign of 1932, Franklin D. Roosevelt
strongly denounced Smoot-Hawley and pledged to dismantle
trade barriers imposed by Presidents William McKinley, War-
ren Harding, Calvin Coolidge, and Herbert Hoover. True to his
promise, he prodded Congress to pass the Reciprocal Trade
Agreements Act in 1934, authorizing the President to negotiate
mutual tariff reductions of as much as 50 percent.

The 1934 trade law, renewed several times through the 1940s
and 1950s, dramatically changed not only the direction of trade
policy but the process by which the two branches dealt with the
issue. Congress assumed an oversight role to maintain its constitutional responsibility to "regulate commerce with foreign
nations," but gave the Executive the authority to carry out
day-to-day trade policy and consummate trade agreements with
other governments.

President Roosevelt, committed to rebuilding the world trading system, gave his secretary of State, Cordell Hull, free rein
to restore trade among nations. Both feared that unfair eco-

nomic conditions or restrictions on trade would lead to geo-political conflicts and another war. Beginning in 1934, they gradually phased out tariffs in favor of bilateral agreements and efforts to establish multilateral institutions to stabilize economic and trade relations among nations.

FDR preferred going full swing with multilateral negotiations, but a reluctant Congress and world economic conditions in the Depression years would not permit it. By 1945, however, the United States had concluded twenty-eight bilateral agreements, and the average U.S. tariff had fallen by nearly 60 percent.

During the 1950s, the South and Northeast began feeling the pressure of foreign imports, causing labor and party leaders to push for import restrictions. Southern descendants of the original free traders in cotton, tobacco, and sugar moved over to the protectionist side of the debate to assist their beleaguered textile industry. New Deal Democrats called for protection of affected industries in their districts. On one occasion, the House barely passed a three-year extension of the Reciprocal Trade Act only after the pro-trade leadership intervened. Speaker Sam Rayburn, using his familiar admonition, sternly counseled freshman members about to vote on the trade bill, "If you want to get along, go along." To avoid an embarrassing defeat, Rayburn finally had to call in Minority Leader Joseph Martin to get enough Republican votes to win.

In the early 1960s, protectionism had grown stronger among some Democrats, but Kennedy was able to appease Southern textile interests and won an overwhelming 210–44 Democratic vote for the Trade Expansion Act of 1962.

In 1963, Raymond Bauer gave this description of the political scene:

A combination of a general decline in protectionist ideology, a widespread malaise about the prospects of American export trade in the face of the Common Market and the administration's calculated and massive individualized approach to such industries as chemicals and textiles cut the protectionist coalition to shreds.[4]

At the same time, the Democratic Party platforms continued to stress open trade. References to the "tradition of Cordell Hull" and FDR's liberal trade policies were common in party platforms through the 1960s. But ten years after Kennedy's victory on the Trade Expansion Act, the Democrats had moved noticeably toward protectionism. I. M. Destler writes that "only when organized labor left the liberal trade camp in the late 1960s did substantial numbers of northern Democrats begin to defect."[5]

Democrats opposed 1973 legislation authorizing trade talks by a margin of 121 to 112, a profound shift from the 210–44 Democratic vote for the 1962 bill. The bulk of the defectors were northern Democrats, who voted 141–7 *for* the 1962 bill and 101–52 *against* the 1973 legislation.

By 1975, the Democratic Party's free-trade philosophy was being compromised by calls for selective protectionist actions, although support for "liberal" trade and "reciprocal reductions" of barriers were still prominently mentioned in the party's platforms.

Finally, in 1980–1984, the Democratic Party platform reflected the growing trade deficit and the tension between the party's traditional free traders and the new calls for protection by union leaders. The now familiar call for "free trade, but fair trade" appeared in the Democratic platform in 1980.

In 1984, the Democratic Party diplomatically called for trade that would "assure a fair playing field for American business and consumers." The 1984 platform stressed that where foreign competition is fair, no government assistance is called for, but that "where it is unfair, we must respond powerfully, using trade laws and international negotiations."

Obviously, new political forces were reshaping Democratic

thinking on international trade toward positions that emphasized local concerns over the global view. Organized labor, traditionally supportive of the Democratic Party's stated opposition to protective tariffs, began calling for protectionist measures in the early 1960s to stem the tide of lost jobs.

Labor concern was heightened during 1984 when Congress considered domestic content legislation to restrict auto imports and require that all imported vehicles contain certain levels of American-made parts. The partisan split is evident in the final vote: Democrats favored domestic content 187–68, while Republicans opposed the bill 131–32.

Domestic content was viewed more as a labor issue than a trade issue. It profoundly influenced Democratic congressmen who had not given much thought to international trade but cared about protecting jobs in the automobile and related industries.

Auto imports were not the only threat that concerned organized labor in 1984. Garment workers reeling from the massive surge of foreign textiles and clothing from Asian countries, the devastated leatherworks industry in the Northeast, machine tool and steel workers, were all seeking legislative remedies to protect their industries and the jobs they represented.

Organized labor had legitimate reasons to be concerned about the job losses that came with the globalization of the U.S. economy. In 1984, between 1.2 and 1.8 million non-oil manufacturing jobs disappeared; in 1985, another 1.2 to 1.9 million jobs were lost. Non-oil imports accounted for 17 percent of U.S. goods purchased in 1984 and 18.4 percent in 1985.

According to Commerce Department figures, imports displaced 632,000 American jobs in 1984. In 1985, that figure soared 49 percent to 942,000. While the Reagan administration liked to point out that new jobs were being created in high-technology fabrication and service industries, these jobs were often less than full time and offered much lower wages.

The picture was not much better on the export side. The

decline of U.S. exports to the developing countries resulted in 1.6 million fewer jobs, representing 19 percent of official unemployment in 1985. Using the rule of thumb that every billion dollars of the trade deficit represents about 25,000 lost jobs, the 1986 trade deficit of $156 billion represented nearly 4 million jobs lost or forgone. Labor's alarm was understandable.

In an unusually blunt article in the *New York Times* in 1986, AFL-CIO president Lane Kirkland wrote that "scores of industries, thousands of companies and millions of workers are drowning under a flood of imports generated by foreign government initiatives and Washington's neglect." He cited stagnant living standards, falling wages, and the fact that half our nation's displaced workers must accept part-time work or greatly reduced pay.

According to Kirkland, free trade is a dead theory. If it benefits anyone, "it is the manipulators who depress wages in order to inflate profits." He disparaged "free trade evangelists who say that our 'overpaid workers' have priced themselves out of the market." Obviously not impressed with the world trading system, the labor leader charged that much of the world "disavows a market economy."[6]

United Auto Workers President Owen Bieber echoed Kirkland's view before a 1986 conference on Labor Rights and Trade.

> The U.S. workers are often left with a closed plant, a depressed community and no chance of finding jobs at a level of pay comparable to those lost. This waste of valuable resources has occurred despite the assurances of the promoters of free trade that resources will easily move to industries in which the U.S. has an international advantage.
>
> Millions of American workers have been hurt by this process and, today, the job prospects of many more are dimming. There are still eight million Americans officially unemployed and more than five million working part-time for economic reasons.
>
> Meanwhile, imports from countries abusing the rights of

workers flood into our markets, using high technology production techniques as well as basic manufacturing methods.

There is something grossly unfair about a system that expects workers to sacrifice their jobs and lower their living standards so that companies can be free to take advantage of oppressive working conditions to fatten their profits. Yet that is the situation our members face today.[7]

While corporate management found ways to cope with domestic and global adjustments, there was little hope for the displaced worker. In the 1970s, when many large companies moved their production abroad to seize the benefits of cheaper labor costs, the impact was devastating to the workers and communities left behind. Unemployed, with no immediate job alternatives and no skills to rebuild their futures, displaced workers were a graphic symbol of what was happening to the U.S. work force. At the time, government was adding insult to injury by cutting back on education, training, and trade adjustment assistance programs. Responsible union leaders could not ignore the plight of their membership under such conditions.

What was once written off as labor retrenchment on trade soon became widespread national sentiment favoring their positions. Suddenly protectionism was not such a bad word if it meant preserving U.S. plants and jobs. Even some trade associations rallied behind the call for retaliation against countries that maintained high tariffs on U.S. products. The National Association of Manufacturers and the Chamber of Commerce were among the major business organizations whose members were deeply split on the trade subject, depending on whether they had a stake in export markets or were being harmed by imports. Consensus was as elusive for these groups as it had become for the political parties.

For many Democrats, the appeal of protectionism was irresistible. Democratic congressmen began favoring proposals to restrict imports and force other nations to open their markets. It allowed them to identify with economic problems in their districts, expanding their support among business leaders. And it provided them with a viable campaign issue at a time when Democrats had few alternatives to offer to President Reagan's economic policies.

Deep in the party's consciousness, however, protectionism was a troubling issue. From FDR's dismantling of the Smoot-Hawley tariffs and Harry Truman's postwar aid measures to Europe and Japan to more recent Third World assistance, the Democratic Party had traditionally prided itself on taking an outward-looking, international view.

Many of today's Democratic leaders lean toward more long-term policies, rather than the expediency of protectionism. They stress increased competitiveness through export promotion, research, training, advanced education, better corporate management, and greater productivity. They also fear retaliation that could disrupt the world trading system and undermine U.S. security and foreign policy objectives. Recognizing that trade brings countries closer together, they aspire to more global economic integration to further peace among nations.

Former U.S. Senator Paul Tsongas, in his book *The Road from Here,* devoted his chapter on international trade to debunking the idea of trade barriers, saying that they invite retaliation and put off decisions necessary to be competitive. He concluded that such action should be a last-ditch effort only after repeated attempts to forge a more comprehensive trade policy.

The lack of any coherent party position on trade is clearly illustrated by the widely divergent views of the Democrats who threw their hats into the 1988 presidential ring. Nearly a dozen candidates began the race in 1986, representing at least that many different views on trade matters. Former Senator Gary Hart of Colorado and Massachusetts Governor Michael Dukakis represented the free-trade side of the spectrum, while Congressman Richard Gephardt of Missouri was the most visible advocate of tougher trade measures.

Senator Bill Bradley of New Jersey is one of the acknowledged Democratic leaders in the U.S. Senate on fiscal and macroeconomic issues. Having taken on the formidable issues of
LDC debt and the need to revamp the international rules governing trade, Bradley is charting perhaps the most forward-
looking course for Democrats on trade issues.

Many Democrats want to have it both ways on international
trade. They maintain their free-trade philosophy, then support
protectionist measures. While generally advocating bilateral
negotiations to foster global economic growth, Democrats in
large numbers vote for legislation to restrict severely imports of
textiles, automobiles, and other goods.

Democrats are not being any more honest with the issue than
the Reagan administration, which emphatically labels every
trade bill in Congress as protectionist. They usually begin a
speech with "I am for a free and open trading system" but end
with a call for retaliation against other countries and protection
for U.S. workers at home. When it comes to specific issues or
concrete votes, the lack of a coherent party position leaves
individual congressmen to wrestle with these contradictions in
light of the economic pressures in their districts.

GOP: The Road from Protectionism

Like their political opponents, the Republicans have also
turned their trade positions inside out over the last sixty years.
The Grand Old Party generally supports policies that are pleas-
ing to business. Its members strongly back fiscal policies that
foster growth and oppose government activity in the marketplace. But while the Democrats have traditionally advocated
free trade, Republican administrations have championed protectionist causes since the days of Abraham Lincoln. For most
of this century, Republican leaders have not hesitated to use
government intervention to protect industries challenged by
foreign imports.

Republicans proudly carried the protectionist banner throughout the 1920s. It was a recurring theme in the GOP platform,
which boldly proclaimed in 1928, "We view a protective tariff
as a fundamental and essential principle of our economic life."
As historian E. E. Schattschneider argued, "The dominant position of the Republican party before 1932 can be attributed
largely to the successful exploitation of the tariff by this party
as a means of attaching itself to a formidable array of interests
dependent on the protective system and intent upon continuing
it."[8]

Candidate Herbert Hoover promised "limited tariffs" in the
campaign of 1928. On his election, he and the GOP Congress
pushed through the biggest tariff bill in the nation's history.
Tariffs were increased on 20,000 imported items, and the world
trading system deteriorated rapidly. Even so, the GOP platform
continued to stress protectionism for many years.

Two years after Smoot-Hawley was implemented, the GOP
platform proclaimed that "the Republican Party is a staunch
supporter of the American system of a protective tariff." Even
in 1940, ten years after the tariff act wrecked the world economy
and the Democrats had become the major party, the GOP
platform was still embracing protectionism: "We believe in
tariff protection for Agriculture, Labor, and Industry as essential to our American standard of living."[9]

By the mid 1940s, Republican support of protective tariffs
yielded to a growing desire to "promote world-wide economic
stability," though there were lingering calls for import tariffs to
"protect our standard of living."[10]

Finally, in 1948, the GOP abandoned its traditional call for
protective tariffs on foreign products and threw its support to
reciprocal trade agreements. "We shall support the system of
reciprocal trade," the 1948 GOP platform announced. "Barriers
which impede international trade should be reduced on a gradual, selective and *reciprocal* basis."[11]

President Dwight Eisenhower steered the Republican Party

toward an open world trading system in the 1950s. Eisenhower's international view split the Republican Party on the issue during the fifties. When the President's prepared draft of the Reciprocal Trade Act renewal arrived at the House Ways and Means Committee, the protectionist chairman, Dan Reed, reportedly tossed it on the table and said, "Who wants to take this?" After a long pause, Congressman Robert Kean of New Jersey, the fourth-ranking member, reluctantly said, "I will." No higher-ranking Republican would touch it.

Reed tried to kill the bill. Drew Pearson of the *Washington Post* wrote, "Uncle Dan Reed . . . has secretly offered to help put the President's Social Security program through Congress if the President, in turn, will abandon his campaign to liberalize the reciprocal trade agreement. . . . So far—no answer." The bill eventually passed only because the outbreak of war in Asia prompted the need for negotiations with Japan.

The Republican Party softened its enthusiasm for tariffs in party platforms throughout the 1960s and 1970s, but in 1972 cautioned that "as we create a more open world market, we are not unmindful of dangers to American workers from dislocation by the changing patterns of trade. We have several agreements to protect these workers."[12]

In 1976, the GOP moved closer to a free-trade stance, calling for negotiations to "protect our domestic textile industry," but warning of the need to "guard against protectionism."[13]

By 1980, the GOP platform came full circle by including strong language promoting free trade and warning about protectionism.

> Trade, especially exporting, will be high on our list of priorities . . . Republicans will emphasize a policy of free trade, but will expect our trading partners to do so as well . . . Protectionist legislation has engendered "beggar thy neighbor" policies.

The 1984 GOP platform confirmed the new position of the Republican Party:

[The party remains] committed to a free and open trading system. But free trade must be fair trade . . . The greatest danger today to our international trade is growing protectionist sentiment.[14]

Ironically, both parties used the code words "free trade but fair trade" in their party platforms throughout the 1980s, an indication of their ambivalence and division on key trade questions.

RONALD REAGAN: FREE TRADER OR FAIR TRADER?

If Dwight Eisenhower's presidency signaled the GOP's turn away from protectionism, Ronald Reagan's two terms in the White House have led the Republicans into previously uncharted territory on the path toward free trade. Reagan's free-trade policies and rhetoric have forced many Republican congressmen to choose between their President and their constituents who are affected by international trade. If the voters blame foreign imports for plant closures and lost jobs, free-trade theory will not help. The congressmen will most probably lean toward a protectionist solution.

As with most issues, Ronald Reagan has not been totally pure on trade. The President and his cabinet secretaries have preached the gospel of free trade but have occasionally yielded to the temptations of protectionist action. But no one can doubt that Ronald Reagan has fundamentally altered the Republican Party's position on one of the most important issues of its hundred-year history.

Reagan's trade philosophy is deeply rooted in his memory of the Great Depression, as he himself noted in a talk to the National Association of Manufacturers in 1986.

Having celebrated my thirty-ninth birthday thirty-six times now, I've been around to witness a sizable chunk of this century.

I well remember that anti-trade frenzy in the late twenties that produced the Smoot-Hawley tariffs, greasing the skids for our descent into the Great Depression and the most destructive war this world has ever seen. That's one episode of history I'm determined we will never repeat.

Reagan is just as convinced that America's postwar prosperity is the result of reestablishing an international trading system.

I also remember that after the war, the peoples of the free world pulled themselves from the ashes and swore it would never happen again. From their vision and determination came a great act of statesmanship. With the unimpressive title of the General Agreement on Tariffs and Trade, the global trading system was opened up and the free world entered an era of cooperation and prosperity unparalleled in human history.[15]

Ironically, Ronald Reagan's views are a rebuff to past Republicans and a ringing endorsement of the trade policies of his Democratic predecessors. On trade matters, Ronald Reagan is an unabashed admirer of Franklin Roosevelt.

In every edition of the *Economic Report of the President* since his presidency began, Reagan has asserted his belief in free trade.

1982 I reaffirm my Administration's commitment to free trade.[16]

1983 I am committed to a policy of preventing the enactment of protectionist measures in the United States, and I will continue working to persuade the other nations of the world to eliminate trade distorting practices.[17]

1984 Despite these problems, I remain committed to the principle of free trade as the best way to bring the benefits of competition to American consumers and businesses.[18]

1985 Our goal is a system of free and fair trade in goods, services, and capital. We will work toward this goal through both bilateral and multilateral agreements.[19]

1986   Our international trade policy rests firmly on the foundation of free and open markets. The benefits of free trade
are well known: it generates more jobs, a more productive
use of a nation's resources, more rapid innovation, and
higher standards of living both for this nation and its
trading partners.[20]

1987   Protectionism is antigrowth. It would make us less competitive, not more. It would not create jobs. It would hurt
most Americans in the interest of helping a few. . . . In
the long run, protectionism would trap us in those areas
of our economy where we are relatively weak, instead of
allowing growth in areas where we are relatively strong.[21]

1988   We also must resist efforts to push the Nation into protectionism. . . . It would be a tragic mistake to attempt to
close the trade gap by closing our markets. Isolating U.S.
markets could only lead to a global downward spiral in
trade and economic activity.[22]

While Ronald Reagan has announced his commitment to
free trade at almost every opportunity, his actions do not always agree with his rhetoric. Norman Tebbit, Great Britain's
secretary of State for Trade and Industry, charges that the
Reagan administration has "preached free trade while stepping
into protectionist practices."

On virtually every tough trade decision before the administration, free trade has given way to old-fashioned pragmatism
at best and political expediency at worst. In a number of cases,
the President has tempered his free-market philosophy and
either imposed tariffs or quotas or negotiated voluntary restraints to limit imports. These quasi-protectionist actions include the following:

Automobiles: The administration imposed voluntary export restrictions on Japanese autos to mollify U.S. carmakers and
avoid domestic content legislation.

Motorcycles: The administration imposed steep tariffs on imports of large motorcycles, under Section 201, to save Harley-Davidson.

Specialty Steel: Again, under Section 201, imports of specialty steel were restricted for a period of four years.

Steel: In 1984, under the threat of legislated import quotas on steel, the President launched an effort to secure "voluntary" restraint agreements on all categories of steel from all major steel-exporting countries.

Textiles and Apparel: After vetoing the textile bill, the administration negotiated the most restrictive multifiber arrangement ever and followed up with severely restrictive bilateral agreements with Taiwan, Hong Kong, China, and Korea.

Shakes and Shingles: The President imposed a 35 percent tariff on imported shakes and shingles, as recommended by the ITC in Section 201 proceedings.

Agricultural Products: The President authorized the use of subsidies to push exports of U.S. agricultural commodities, even though several of our principal competitors were not guilty of subsidizing exports.

The Reagan administration's international economic and trade policies are fueled by two often contradictory internal forces. One camp is composed of the political ideologues and supply-side adherents promoting fair and open trade. They believe that government intervention is warranted only if security matters, such as placing restrictions on technology transfers to Eastern bloc countries, are at stake or to achieve foreign policy objectives.

In the early days of the Reagan administration, this laissez-faire philosophy dominated on international finance and trade issues. So what if the country is piling up a massive trade deficit or becoming a debtor nation? The Reagan conservatives accepted the shaking-out theory, namely, if some industries were no longer competitive, they should disappear. These advocates prevailed throughout 1981–1984, even as the dollar soared against other currencies, American firms lost export markets overseas, and a flood of artificially cheap imports quadrupled our nation's trade deficit.

Reagan's other camp is populated by officials with a more pragmatic, less ideological perspective. These elements began to prevail in 1985, as James Baker took over from Donald Regan as Treasury secretary. One of Secretary Baker's first actions was to issue a new policy statement on the overvalued dollar, signaling a belated recognition of its connection to trade imbalances. Baker's statement was directly at odds with departing Undersecretary Beryl Sprinkel's repeated praise of the strong dollar and apparent disregard for the growing U.S. trade deficit.

The conflicting policies and personalities within the Reagan administration made a clear strategy for handling the trade deficit impossible. The President would favor one camp, then the other, depending on the issue. The administration's policy was comparable to a driver who keeps one foot on the accelerator and the other on the brake.

Little wonder, then, that as Congress took up trade legislation it had little direction or political accountability. The President's advisers were split on the subject, and neither party had reconciled its past trade stands with the current economic and political realities.

At the Crossroads: The Comprehensive Trade Bill

On a bright but chilly afternoon in March 1985, a chartered train made its way through the small communities that dot the picturesque landscape of West Virginia. The crowded passengers, absorbed in political talk, were oblivious to the pleasant scenery rolling by them. More than one hundred Democratic congressmen, along with staff and sponsors, were returning to

Washington, D.C., from the first Issues Conference, at the Greenbrier resort, organized by Richard Gephardt, the newly elected chairman of the House Democratic caucus.

In three days, the Democrats had covered the whole range of national issues, including a panel discussion on trade and competitiveness. Two highly regarded trade specialists, Robert Hormats and Charles Levy, had made presentations and fielded questions, but it was the luncheon speech by Chrysler Chairman Lee Iacocca that started everyone talking about America's declining competitiveness and the coming trade crisis.

Not many corporate chief executive officers (CEOs) could excite Democrats, but Iacocca, a maverick among his peers, is no ordinary industrialist. He punctuated his speech with barbs at Reagan administration policies and the country's rapidly fading economic position in the world:

> President Reagan says we're about to have a "New American Revolution." Well, I want him to remember why we had the first one. It was because we didn't want to be a colony anymore. We threw the tea in the harbor, remember?

Just one day before Iacocca's speech the Reagan administration had announced it would not extend the voluntary limits on auto imports. This announcement prompted Iacocca to unload on the Japanese:

> Why are we letting the Japanese test our threshold of pain? What are we, masochists?
>
> By the way, for you the threshold of pain comes when we cancel a plant in one of your districts. And a few of you are going to reach it very soon.
>
> We've got a $37 billion trade imbalance with Japan. Our doors are wide open and theirs are practically locked. Does anybody want to argue that Japan isn't protectionist?
>
> Sure, they buy raw materials, because that creates labor. But they won't take finished goods, because that's our labor.

Potatoes, yes; potato chips, no, because that's labor.

Tomatoes, yes; tomato puree, no.

Oranges, yes; orange juice, no—don't squeeze the oranges because that's value added.

Don't worry about starting a trade war: We're already in one. When the other guy is shooting at you, aren't you allowed to shoot back?

The Japanese have made it perfectly clear that they don't intend to open their markets. They aren't being devious about it. They've said it.

So, I don't blame the Japanese for what's happening. Hell, I admire them. They're smart enough to know they're in a trade war and tough enough to win it.

Obviously frustrated with Reagan ideologues who were not coming to grips with economic and trade realities, the Chrysler chairman pulled no punches before his highly partisan audience.

Don't expect any help from the administration, because they're all ideologically committed to inaction. They believe in the "invisible hand" that will reach down and right all wrongs. Well, it's become an iron fist, and it's pounding us into the ground.

But then he laid down the gauntlet to the Democratic leaders at the Greenbrier, challenging them to reject Reagan policies and come up with tough alternatives.[23]

Iacocca's speech had an uncannily persuasive quality, but it sparked more controversy than consensus. Some thought he'd be a good nominee for President in 1988, or at least an excellent choice for a cabinet position. Others felt that his remarks bordered on racism. What he said and the way he said it were deliberately provocative, but he got everyone thinking and talking about trade.

On the train back to Washington, D.C., then Majority Leader Jim Wright of Texas and I talked about how international trade was damaging the American economy and how

Ronald Reagan had failed to address the issue. Trade was a timely issue for Democrats, yet there was potential for divisiveness within the party. Our colleagues were aroused, but no one knew quite how to tackle the trade problem. Were we prepared to advance an alternative trade policy?

The train ride began the Democrats' three-year journey toward enactment of a national trade policy. Back in the nation's capital, Jim Wright convinced retiring Speaker Tip O'Neill to appoint a Democratic trade task force. The twenty-one-member panel was broadly representative of committees with jurisdiction on trade and every region of the country. Membership ranged from ardent free traders to self-described protectionists, which made consensus a difficult goal. The Speaker appointed me chairman and Congressman Sam Gibbons of Florida, the respected chairman of the Ways and Means Trade Subcommittee, vice chairman.

It took six months for the task force to hammer out a sweeping trade plan. The October 1985 report, *A Democratic Program for Trade,* identified the major trade problems facing our nation, compared the positions of the Reagan administration and Democrats, and offered the most detailed and comprehensive legislative proposal to date.[24]

The task force somehow managed to resist the temptation of resorting to quick fixes to protect domestic jobs and instead charted a long-term competitiveness strategy. According to the *Los Angeles Times,* the report "contained none of the tariffs and quotas included in several earlier trade bills" and hinted that the Democrats were backing away from the "protectionist position embraced by their leaders."[25]

In many ways, hammering out the framework of the package was the easy part. The bill still had to overcome hurdles that had doomed previous bills of such magnitude—complicated House procedures and multiple committees, each jealously guarding its own jurisdiction. Even if a bill emerged from this procedural gauntlet, it might still face protectionist amendments on the House floor, which could spell a presidential veto or complicate Senate consideration.

To avoid jurisdictional disputes and other problems, the Speaker assembled the principal committee chairmen in his office and directed them to report out separate bills by the week of 5 May. The Majority Leader's office was charged with resolving any differences and packaging the bill for debate on the House floor.

With the procedural roadblocks cleared, the eight major committees with trade jurisdiction met the Speaker's deadline. The Trade and International Economic Reform Act of 1986, introduced by Jim Wright on 9 May 1986, was a 458-page document covering nearly every aspect of the trade and competitiveness issue.

To enhance U.S. exports, the bill increased export promotion and export financing programs and outlined steps to bring down the overvalued dollar. To deal with unfair trade barriers overseas, the bill tightened up U.S. trade laws. To promote long-term competitiveness, the bill increased funding for education, job training, and research.

The so-called Gephardt amendment, which mandated import restrictions on countries whose "excessive trade surpluses" were caused by "unjustifiable or discriminatory" trade practices, quickly became the most controversial aspect of the bill. Under this formula, at least four countries would be singled out for retaliatory action: Japan, South Korea, Taiwan, and West Germany. The Gephardt language called for negotiations and gave the President the ability to waive restrictions if they harmed U.S. economic interests but the amendment was nonetheless labeled protectionist by its critics.

As the bill moved toward House consideration, various members proposed protectionist amendments covering everything from lumber to lambs. These were rejected by the House Rules Committee, preventing an orgy of protectionism during floor debate on the trade bill.

Meanwhile, the Republicans were mapping their own strategy. Their trade package, issued on 8 October 1985, paralleled the Democrats' bill in many respects but stopped short of measures to force Executive Branch action against nations that maintain import barriers.

In late May 1986, after five days of House debate, the Democratic package passed virtually intact. GOP attacks on specific provisions attracted few supporters, and the Republican substitute was rejected by a vote of 145–265. On final passage, 59 Republicans deserted their President, providing a decisive 295–115 vote in favor of the omnibus trade bill.

Predictably, the Reagan administration viewed the House-passed bill as an affront to its trade policies. During the week the House debated trade legislation, the White House announced a flurry of new "get tough" trade actions. It blasted Brazil's informatics policy of protecting its computer industry, then threatened to place a 200 percent tariff on European pasta and cheese unless the pasta-citrus dispute was resolved, and finally dusted off a three-year-old case involving U.S. machine tool manufacturers to show it was getting tough with Japan. On the day of the vote, the President slapped a 35 percent tariff on Canadian shakes and shingle products, but House members were not impressed. Despite the volley of trade actions and heavy lobbying by President Reagan and his cabinet officers, the House of Representatives went its own way.

President Reagan wasted no time in attacking the House bill. In a speech before the National Association of Manufacturers (NAM), he called it "kamikaze legislation that would take their jobs down in flames . . . an ominous antitrade bill that could send our economy into the steepest nose dive since the Great Depression." He warned that "the reactionary legislation would force the American consumers to pay billions in higher prices, throw millions of Americans out of work, and strangle our economy as foreign markets slam shut in retaliation." He called the trade bill "destructionism" and "defeatism" and pledged a veto when it reached his desk.[26]

This was a 180-degree turn from the days of his predecessor and hero, Calvin Coolidge, whose party platform declared, "We reaffirm our belief in the protective tariff as a fundamental and essential principle of the economic life of this nation."[27]

Ironically, the President's NAM speech received a lukewarm, if not skeptical reception from industrialists. The chairman of that organization's trade committee, R. E. Hecket, CEO of E. I. du Pont de Nemours, said the flurry of administration trade actions during House debate on the legislation "reflects the continuing dynamics of trade policy in our government: Congress acts, the Administration reacts." After the President's speech, NAM's president, Sandy Trowbridge, added, "For all its faults, the House bill makes this important contribution to U.S. policy. It recognizes that the United States has an enormous trade problem of special concern to manufacturers."[28]

But President Reagan's position was supported by the nation's leading newspapers, which took special delight in lampooning the trade bill. Editorial headlines read, "Take That, Foreigners!" and "A Shin-Kicker Bill." The *Wall Street Journal* labeled it "outrageously protectionist," the *Washington Post* described it as "an anthology of Congressional grievances and irritations," and the *New York Times* said, "It would shoot American consumers in the foot." The *Times* went on to say "The enthusiastic support the proposal has received shows how myopia and mediocrity mar Congressional thinking about trade" and concluded, "Like soldiers refighting old wars, we snipe and dodge and plot to teach the wily foreigners a lesson. Meanwhile, the political and economic institutions that insure our prosperity grow feeble from lack of exercise."[29]

With House action on a trade bill completed in May 1986, the spotlight turned to the Republican-controlled Senate. Unlike the House, which had developed a process to ensure orderly consideration and passage of trade legislation in 1986, the Senate had little direction from its leaders and no enthusiasm for confronting the White House on a trade bill.

Thus, the Ninety-ninth Congress ended without Senate action on trade legislation. Senator Lloyd Bentsen of Texas, the ranking Democrat of the Finance Committee, told the *Washington Post* on 26 September, "It's a real shame the Senate has failed to act this year. It will be easier to pass and demand a trade bill next year because of the enormity of that trade deficit."[30]

When the One Hundredth Congress convened in January 1987, the political landscape had changed. Democrats controlled both the House and the Senate. House Speaker Jim Wright and Senate Majority Leader Robert Byrd of West Virginia both proclaimed trade the number one legislative issue for the session. Republicans, frustrated over escalating trade deficits and impatient with White House inaction, were also eager to address the issue.

The House began work immediately. The bill number assigned to the Trade and International Economic Policy Reform Act of 1987, H.R. 3, signified its high priority with the House leadership. The bill was nearly identical to the package that had cleared the House the previous year, sparing committees the grind of formulating new legislation.

Like the 1986 trade bill, the 1987 version included a number of provisions aimed at toughening U.S. trade laws, limiting the President's discretion, dismantling unnecessary restrictions on high-tech exports, increasing U.S. export promotion, and improving our education, training, and trade adjustment programs.

The bill once again contained several items the Reagan administration wanted, such as renewed negotiating authority for the new round of international trade talks, strengthened protection of U.S. intellectual property rights, and language to seek agreements that would achieve "fully competitive market opportunities" for U.S. telecommunications exporters and their subsidiaries.

There was one major distinction. Chairman Dan Rostenkowski of the Ways and Means Committee preempted his colleague Dick Gephardt on the issue that had dominated the debate the previous year. The chairman adopted a provision very similar to the 1986 Gephardt language that singled out countries which engaged in "a pattern of unjustifiable, unreasonable or discriminatory trade policies" and enjoyed "excessive trade surpluses" against the United States, but his proposed penalty stopped short of protectionism.

As in the earlier Gephardt amendment, these countries would be subject to short-term negotiations aimed at lowering their trade barriers. If the talks failed, the President could reduce imports from these nations, but only *by an amount equal to their documented unfair trade practices.* It was clearly a coup for Chairman Rostenkowski. By adopting much of Gephardt's language but limiting the potential sanctions to a legitimate level, he defused the opposition to the Democratic trade bill.

At the same time, Gephardt and his allies were developing a "new" Gephardt amendment, which was nearly identical to the Rostenkowski provision except for one critical feature. Once a nation was targeted by the bill's formula, Gephardt's new amendment mandated a 10 percent annual reduction in America's trade deficit with that nation for the next five years. While Gephardt defended the new language as necessary "verification" for tough trade action, others objected to the arbitrary standard of punishment. "Gephardt II" quickly became an easy target for the President, the press, and other critics of the trade bill.

Debate on the House floor paralleled the arguments that had been tossed around the year before. Once again the most visible controversy was over the Gephardt amendment. After intense debate and heavy lobbying on both sides, the House adopted the new Gephardt amendment by a razor-thin 218–214 vote.

The House proceeded to pass the Trade and International Economic Policy Reform Act on 30 April 1987 by a vote of 290 to 137, easily surpassing the margin needed to override a presidential veto.

Once again, the ball was in the Senate court. Unlike 1986, however, with the leadership of Majority Leader Byrd and Senator Lloyd Bentsen, the Senate was ready to act. To speed things up, many Senate committees borrowed liberally from the House bill.

While the Senate crafted language to put more bite into the nation's trade laws, it stopped short of approving a Gephardt-type amendment. Instead, it embraced a bipartisan proposal to require action against countries whose trade policies violate international trade agreements. The Senate rejected any triggering mechanism based on a country's excessive surpluses and relied on existing procedures to carry out sanctions against an offending country.

When the bill reached the Senate floor, a number of amendments were added, including over one hundred offered on the final day's action. The Senate adopted provisions requiring plant closing notification and modifying windfall profits taxes and a number of sector-specific measures, many strongly opposed by the Reagan administration.

In the end, however, the Senate omnibus trade bill won approval by a convincing 71–27 vote, with 19 Republicans and 52 Democrats voting in favor of the bill. The administration's hope for 34 GOP no votes never materialized.

Never before had a Senate-House conference faced such a wide-ranging piece of legislation. Each bill totaled close to one thousand pages. Over two hundred conferees from twenty different committees were assembled to hammer out the differences between the two bills, making the conference itself a logistical nightmare.

The sheer complexity of the bill and the scope of the conference made final action difficult in 1987. After efforts to curb the budget deficit intensified following the stock market crash in October, time simply ran out before Congress could finish its work on the Omnibus Trade bill in 1987.

When Congress reconvened in 1988, House and Senate conferees tackled the trade bill with renewed vigor. In short order, many controversial items were removed from the bill or greatly modified.

The House leadership delayed final resolution of the Gephardt Amendment until after the March 7 Super Tuesday primaries, out of deference to the Missouri lawmaker's presidential campaign. Although Gephardt did not fare well on Super Tuesday, the decision to drop his provision from the trade bill actually had been made weeks earlier.

While the conferees resolved most of the President's concerns about the bill, Congress refused to yield on one provision: plant closure notification. This section of the trade bill, originally added by the Senate, required large firms to give their workers sixty days advance notice before a plant closing or mass layoff.

Supporters of the provision pointed out that organized labor had lost nearly every section of the trade bill they cared about except plant closure, but opponents howled that the new requirements would place an unfair burden on American firms. President Reagan vowed to veto the entire 1100-page trade bill over this single provision.

Once the conferees had hammered out the differences between the two bills, both the House and Senate had to approve the final version. Passage was virtually guaranteed in both chambers; the real question was the size of the margin. Could the House and Senate both muster more than the two-thirds necessary to override the anticipated veto by the President?

The House left no doubt with an overwhelming 312–107 vote,

which saw 68 Republicans desert their leadership to support the bill.

The Senate, however, was the real battleground. After four days of highly charged debate and intense behind-the-scenes lobbying, the bill passed 63–36. The victory was misleading, for the margin fell 4 votes short of the 67 needed to override a veto.

True to his word, President Reagan vetoed the bill, largely because of his opposition to the plant closure notification provision. On the very same day, the House overrode the veto by a comfortable margin, but the Senate faced a much more difficult battle.

The President's veto confronted congressional leaders with an extremely difficult dilemma. Some felt the need for a trade bill was so great that Congress should strip out the plant closure notification provision and send the President a clean bill. Others reviled at this suggestion, saying Congress had already met the President more than halfway, by dropping major parts of the trade bill which the White House opposed. A few wanted to use the President's inaction on trade and insensitivity to displaced workers as a political issue in the November elections.

Whether or not Congress and the President reached an accommodation, the three-year odyssey of the trade bill illustrates that Congress can approach a complex and emotional issue like trade in a far-sighted, responsible way. It also demonstrates how ideological differences can undermine a bipartisan effort to deal with a national economic crisis.

The differing agenda between the White House and Congress, and within Congress itself, delayed passage of a badly needed trade bill for three years. During that same three years, the United States had piled up $450 billion in trade deficits, millions of Americans had been denied job opportunities, and our nation had fallen further into industrial decline.

The Road to Competitiveness

If the road for Republicans has been from protectionism and for Democrats from free trade, it appears that both these familiar paths are no longer comfortable routes. The dilemma for Republicans and Democrats alike in the late 1980s is how to deal with unfair trading practices and pry open foreign markets. Party leaders, heeding the warning signs ahead, prefer to find new and more appealing directions to deal with the trade crisis. Trade will continue to be a dominant national issue in the future, but the debate has been altered as congressional leaders look for a common ground. For Democrats and Republicans alike, the new road leads to competitiveness.

Even the Reagan White House, after two years of confrontation with Congress, has signaled a more pragmatic approach that would emphasize competitiveness. The new strategy, endorsed by the cabinet-level Economic Policy Commission, includes trade adjustment assistance for workers displaced by imports and a program to revamp government aid for research and development. The administration hoped that offering its own trade proposal might pave the way for some of its priorities and make it a player in the deliberations on Capitol Hill.

The more time that elapsed without comprehensive action on the trade deficit, the more political pressure on Congress intensified. The two political parties have traveled far from their earlier positions on trade and tariff issues, but neither has any clear direction for the future. Competitiveness may be appealing, but it is only a vague long-term goal, not a detailed immediate solution. The U.S. public may press for a short-term fix if restoring our long-term competitiveness takes too long. Meanwhile, world leaders watch anxiously as U.S. policymakers map their route for the remainder of the twentieth century.

FIVE

Perils of Protectionism

FROM HIS "election" to the United States Senate by the Utah legislature in 1903 until his surprise defeat thirty years later, Republican Reed Smoot was a major figure in some of the more bizarre political events of the twentieth century.

Smoot arrived in Washington, D.C., in February 1903, expecting to take his seat in the Senate, only to discover that he was the subject of national controversy. A citizens' protest sparked by church groups accused the senator-elect of polygamy and other criminal activities. The protest was rooted in the newly elected senator's Mormon faith, which, at the time, permitted polygamy. The conflict surrounding Smoot quickly captured the attention of the entire nation. After a lengthy congressional investigation and prolonged debate, Reed Smoot was finally seated in the U.S. Senate on 20 February 1907, exactly one day before the fourth anniversary of his arrival in the nation's capital. Few people now recall Smoot's controversial beginning in the Senate, but his name lives on as cosponsor of the Smoot-Hawley Tariff Act.

Smoot served during an era of relative prosperity in the United States. Except for a brief depression in 1921 and the traumatic effects of World War I on American agriculture, the economy grew steadily throughout the 1920s. But there were early warning signs of catastrophic events to come.[1] The primary basis for the nation's favorable economy at the time was the high level of U.S. production, which accounted for nearly half the world's manufacturing activity. Underlying the eight-year stretch of prosperity was investment of record proportions, which made America's greatest building boom in history possible.

While the 1920s were good years for the country as a whole, prosperity was unevenly distributed. The huge investment that primed the domestic economy finally became saturated. As P. T. Ellsworth wrote in *The International Economy:*

> The capacity of the automobile industry to produce cars by 1929 far exceeded its ability to sell them. The tire industry, too, was overbuilt. Many other producers of durable goods, washing machines, vacuum cleaners, radios, faced a similar situation, and encountered serious sales resistance in 1929. Ever since the beginning of 1928, residential construction had been falling off sharply.[2]

Economic problems were most acute in the nation's farming country. High postwar demand meant higher prices and rising production from 1917 to 1920. These eventually led to surpluses and depressed prices. The United States found itself competing with countries such as Europe, Canada, and Argentina in a world of export surpluses and sagging markets. The resulting foreclosures marred thousands of lives in rural America.

By 1929, agrarian protectionism was on the rise. Farmers were resentful that they were not sharing in the general prosperity of the 1920s. If manufacturing could benefit from a little import relief, farmers reasoned, perhaps they, too, could prosper from some tariff protection. The farmers in the rural West wanted as much protection as that afforded the industrial East.

By the late twenties, the farming problem developed as a serious issue among Republican leaders. Herbert Hoover stressed agricultural tariffs in the 1928 campaign and, on taking office, convened a special session of Congress to consider the issue. While Hoover hoped to limit tariffs to only those farming and manufacturing sectors which were seriously depressed, the door to protectionism was opened. Senators and congressmen seized the occasion to help their constituents. Wholesale vote trading was rampant so that elected leaders could be sure they got on the tariff bandwagon that was moving through Congress. What began as a surgical treatment to assist a few ailing industries turned into free-for-all plundering that went on for a year.

The climate was right for Congress to run amok. Special-interest groups quickly formed national lobbies to push for relief before congressional committees. As one observer noted, "Within recent years these groups have increased and multiplied. More important still, they have become highly organized and are today conducted by shrewd and capable leaders."[3]

New trade associations were formed to promote special legislative treatment for their members. The Chamber of Commerce took the lead in mobilizing businesses to be more politically involved. According to a 1925 Department of Commerce report, over fifteen hundred specialized lobbying groups were organized to represent products and industries in the nation's capital.[4] Commodity interests set up associations to give the farm community better representation. Ordinary working people had a say too, for organized labor emerged as a major political force in the 1920s. Contemporary authors agreed that the actions of lobbyists and special interests were largely responsible for pushing Congress to adopt the tariffs.

The stage was set. As the economy deteriorated and special-interest groups were poised for action, the House Ways and Means Committee and the Senate Finance Committee took up the tariff bill in 1930. On the House side, the Republicans, led by Willis C. Hawley of Oregon, controlled the committee and the process. They created fifteen subcommittees of three to consider a particular tariff schedule—textiles, metals, chemicals.[5] Each member gravitated to the subcommittee that reflected his constituents' interests. What followed was an unbridled frenzy of log-rolling, each member letting the others have their way, provided his own proposals were not interfered with. The resulting bill contained specific tariff schedules for more than twenty thousand products.

The Senate procedure was different, but the result was much the same. Reed Smoot, chairman of the Republican-controlled Senate Finance Committee, traded support of higher tariffs on imported industrial goods for increased agricultural duties to benefit farmers in his native state. After a series of hearings, the senators met informally and drafted a tariff bill that included hundreds of amendments to the House legislation. Once the bill hit the Senate floor, there was no holding back the stampede as more than twelve hundred amendments were eventually adopted.[6]

"I might suggest that we have taxed everything in the bill except gall," Senator Thaedeus H. Caraway, an Arkansas Democrat, told his colleagues.

"Yes," Senator Carter Glass, a Virginia Democrat, replied, "and a tax on that would bring considerable revenue."

In the end, they all got what they wanted. Congress showed no restraint and the President didn't try to curb the excesses. While he asked for "limited revision" on a tariff measure, President Hoover exerted no leadership in checking the process that clearly was out of control, nor did he threaten a veto if the final product were unsatisfactory. The result, said one senator, was the "worst tariff bill in the nation's history."

Satisfied that there was nothing left to add to the bill, Congress sent the voluminous document to the President for his signature.

Alarmed that such a bill had passed Congress, 1028 of the nation's leading economists signed a petition urging President Hoover to veto the measure. Printed in the *New York Times* on

5 May 1930, it carried signatures from 46 states and 179 universities.[7]

Economists warned that imposing high duties would raise prices for American consumers and most certainly invite foreign retaliation. The President tried to mollify his critics by declaring that even though the bill imposed higher tariffs, it established explicit procedures. Having campaigned for tariffs on agricultural imports and called the special session of Congress, the President felt he had no choice but to sign the bill, and citing the Republican Party platform, he did.

In all, the ordeal took fourteen months from the time President Hoover called a special session to his signing the Smoot-Hawley Tariff Act. The record of public hearings totaled twenty thousand pages.

The new tariff schedule under Smoot-Hawley included every conceivable item, from major commodities such as wheat, textiles, and sugar to petty goods like pocketberries, tennis balls, and firecrackers. Cheap celluloid dolls faced a duty increase of 160 percent. The duty on women's leather gloves, "embroidered or embellished," went from 70 percent to 140 percent. Farm groups had their own extended line of protected goods, which included cabbages, celery, eggplant, lettuce, green peas and beans, tomatoes, clover seed, blueberries, plums, and prunes.[8]

The reaction abroad was quick and fierce. Within months, the United States' leading trading partners—Canada, France, Mexico, Italy, Spain, Cuba, Australia, and New Zealand —raised their tariffs on U.S. products. By the end of 1931, twenty-six countries had retaliated.

The Smoot-Hawley Act did more than provoke official criticism from foreign governments. Twenty thousand French lace workers marched in the streets of Calais and fifteen thousand Swiss clock- and watchmakers protested in Bienne to demonstrate worldwide disgust over the American tariff measure. Public opinion abroad heightened efforts to boycott American goods and led public officials to denounce two-way trade with America.

Senator Smoot shrugged off criticism, saying that other nations had begun to revise their tariffs even before Congress had acted. "Only the purblind egotist can suggest that the world turned to protection in retaliation against the American tariff," he wrote.[9] True, protectionist pressures were not limited to the United States, and countries had been adopting tariff increases between 1925 and 1929. But a single stroke of Herbert Hoover's pen on the Smoot-Hawley Tariff Act unleashed a tidal wave of retaliation that jeopardized international finance and trade markets.

At home, the new tariff law increased by almost half the average duty on imports, which shrank by 77 percent between 1929 and 1930. U.S. producers welcomed the protection but also felt the pain of retaliation. U.S. exports of food products, for example, dropped 66 percent.[10]

World trade plummeted by more than half of pre-1929 totals. The U.S. economy limped toward a state of paralysis, and in a matter of just a few months, the entire world trading system came to a near standstill.

Smoot-Hawley also undermined the stability of the international financial and monetary system. Financial institutions were unable to make the normal balance-of-payments adjustment because of the economic pressures caused by tariffs. Many countries had to give up their gold reserves to pay the higher duties. This added considerably to America's gold stock and strengthened the dollar but severely undermined the stability of currencies abroad. As foreign countries were pressed to defend the convertibility of their currencies because of declining reserves, they eventually went off the gold standard. The devaluation cycle of the 1930s was under way.

The disintegration of the gold standard coincided with the collapse of foreign lending, which was vital to international commerce. During the 1920s, the United States and the United

Kingdom possessed most of the lending capital, but the protectionist measures worsened the difficulties borrowing countries faced in paying their debts. Without access to capital and facing certain default, these countries could not purchase goods and services from the United States or anyone else. Since the United States was consuming nearly half the products of the leading industrial economies, it would suffer most.

The 1932 election saw the defeat of Senator Reed Smoot, Congressman William Hawley, President Herbert Hoover, and a host of others who had voted for the Smoot-Hawley Tariff Act. A report by the American Enterprise Institute has likened the Smoot-Hawley Act of 1930 to the Munich agreement of 1938: "Hailed at the time, both decisions soon betrayed their promises, and they remain indelibly imprinted on the consciousness of the world as historical errors of such magnitude that every generation of leaders has pledged to avoid repeating them."

The year 1932 was a political and economic watershed. Out went the Republican platform that extolled the virtues of protectionism, defense of the Smoot-Hawley Act for keeping agricultural prices high, and promises of high tariffs. In came the Democratic platform calling for reciprocal tariff agreements with other nations and an international conference to restore trade relations. The Democrats took firm control of the White House and Congress, laying the groundwork for dramatically innovative domestic and trade policies for the next fifty years. The Reciprocal Trade Agreements Act of 1934, framed as an amendment to the Smoot-Hawley Act, relied on bilateral negotiations with a heavy emphasis on lowering tariffs. From 1945 to 1967, the United States pushed for multilateral trade negotiations and, during the 1970s and 1980s, led efforts to harmonize and reduce non-tariff barriers. In the postwar period, successive American presidents continued to support international efforts to reduce tariff and non-tariff barriers.

Almost every president since FDR has steadfastly promoted

liberalized trade and at the same time worked to protect vital manufacturing and agricultural sectors from foreign competition. It became the custom of American presidents to embrace free trade while yielding to domestic pressures on specific cases.

That was the case when Dwight D. Eisenhower launched a new program of "voluntary" restraints on Japanese cotton textile exports and John F. Kennedy established voluntary, then mandatory, controls on oil imports. Lyndon B. Johnson found a legal way to restrict meat imports. Richard Nixon set up a series of restraints on imported steel and tighter restrictions on textiles. After the Tokyo Round of multilateral trade negotiations, Jimmy Carter further restricted steel, textiles, and footwear.

For each successive president, the goal was to ease the pain for important U.S. industries that had to cope with stiff new competition and adjust to the realities of a global economy. Steel, textiles, footwear, and automobiles are visible cases of aging industries' needing relief to stay in business or retool for new market demands. In some cases, like specialty steel, the industry may never recover, but some, like the auto industry, may again be competitive following bold changes.

For the most part, Congress avoided protectionism for fifty-five years. Content to let the Executive manage the trade front, legislators rarely invoked their constitutional power to "regulate" foreign commerce. Congressional indifference on trade matters gave way to intense interest by the 1980s, largely because of the deep recession of 1981–1982. In 1985 alone, over three hundred trade bills were introduced in the House, many of them protectionist. These bills ranged from minor tariff adjustments and trade law reforms to stiff penalties meant to protect specific industries. Their effect was to put the rest of the world on notice that political sentiment to act on the import problem was building in this nation.

As imports increased and spread throughout every part of the country, American plants shut down and workers were laid off. Bills to relieve the situation multiplied rapidly. The House Ways and Means Committee suddenly faced protectionist bills on automobiles, specialty steel, textiles, lumber, copper, footwear, and a number of agricultural goods.

Our biggest bout with protectionism since the Smoot-Hawley Act came in the second session of the Ninety-ninth Congress with the Textile and Apparel Trade Enforcement Act. The measure, adopted by wide margins in the House and Senate in late 1985, was vetoed by the President and nearly overridden in the House. Had the Congress prevailed, the United States would unilaterally have broken thirty-four trade agreements. The textile vote is vivid testimony to the strong protectionist impulses of the U.S. Congress in the 1980s.

The textile issue was extraordinary for several reasons. First, the textile and apparel industry already enjoyed considerable protection. With tariffs four times higher than the average rates for other sectors of the economy and severe import limits imposed by a complex international quota system, the industry still had difficulty competing with foreign producers. Since 1981, imported textile and apparel doubled, capturing half the U.S. market.

The textile and apparel industry was not only the most protected, it was also the most powerful. Allied with organized labor and armed with lobbyists who had clout in Washington, D.C., its members were an irresistible force in the corridors of Congress. "The textile and apparel boys have street smarts in dealing with government. Their method is to ignore GATT, ignore the existing law, ignore the International Trade Commission," said a senator who first opposed the textile bill and later voted to override the veto.

The textile vote revealed serious fault lines in the way Congress deals with trade issues. In the House, where the leadership controlled the process, no floor amendments were permitted, so members voted yes or no on a "clean" textile bill.

The system works differently in the Senate. Unable to get

action in committee, Senate sponsors tried to attach a textile amendment to bills moving to the floor until, reluctantly, Majority Leader Robert Dole of Kansas was forced to take it up for debate. Once that happened, amendments were quickly added to limit footwear imports and to negotiate limitations on worldwide production of copper. When the bill was delivered to the White House, the President, as promised, promptly vetoed the measure.

Protectionism reared its head again in 1985, when three leading Democrats proposed legislation that would impose a 25 percent import penalty on countries that had amassed trade surpluses by employing trade barriers. According to the formula devised by Senator Lloyd Bentsen and Congressmen Richard Gephardt and Dan Rostenkowski, Brazil, Japan, and Korea would be hit with the automatic import tax. At home and overseas, the reaction to the plan was fast and fierce, and the Democrats came under attack for protectionism. Eventually, all three congressmen backed away from their controversial proposal.

A later Gephardt proposal, included in the House trade bill in 1986, applied a similar formula for singling out "offending" countries, but the emphasis was on negotiations rather than mandated actions. Chairman Rostenkowski incorporated the Gephardt formula in the 1987 trade bill, forcing Gephardt to sponsor a drastic 10 percent mandated import reduction on countries that maintain excessive trade surpluses against the United States. Not all attempts at protectionism are as immediately recognizable as the textile bill or the Gephardt market-access proposals, but the effect is the same — to protect a domestic producer. Two such examples of hidden-agenda protectionist measures are import surcharges and "buy-American" requirements. The idea of imposing an import surcharge gained much congressional attention in 1985–1986 as a politically acceptable way of simultaneously shrinking the budget and trade deficits. Republican Congressman Newt Gingrich of

Georgia floated the idea of a surcharge on products from less developed countries to make up for the "advantage" they enjoy because of their lower wage rates. Conservatives like Gingrich, who back lower taxes and more spending for defense, are attracted to an import surcharge that would generate additional revenues to balance the budget without confronting other parts of the fiscal equation.

The Reagan administration also toyed with the idea of a generic import surcharge. In 1986, the President asked for an increase in Customs Service user fees, ostensibly to pay for processing costs but really designed to reduce the budget deficit. Motorola is one of several U.S. firms that endorsed the import user fee, claiming that Japan and Germany could absorb the fee, which would help make U.S. products more price competitive at home. Industry officials felt that a surcharge could easily be absorbed by our trading partners and provide revenue at the same time.

How do you distinguish between a backdoor tariff and legitimate Customs fees? The General Agreement on Tariffs and Trade does not allow tariff surcharges beyond the costs of administering normal port and Customs fees, and it specifically prohibits Customs fee taxes' fiscally benefiting the budget. Support for an import tax will gain momentum as Congress copes with structural budget deficits. However, once such a tariff is imposed, it would be extremely difficult to remove, since it must be offset by spending cuts or tax revenue from other sources.

Another form of protectionism evoking nationalistic sentiment is buy-American provisions in appropriations bills. Proponents try to rationalize these restrictions as merely requiring the U.S. government to spend its tax dollars at home, but buy-American requirements are nonetheless a form of protectionism. The U.S. government itself assails buy-at-home provisions of foreign governments as an unfair trade practice. Congressional sponsors of buy-American amendments rarely talk about "protecting" U.S. producers; instead, they emphasize keeping government purchases at home. Behind the rhetoric, however, one can usually find a specific industry that would directly benefit from government protection.

In the United States' first two hundred years, trade policy consisted mostly of tariffs that increased or decreased, depending on Congress's state of mind at any given time. Traditionally, tariffs were used as a means of raising revenue for the country. Until enactment of corporate and personal income taxes, tariffs were the principal source of revenue for the national treasury.

The Smoot-Hawley Tariff Act of 1930 was designed not to raise revenue, but to "protect" threatened domestic producers; the threat came less from foreign imports than the approaching depression. Today, import restrictions are being used or considered for a variety of reasons—to shield local industries, to protect workers and communities from the pain of unemployment, to promote national security, to pry open other markets, to raise money for deficit reduction, to counter subsidies and dumping practices. While many of these are laudable goals, in the eyes of other nations it all spells protectionism.

The term "protectionism" is always present in the political debate on trade, and its use is often fuzzy. Leaders in both political parties have flirted with protectionism, but the label has stuck with the Democrats in the wake of Walter Mondale's endorsement of the domestic-content legislation in the 1984 presidential election and the proposal by some Democrats to slap import restrictions on countries that maintain trade barriers while running up big surpluses with the United States. Ronald Reagan's attacks on the Democratic trade bill in 1986 helped to polarize the debate on trade and competitiveness issues.

What is and is not protectionism has not been properly defined. Legislatively imposed or industry-specific import restrictions are obviously protectionist, but there is no standard on what constitutes protectionism when a country tries to use retaliation to pry open foreign markets. A credible and widely accepted definition of protectionism is badly needed. Not only would it clarify the debate on trade policy, but it could set appropriate parameters for the Congress and the President in dealing responsibly with trade issues. A definition would minimize confusion within the Congress and abroad on the intentions and policies of the U.S. government.

An implicit definition of protectionism can be found in a variety of existing laws that allow the President to impose sanctions on goods from other nations for a variety of reasons. For example, Congress has given the President authority to restrict imports to protect U.S. national security, to give a limited number of import-ravaged industries temporary relief, and to combat foreign subsidies or unfair pricing schemes that distort the U.S. market. These non-protectionist trade procedures do not clearly describe what constitutes protectionist action, but they can help to shape our definition.

As the One Hundredth Congress convened, members appeared to be backing away from a protectionist mentality in favor of export promotion and competitiveness. But legislative leaders did little to ease fears of protectionism. Political sentiment for protecting import-scarred industries or increasing revenues at the borders was well established in both the Senate and House.

The ghost of Smoot-Hawley is enough to frighten any free trader, but most of today's congressional leaders have scant memory of the damaging effects of earlier protectionism. Legitimate concerns about America's industrial decline and the hardships facing our workers could tempt our political leaders to take hasty and ill-conceived actions. A turn toward protectionism would hurt our own economy in the long run and put America on a collision course with the needs of a peaceful global community.

SIX

Tensions with Trading Partners

THE UNITED STATES has avoided an all-out trade war, but fierce competition and economic strains threaten our relations with a number of countries. Along our northern border, efforts to negotiate a free-trade agreement with Canada highlighted the serious trade frictions between the two countries. Across the Atlantic, tense negotiations have been necessary to defuse confrontations over Europe's trade and economic policies. In Asia, unfair trade practices and dynamic growth have created lopsided trade imbalances and sparked calls in Congress for retaliation. The Latin American debt crisis threatens economic ties throughout the hemisphere.

Trade tensions are inevitable in today's world, given the contradictory goals of individual nations and the intense political pressures world leaders face at home. How the United States deals with these tensions will test our nation's bilateral relations and shape the economy we leave for our children.

Europe: All Is *Not* Quiet on the Western Front

When six European nations gathered in Rome in 1957 to create a more unified Europe, the United States heartily endorsed the idea. We had no idea that thirty years later, a twelve-nation European Community (EC) would be such a formidable competitor, restricting our sales in the European market and elbowing our firms out of traditional markets in other parts of the world. Despite our political, legal, and cultural bonds, the United States and the European Community are constantly at each other's throats when it comes to trade policy.

Our trade with Europe in 1986 totaled $132.6 billion, roughly one fifth of all U.S. trade, but the United States posted a $26 billion trade deficit. When you consider that we had a $19 billion trade *surplus* in 1980, our falling trade balance with Europe has actually outpaced our growing imbalance with Japan. Europe's share of America's exports has fallen from 35 percent to 18 percent, and Europe is capturing many of our former markets around the world.

U.S. policymakers blame the European Community's subsidy policies for upsetting the trade equilibrium in agriculture, aircraft manufacturing, and numerous other goods. Europeans view U.S. free-trade statements as largely hypocritical, pointing to our own agricultural and defense-related subsidies, our budget deficits that distort currency values, and our occasional imposition of tariffs or quotas.

One of the largest areas of dispute is agricultural policy. Both sides have a history of generously subsidizing their farmers through production incentives, protective tariffs, and, more recently, targeted export subsidies. Today's oversupply of basic foodstuffs has both sides fighting to unload their surplus wheat, corn, sugar, and dairy products in the few remaining world markets.

The European Community's aggressive policies have upset the world's supply-demand equilibrium, largely at U.S. expense. In many commodities, Europe has displaced the United States as the dominant producer.

· EC wheat and flour exports have increased fivefold during the past 14 years, to an estimated 17 million metric tons in 1984–1985. It is now the world's third largest wheat exporter.
· The EC has gone from a net importer of white sugar in 1976–1977 to the world's largest exporter today, with exports totaling 5.4 million metric tons in 1986.
· Prior to 1973–1974, the EC was a net importer of beef and veal. Today the EC is the world's largest exporter.
· In poultry meat, the EC has moved from being the world's largest importer in the mid-1960s to the world's largest exporter, now accounting for 36 percent of world poultry trade.
· The EC is the world's largest dairy exporter, accounting for 60 percent of the trade. EC imports of processed fruit and vegetable products today are negligible, while exports of canned fruit are penetrating foreign markets.
· The EC is now the world's largest egg exporter, shipping 2.7 billion eggs in 1984. Prior to 1967, Europe was the world's largest egg importer.[1]

While new technology and better marketing have helped to improve Europe's export picture, it's the lavish subsidies that keep its inefficient farmers protected at home and successful in international markets. Over 80 percent of the EC budget goes for the Common Agricultural Policy, which provides a wide range of subsidies and coordinates farm policy among the twelve nations.[2]

The Common Agricultural Policy guarantees European farmers prices that exceed world market levels. If a commodity's market price drops, the government intervenes to purchase domestic production and bolster prices. European farmers are also protected from cheaper foreign imports by a variable levy system that raises prices for consumers.

These policies have stimulated excess production and massive surpluses of butter, sugar, grains, wine, olive oil, and milk powder. The stockpiles must be disposed of outside the European Community through subsidized exports. Not surprisingly, the EC has become the world's second largest agricultural exporter, displacing the United States in many Third World markets.[3]

By 1986, economic conditions worldwide had set the stage for confrontation. A long-simmering trade dispute over citrus fruit brought the issue to a head. For seventeen years, the United States had objected to the EC's preferential treatment of citrus from Mediterranean countries. Finally, the United States announced that it was imposing hefty import fees on European pasta. Angry European officials retaliated with additional tariffs on U.S. limes and walnuts. After months of intense negotiations and the near collapse of ongoing trade talks, an agreement was reached in late 1986 that guaranteed improved market access to U.S. citrus growers in exchange for withdrawal of the new tariffs on European pasta.

No sooner had the citrus-pasta controversy been settled than trade negotiators confronted an even knottier problem. Spain and Portugal joined the European Community in January 1986. Since EC policy requires member countries to purchase commodities from other EC nations, tariffs on many of our major exports to Spain and Portugal jumped from 20 percent to as high as 140 percent. The stakes were high. The two nations represented a $1 billion market for U.S. farmers.[4]

The Reagan administration, after repeated warnings, announced that it would sharply increase duties, up to 200 percent, on a host of European products, including wine, spirits, and specialty cheeses. French brandy producers and British gin distillers were high on the list of targets.[5]

EC Commissioner Willy DeClercq denounced the American action and promised equivalent measures on U.S. corn, gluten, feed, wheat, and rice. Only a last-ditch postponement of the retaliatory measures gave negotiators enough time to work out a truce that permitted U.S. producers limited access to Spanish and Portuguese markets and lowered EC tariffs on other products covering about $40 million in U.S. exports.

While the United States and Europe managed to defuse these crises, agricultural trade conflicts will undoubtedly continue as long as both sides subsidize overproduction and protect their producers. The two agricultural giants are in a no-holds-barred struggle to dominate what's left of the world market.

As one British diplomat observed, there is something quaintly charming about the ongoing U.S.-European battles over farm policy. The antagonists resemble two incurable alcoholics propping each other up while discoursing vehemently on the virtues of temperance. As with most addictions, there is little hope for cure short of a total commitment to reform, which is unlikely given the strong farm lobbies on both sides and the degree of mutual mistrust.

Our negotiators have also been tested by disputes over such nonagricultural commodities as aircraft, steel, machine tools, and telecommunications equipment. The commercial aircraft industry is one of the few remaining sectors in which the United States maintains a favorable trade position, but our firms cannot compete for long against predatory pricing in world markets.

While our major aerospace firms are private companies like Boeing and McDonnell Douglas, the European Community nations have pooled their resources to form Airbus, a giant government-supported aerospace consortium. The stakes are high on both sides. By the year 2000, the civilian aircraft market is projected at $222 billion in sales.[6]

For years, Airbus has enjoyed heavy government support. Billions of dollars of public funds have been poured into design and production of its aircraft over the years. Until a recent "gentlemen's agreement" between the United States and the European Community, Airbus had relied upon government-subsidized below-market loans to undercut U.S. manufacturers and win lucrative contracts.

Even with settlement of the export financing problem, Airbus continues to enjoy sweeping production subsidies. U.S. manufacturers complain bitterly about below-market loans to Airbus by European governments for capital investment and operating expenses and the lack of any concrete timetable for repayment of that assistance. Without a payment schedule, Airbus is free to overproduce aircraft, then slash prices—even below construction costs—to maintain employment. Europeans counter that Pentagon defense contracts are a form of subsidy that provides U.S. aircraft manufacturers with a constant stream of avionics improvements and design ideas, but this indirect support pales in comparison to the $10 to $15 billion in direct subsidies enjoyed by Airbus.[7]

While U.S. negotiators have succeeded in curbing subsidized financing on aircraft sales, Europe's export financing practices are a pervasive problem in most other high-priced, capital-intensive sectors. For years, European governments have used mixed credits or tied aid to give their firms a strategic advantage, especially in the developing world.

The process is simple: when firms from two or more nations are bidding on a large contract, the European nations offer a foreign-aid grant or concessionary financing to sweeten the package and win contracts that otherwise would go to American bidders.

The United States has always opposed the use of mixed credits and has rarely used foreign-aid money to advance its commercial opportunities abroad. U.S. government officials have complained, negotiated, threatened, and pleaded with European countries to end the practice, but our efforts have been ignored. Finally, in 1983, Congress set up its own mixed-credit program, combining foreign aid with direct loans from the Export-Import Bank to enable our exporters to compete on roughly equal footing with European firms.

The United States and Europe are also sparring over broader economic policies. The United States particularly resents West Germany's tight-fisted, slow-growth policies that hold domestic consumption down but stimulate their export industries. Conversely, European leaders constantly harp on U.S. budget deficits that affect foreign investments and currency values and accuse both Congress and the President of protectionist actions.

Taken individually, each of these trade disputes represents a serious but manageable threat to U.S.-European relations. Taken together, they signal real trouble ahead for the Western alliance. Continuing trade imbalances, government subsidies, and growth differentials could erupt into an all-out trade war, especially if there is a worldwide recession. Small trade skirmishes could trigger retaliation, leading to major conflicts. It will take extraordinary diplomatic skills and all our deeply rooted cultural ties to avert a major trade crisis.

Leaders on both sides of the Atlantic need to recall the good counsel of Jean Monnet, architect of the European union, who cautioned, "Nothing would be more dangerous than confusing difficulties with failure."[8]

Canada: Free-Trade Zone or Trade Combat Zone?

After negotiating tirelessly for months, U.S. and Canadian officials finally agreed on a free-trade pact that would substantially reduce tariffs on both sides of the border. The formal agreement was submitted to the Congress and the Canadian Parliament for what was expected to be fiery debate between the free traders and protectionists in both countries.

The year was 1911.

The give-and-take in the U.S. House of Representatives was punctuated by laughter and applause, as well as heated exchanges. Congressman Champ Clark of Missouri, soon to be Speaker of the House and always one of its most colorful orators, portrayed the trade accord as something more than lower tariffs and expanded markets.

"I am for it," intoned Clark, "because I hope to see the day when the American flag will float over every square foot of the British–North American possessions clear to the North Pole."[9]

When news of Clark's speech hit Canada, the agreement was doomed. The Canadian Parliament rejected the proposal with a vengeance, and the opposition party rode to power in the following election with the slogan "No Truck nor Trade with the Yankees."[10]

Champ Clark's "manifest destiny" speech is now a footnote in U.S. history, but Canada's latent fears of free and equal trade were revived in 1985 when the two nations' leaders met in Quebec City to launch a new initiative on trade cooperation.

President Ronald Reagan and Prime Minister Brian Mulroney, both popular conservatives of Irish ancestry, signed a communiqué on Saint Patrick's Day that pledged the two countries to achieve a free-trade agreement. The two leaders instructed their trade ministers to pursue negotiations "to reduce and eliminate existing barriers to trade" at a time when irritating trade disputes threatened to turn the proposed free-trade zone into a combat zone along the three-thousand-mile border.[11] In time, their respective positions on trade would cost them in popularity, but each steadfastly clung to the idea of free and open trade between the two nations.

U.S.-Canadian free trade has been an elusive goal for over a century. The two countries had the equivalent of a free-trade arrangement during the period of "reciprocity" from 1854 to 1863. Canada fought a landmark election over free trade in 1911, when its Liberal Party went down to defeat over the issue. Periodic attempts to secure a free-trade agreement occurred in the late 1930s and early postwar years. In 1944, Prime Minister Mackenzie King negotiated an agreement to end tariffs, phase out quotas, and set up a bilateral commission but later lost his nerve to follow through, doubtlessly looking back to what had happened in 1911.

The Shamrock summit in 1985 marked the first time in forty years that the two sides had seriously considered efforts to level the playing field across the border. While tariff barriers have been declining over time, non-tariff barriers, subsidies, and retaliatory actions have alarmed leaders in both capitals. Escalating trade irritants, plus their own irrepressible optimism, launched Reagan and Mulroney on a free-trade mission against the odds of history.

The risks were high on both sides. United States trade with Canada in 1987 totaled $131 billion, compared with $116 billion with Japan and $145 billion with the European Community. In 1984–1985, Canada bought 22 percent of U.S. exports, nearly twice the level sold to Japan. Fully 80 percent of Canadian exports are destined for U.S. markets. Merchandise exports constitute 25 percent of Canada's GNP, making the Canadian economy heavily dependent on the U.S. domestic market.[12]

Within two such large and integrated economies, trade problems are bound to occur. America's $20 billion trade deficit with Canada in 1986 was larger, on a per capita basis, than our shortfall with Japan. In recent years, trade disputes have involved a variety of sectoral areas — wood products, live swine, malt beverages, corn, fish, and potatoes and other vegetables. Canadians dislike U.S. trade remedy laws that permit our industries to seek import relief against unfair trade practices. U.S. firms are testy over what they feel are subsidies that give Canadian producers an advantage on both sides of the border.

Both countries are feeling the pressures of a more competitive global economy. The economic tidal waves from across the Pacific are battering all North American manufacturers. Canadian and U.S. farmers alike feel the pain of European agricultural subsidies, shrinking markets in developing countries, and depressed prices.

Trade problems mounted in the early 1980s as the U.S. trade deficit soared and our competitive position declined. The strong dollar gave Canada and other foreign exporters a larger share of the U.S. market while U.S. exporters were losing ground abroad. U.S. producers could do little about exchange rates, so many petitioned government agencies for relief through tariffs on Canadian imports. U.S. remedy laws permit such action if the government determines that subsidies, dumping, or certain other unfair trade practices are the cause of the injury.

Facing the prospect of numerous countervailing tariffs and recurring calls for protectionism in the U.S. Congress, Canadians feared their sizable U.S. market share might be jeopardized. Canadian officials felt a bilateral accord might be the best way to protect their access to the U.S. market. On the U.S. side, the idea was met with indifference, except as to how such an agreement would affect pending import relief petitions.

On both sides, the largest issue involved Canadian lumber exports to the United States. By 1985, Canadian mills had captured over 30 percent of the U.S. market at a time when U.S. mills were facing hard times. From 1977 to 1984, more than 600 U.S. lumber mills shut down, throwing 30,000 people out of work. By contrast, 85 new mills were opened in Canada.[13] While the strong dollar and the decline in U.S. housing starts both were partly responsible, industry representatives charged that Canadian provinces were subsidizing their timber industry, giving them an unfair advantage in the U.S. domestic market.

In 1982, a small segment of the U.S. timber industry took its case to our federal government, arguing that the provinces owned over 90 percent of the timber and sold cutting rights to Canadian timber companies at far below the market value. The industry asked for a 30 percent tariff or countervailing duty to compensate for the value of the Canadian subsidy. While the International Trade Commission ruled that Canadian imports were indeed damaging U.S. lumber mills, the Department of Commerce ruled that subsidy was not a major factor.

Over the next few years, the Canadian share of the U.S. market continued to increase. As a result, in 1986 a much broader coalition of U.S. lumber manufacturers filed a second complaint against Canadian timber pricing. This time, the administration reversed its earlier decision and imposed a preliminary 15 percent tariff on Canadian lumber imports. Canada, rather than face a U.S.-imposed tariff, put an equivalent border tax on all lumber shipments to the United States.[14]

Between 1980 and 1986, over sixty such claims were filed against Canadian imports by U.S. companies and trade associations, covering a broad range of products from logs and hogs to suds and spuds. Tough new trade measures were introduced in both the U.S. Senate and the House of Representatives. Canadians, fearing action that would cripple their exports to the United States, were clearly not amused. The Tory government, convinced that a free-trade deal would be in Canada's interest, began pushing the idea of unrestricted trade as early as 1982.

Meanwhile, preliminary steps were being taken in Washington, D.C., when Congress gave its blessing to free-trade talks with both Canada and Israel in the Trade and Tariff Act of 1984. U.S. officials had been toying with the idea of trade agreements with countries in the hemisphere since 1979, but a U.S. Trade Representative report concluded that such agreements ought to be pursued separately rather than on a broad regional basis.

Congress endorsed free-trade talks with Canada but made certain it could check the progress and nix any agreement not to its liking. On a test vote in early 1986 on whether to allow expedited consideration of any eventual agreement, the Senate Finance Committee nearly derailed the negotiations with a 10–10 vote of disapproval. Only President Reagan's personal intervention, in a letter to committee Chairman Robert Packwood of Oregon, saved the day. The chairman and other timber-state senators were wary of any trade negotiations without first settling the Canadian lumber issue.[15]

The close Senate committee vote was a warning to negotiators that any trade accord must fit the mindset of the U.S. Congress. Settlement of the lumber case in late 1986 removed one major logjam preventing a free-trade agreement, but many difficult issues remained. The bottom line for Canada was a blanket exemption from U.S. trade remedy laws that permit U.S. industries or trade associations to bring action against subsidized or dumped Canadian goods. Such a waiver was unacceptable to U.S. negotiators and to nearly every member of Congress.

Across the border, opposition was mounting. The provinces, angered by the bilateral settlement of the wood products issue, demanded a participatory role in any pact that would affect their sovereignty. While Ottawa negotiated and signed the agreement, the Canadian provinces enjoy far-reaching powers and hold a de facto veto over any final agreement. The premiers of Canada's two most populous and industrially developed provinces, Ontario and Quebec, pledged to resist any pact threatening employment.[16]

A powerful group, Pro-Canada Network, vowed to fight any agreement that, in its view, would diminish Canada's "economic independence" from the United States. Led by the Canadian Labor Congress, Pro-Canada Network placed a series of advertisements in Canada's leading newspapers, accusing the prime minister of plotting to "sell out" Canadian independence. Opposition was not limited to political groups. Polls taken in 1986 revealed growing Canadian skepticism of a free-trade agreement, notably in the populous province of Ontario.[17]

To make matters worse, the Canadian press had its own concern with any new trade pact: cultural sovereignty. In their view, the United States posed serious threats to Canada's cultural independence and way of life. Canada's leading TV stations and newspapers heavily covered, unfavorably, U.S.-

Canadian trade disputes and the bilateral free-trade talks. Brian Mulroney's popularity, already in decline, was certainly not helped by media criticism of his efforts to achieve a free-trade pact with the United States.

Some Canadians complain that "60 percent of everything that enters a Canadian's head is made in America."[18] Canadian opponents of the agreement also worry that provisions which give the United States more dependable access to Canadian energy resources relinquish too much control over their own natural resources.

Canada's fear, understandably, is possible loss of sovereignty. While few, if any, U.S. citizens these days speak of the Stars and Stripes flying all the way to the North Pole, Canadians intuitively share former Prime Minister Pierre Trudeau's view that Canada's relationship with the United States is like sleeping next to an elephant: no matter how good-natured the beast, one does tend to notice every grunt and sniffle![19] Yet Canada's government stood the course on a free-trade agreement and even invited the U.S. President to address the Canadian Parliament on the subject in early 1987.

In late September, the negotiators were working frantically to meet their deadline, tackling some of the toughest issues, when the chief Canadian negotiator suddenly stormed out of the talks. Analysts disagreed as to whether the Canadian move reflected substantive concern or was merely a bargaining ploy, but only last-minute intervention by top officials on both sides revived the discussion. Just minutes before the deadline, at midnight on 3 October, the negotiators initialed the principles of a hastily drafted trade document.[20]

Under the agreement, both sides could claim victory on the sensitive issue of unfair trade remedies. U.S. firms will retain the right to file petitions against alleged Canadian subsidies, unfair pricing schemes, and other practices. Canadian firms that feel they have been unfairly penalized will no longer have to file costly, time-consuming appeals in our courts; they can seek a judgment from a bilateral tribunal. Tariffs on both sides will be phased out over a period of time.

But as 1911 demonstrated, agreement at the negotiating table does not guarantee success. No sooner had the trade pact been announced than Canada's ten provincial premiers denounced it. Leaders in two other provinces expressed serious reservations. Premier Richard Hatfield of New Brunswick, who supported the agreement, suffered a crushing defeat at the polls within a week of the initialing. In Ottawa, both opposition parties attacked the bilateral free-trade agreement stridently, accusing the Mulroney government of "putting Canada up for sale."

Reaction in the United States was predictably more muted. Congress generally saw the agreement in a positive light but kept a wait-and-see attitude on the fine print before giving the green light. U.S. industry and labor, while not happy with everything in the agreement, recognizes the potential benefits of freer trade with Canada.

The agreement was as good as could be expected for both sides. Canada's Finance minister, Michael Wilson, called it a "win-win" situation, in which both sides will see increased economic growth and employment.[21] Economists estimate that GNP will grow by one percent in the United States and 5 percent in Canada. By eliminating tariffs—an average of 10 percent in Canada and 4 percent in the States—the agreement should stimulate sales for both countries of goods ranging from agricultural products to zinc.[22]

Will history repeat itself? Canada has twice before backed out of free-trade pacts at the last minute, and in 1930 it was the first to retaliate against the Smoot-Hawley Tariff Act. The two countries are as closely allied—politically, economically, and culturally—as any in the world. No two leaders have been as fully committed to pursuing a free and open trade arrangement as Ronald Reagan and Brian Mulroney. Whether they succeed will be a test of their political leadership and the strength of our bilateral relationship.

Asia: Trade Storms in the Pacific

In July 1984, *U.S. News and World Report* ran a banner story entitled "Pacific Rim: America's New Frontier." In many ways, a more fitting title for the story would have been "The Pacific Rim's New Frontier: The United States."[23]

America's trade deficit with Pacific Rim nations, which had risen steadily during the 1970s and 1980s, approached the $100 billion figure in 1987. Led by Japan's astounding $60 billion surplus, over 60 percent of the U.S. merchandise trade deficit in 1986 was with Asian countries.[24] Considering that just ten years ago the United States had a favorable trade balance with Pacific Rim nations, it was a remarkable turnaround.

In just twenty-five years, the Asian Pacific Rim has been tranformed into a major center of world commerce, industry, and economic activity. It rivals North America and Europe in most dimensions of economic power. The region's spectacular economic achievements have forced governments and firms in Western industrialized countries to reexamine their own policies. Many analysts predict that Pacific Rim countries will eclipse North America and Europe as the center of world power and economic dynamism in the twenty-first century.

In 1965, Asian Pacific countries produced a total of $183 billion in goods and services, just over one third of Europe's production and only one quarter of North America's output. By 1983, Asia's explosive growth had increased total production eightfold to $1.7 trillion, fully one half of North America's production and more than two thirds of Western Europe's output.[25]

At this pace, Asian Pacific economies will account for 25 percent of the world's production by the year 2000, compared with less than 30 percent for North America.[26] The interaction of these two regions will account for over half the world's total production, and determine the international economic order for decades to come.

For a region once plagued by violent revolutionary surges, the relative stability of Asia during recent years has helped usher in an era of unprecedented prosperity. Even more astonishing is what's ahead. As these nations combine the latest technology with low wages and aggressive marketing efforts, they will be in a position to challenge, if not overwhelm, other industrialized countries. Indeed, if current trends persist, Asia's industrial boom could upset the economic equilibrium and play havoc with the world trading system.

Asia is often treated as a monolithic bloc, but the level of development and economic policies vary considerably from country to country. Japan is so advanced that it ranks with the United States and Europe. The newly industrialized countries (NICs)—Hong Kong, Taiwan, Singapore, and South Korea —fall roughly between the developing world and the industrialized nations in terms of their levels of development and per capita income. Thailand and Malaysia are preparing to join the NIC club. China and Indonesia, on the other end of the development scale, are still heavily agrarian but have rapidly growing industrial sectors.

The phenomenal growth of Pacific Rim nations is one of the economic miracles of the twentieth century. While many factors—export-oriented policies, an industrious work force, and aggressive marketing practices—have combined to advance the growth of these countries, direct government action has played a major role in each case. Strong central government is as intrinsic to the Asian culture as Confucianism or Buddhism. With Japan in the forefront, Asian nations have adopted outward-directed trade and industrialization strategies, pushed high rates of savings, promoted key industries, protected domestic markets, and heavily assisted their exporters.

During the 1970s and early 1980s, public sector investment provided the primary force for economic expansion in virtually every country in the region. The investment was financed from a variety of sources: increased oil income in Indonesia and Malaysia; foreign borrowing in the Philippines and Thailand; domestic savings in South Korea and Taiwan; and a combination of savings and export earnings in Japan. The combination of strong central planning, outward-looking economic goals, and heavy capital investment made these nations tough competitors in world commerce.[27]

Few Americans seemed to notice that Asian governments were promoting their exporting industries and shielding domestic producers until U.S. trade deficits became headline news in the mid 1980s. Monthly articles on the U.S. trade deficit frequently singled out the unfair trade practices of Japan and other Asian countries, fueling the protectionist mood in Congress.

However varied their trade policies, all the Asian nations resolutely pushed exports during the 1960s and 1970s as their share of world markets dramatically increased from 7.5 percent to 17 percent. Korea's exports of manufactured products as a percentage of total exports increased from 61 percent in 1965 to 92 percent in 1984. For Taiwan, it was 43 percent to 94 percent; Singapore, 31 percent to 53 percent; and Hong Kong, 93 percent to 95 percent.[28]

The strategy of maximizing exports while erecting barriers to imports succeeded in promoting unprecedented growth in Pacific Rim nations, but it also sparked calls in the United States for tougher trade policies and threatened to undermine trade relations across the Pacific. In the Congress, bills were introduced to punish countries—notably Japan, South Korea, and Taiwan—for their unfair or discriminatory policies that allegedly caused trade imbalances. The textile bill, overwhelmingly approved by Congress but vetoed by President Reagan in 1985, was directed primarily against Asian exporters. Not surprisingly, Asian leaders were offended and worried by such actions.

By 1986, a political backlash was cresting in several Asian countries, which viewed the United States as a rich, powerful, but ungrateful nation that was applying pressure on its underdeveloped, defenseless Asian allies. Asian leaders wondered how the United States could complain about trade barriers while protecting its own market through voluntary restraint agreements and textile import quotas.

By the same token, Americans were being forced to rethink their perceptions of Asia. In the first several decades of the postwar period, U.S. policy had promoted economic growth and democratic institutions throughout Asia. Given our geopolitical goals and the comparative strength of our own economy, we had ignored policies that, over time, resulted in lopsided trade imbalances. By the time U.S. officials recognized the trade barrier problem, domestic expectations on both sides had generated severe political tensions across the Pacific.

During the 1970s, America's economic center of gravity had begun to shift. For most of the century, U.S. economic relations were closely linked to Europe, where capital and trade flows across the Atlantic were rooted in three hundred years of common history and culture. Suddenly all that changed, as Asia became dominant in U.S. trade relations. Trade had never been symmetrical, but in 1980 the growing imbalance began to worry even State Department officials who had been preoccupied with political and security matters in the Pacific.

JAPAN

World War II left Japan in shambles—virtually no industrial base, a debilitated work force, abandoned colonies, disoriented policies, few natural resources, and under occupation by a foreign government. Who would have thought then that Japan would rise to become a global economic power second only to the United States?

America's commitment to rebuilding Japan's economy was not without selfish reasons. Encouragement of a strong, Western-oriented Japan was sound geopolitical strategy for the United States, providing security in the Pacific and a buffer against Communist expansion in the region. In economic terms, however, the plan backfired in ways never anticipated in 1945. Today, disputes over trade and monetary policies threaten to unravel forty years of cooperation.

The most obvious yardstick is the bilateral balance of trade. Japan's surplus skyrocketed from $12.1 billion in 1980 to $60 billion in 1987.[29] Beyond the mere numbers, however, lies a wide range of trade difficulties. The composition of the goods being traded underscores the dimensions of the problem. The United States exports mainly low-value commodities like hides, agricultural goods, and unprocessed logs to Japan while Japan sends mostly high-value manufactured products to the United States. In automotive trade alone, the United States registered a $33 billion deficit in 1986.[30] In capital goods, Japan's surplus jumped from $4 billion in 1981 to nearly $16 billion in 1984.

The incoming flood of Japanese automobiles, motorcycles, tape recorders, cameras, metal fasteners, televisions, VCRs, office machines, and other manufactured goods during the 1970s and 1980s devastated certain U.S. industries and generated intense grassroots pressure for retaliation.

Americans have been irritated by Japan's unfair restrictions on U.S. products, which prevent many of our most competitive industries, such as agriculture, from penetrating the Japanese market. Japan's agricultural import restrictions are rooted in her political system. While farmers constitute only 7 percent of Japan's population, parliamentary representation disproportionately favors rural farming areas.

Rice is the most protected of any agricultural commodity.

Japanese farm unions have threatened leaders of the controlling Liberal Democratic Party that they will switch their support to the Communist Party if the government moves to ease restrictions on rice imports.[31] Japanese consumers pay a heavy price for these barriers. The government forbids rice imports even though domestic rice can cost six or eight times as much.[32]

U.S. and Japanese negotiators have bargained and battled over a wide range of trade issues, from agricultural market access to voluntary restraints on auto imports. The scenario is always the same—U.S. negotiators demand concessions; Japanese leaders call for patience and further negotiation.

In January 1985, in an effort to break the impasse, the U.S. government focused its efforts on several sectors in which U.S. firms are most competitive and Japanese barriers are particularly burdensome—telecommunications products, medical equipment, pharmaceuticals, and forest products. After months of painstaking negotiations, U.S. representatives were able to extract concessions in certain areas, including leather and footwear, semiconductors, veneer and plywood, cigarettes, legal services, and some fisheries products. Despite these sporadic victories, Congress was growing more and more weary of Japanese market barriers. In the 1984 trade bill, Congress gave the President "reciprocity," the authority to limit Japanese imports if U.S. exporters were denied access to the Japanese market.

In May 1986, the House of Representatives passed the Gephardt amendment, which authorized stiff sanctions against Japan and several other Asian countries with high trade surpluses and documented unfair trade practices. Clearly, patience was wearing thin in the Congress. Faith in negotiations to end trade barriers was over, and the pressure for stronger action was mounting.

Another constant irritant in U.S.-Japanese trade relations has been the comparative value of the dollar and the yen. Many analysts noted that the value of the yen was artificially suppressed by the Japanese government during the early 1980s in order to boost Japanese exports, particularly to the United States. Beginning in February 1985, the dollar fell by roughly 50 percent against the yen over two years, but America's bilateral trade deficit with Japan increased.

Japanese exporters stubbornly refused to relinquish their share of the U.S. market. Many sacrificed profits rather than raise prices to accommodate the change in exchange rates. A 1988 Nissan Sentra, for example, retailed for $7850 in the United States compared with $7370 for a 1985 model. Despite a 50 percent shift in the exchange rate, the Sentra sticker price rose by only 6.5 percent.[33]

When the falling dollar and bilateral negotiations failed to reduce the trade imbalance, exasperated U.S. officials called for changes in Japan's domestic economic policies to promote more growth. For months, Reagan administration officials badgered Tokyo to adopt fiscal policies to increase consumer demand, but they were met with polite resistance.

Prime Minister Yasuhiro Nakasone, if anything, moved in the opposite direction. Instead of a tax cut, his government proposed a new value-added tax. Japan showed no signs of shifting the incentives from savings to individual consumption. Nor were Japan's leaders prepared to implement substantial public works programs to stimulate more purchasing. Against this backdrop of frustration over Japan's huge trade surplus and irritation with Japan's intractable market barriers, day-to-day problems quickly boiled over into major trade disputes.

In September 1986, the United States had signed an agreement with Japan in which Japan had agreed to stop dumping semiconductor chips on the U.S. market at below-market prices. The agreement also required Japan to cease dumping in third-country markets and to eliminate import restrictions that prevented U.S. firms from competing in the Japanese chip market.

Many U.S. firms charged that, despite the agreement, Japan continued to maintain protectionist barriers against U.S. chips and continued to dump chips in third-country markets. The U.S. Senate voted 93–0 in favor of retaliation against Japan for its failure to honor the semiconductor pact.

The ax finally fell in March 1987, when President Reagan imposed $300 million in new tariffs on Japanese televisions, word processors, and other electronic goods. The administration's new "get tough" attitude stunned Japanese leaders. Over the next six months, Japan worked to eliminate market barriers and terminate dumping in other markets. A portion of the sanctions was gradually lifted to reward the Japanese government for progress in eliminating its unfair semiconductor practices and provide incentive for further improvements.

The semiconductor problem was replaced by an even more contentious issue: the illegal diversion of highly sensitive military technology to the Soviet Union by Japan's Toshiba Machine Corporation. The Toshiba incident, which also involved a Norwegian firm, was a serious breach of Western technology transfer controls and a major military setback for the United States and its allies. The illegal sales enabled the Soviet navy to gain access to sophisticated milling equipment necessary to produce quieter submarines that could evade U.S. detection.

To make matters worse, Japan's export control laws, poorly administered by the Ministry of International Trade and Industry, allowed Toshiba officials to escape punishment. Democrats and Republicans alike were furious. In Congress, there were angry denunciations of Japan and calls for massive sanctions on imports from Toshiba and other Japanese companies. Pent-up frustration over the loss of American jobs to foreign imports found an outlet in the denunciation of Japan for the Toshiba incident.

Japan's rapidly growing wealth placed enormous strains on her relations with the United States. After thirty years of aggressive and often highly protected industrial growth, Japan had a trade surplus of $83 billion in 1986 alone.[34]

When Japan began investing its huge capital surpluses

abroad in the early 1980s, it placed roughly half in the United States. As America's trade deficit pumped billions in export earnings into Japan's economy, Japanese investors in turn poured a staggering $50 billion back into the United States through the purchase of government and corporate bonds. In 1986, Japanese investors purchased roughly 35 percent of the long-term U.S. treasury notes offered, helping to finance much of the U.S. budget deficit.[35]

This creditor-debtor relationship has made both countries increasingly dependent on each other. The United States desperately needed Japanese capital to finance its public and private debts and keep interest rates down. Japanese investors, realizing that their huge long-term investments were in jeopardy, began to feel they had a stake in the U.S. economy.

The prospect of Japanese investors' turning their backs on the Treasury market in retaliation for U.S. protectionism is a consuming fear for U.S. policymakers. As with mutual nuclear deterrence, each country is in a position to inflict severe damage on the other. What makes the trade and economic conflict between Japan and the United States so menacing is that the two countries seem unable to resolve the difficulties that confront them.

Americans do not understand the nature of the Japanese political economy and thus cannot accept the way it behaves. To most U.S. citizens, Japan owes its superior trade position to subsidies, dumping, and other trade-distorting practices that flood our market with imports but make it impossible for our firms to compete in their market.

Japan, for its part, blames the current trade imbalance on U.S. budget deficits, the strong dollar, and U.S. lack of competitiveness. Japan's repeated excuses and occasional empty promises only convince U.S. business leaders and policymakers that our nation is being deceived.

Public anger and impatience on the American side could easily lead to harsh trade measures aimed at Tokyo. Any U.S.

sanctions could provoke retaliation from Japan that could lead to an all-out trade war. If we are to avoid a trade shoot-out in the Pacific, Americans and Japanese alike must learn to appreciate the causes of the current imbalance and the volatile political situation in both nations.

Ironically, its rapid growth has brought Japan many of the same problems that threaten the U.S. economy. In the late 1980s, Japan is experiencing its highest unemployment rate in four decades. Japan's world-class corporations have begun to move their production abroad to take advantage of cheaper labor and capital costs. While the current balance sheet is tilted heavily in Japan's favor, both nations face serious economic challenges in the years ahead.

The United States and Japan need major structural changes to ease the escalating economic and political pressures that threaten to undermine their bilateral relations. The U.S. government must get control of our runaway budget deficits and restore our competitiveness. Japan must develop the political will to generate enough domestic demand to accept realistic levels of imports from the United States and other nations.

Together, the United States and Japan account for 38 percent of the world's production and trade, nearly $900 billion worth of goods around the globe each year.[36] Much of the responsibility for fostering growth and maintaining stability for the world economy rests on Japanese and American shoulders. Any major disruption between the two nations would set off a chain reaction that could topple the world trading system.

THE FOUR DRAGONS

Japan's economic success has provided the inspiration and the blueprint for other nations in the Pacific, notably Hong Kong, Singapore, South Korea, and Taiwan. Sometimes called the "gang of four," "the four tigers," or the "new Japans," these newly industrialized countries are characterized by strong central governments, strategic planning, export-driven growth, up-to-date technology, and a low-wage, industrious work force.

With 1986 per capita gross national product of $2271 for South Korea, $3748 for Taiwan, $6277 for Hong Kong, and $6516 for Singapore,[37] these nations are easily among the richest in the developing world; Hong Kong and Singapore have emerged as major international financial centers and rival the standards of industrialized nations. Economic growth in all four nations has been nothing less than phenomenal, averaging double or triple the growth rates in the United States and European countries.[38]

The four dragons have developed their industrial bases by importing capital goods and technology and exporting labor-intensive goods. They have relied heavily on government-manipulated exchange rates, subsidies, tax benefits, and other export incentives that gave their industries a comparative advantage in the U.S. market. At the same time, Korea and Taiwan have protected their domestic producers from imports through complex foreign exchange regulations, high tariffs, and other restrictions.

These aggressive policies, coupled with the overvalued U.S. dollar and other factors, have produced lopsided trade imbalances with the United States, which have steadily worsened. In 1987 the United States' trade deficit with the four dragons was larger than our shortfall with all of Western Europe.

For 1987, the United States ran a $24.3 billion deficit with the Old World, compared to a $37.4 billion deficit with the newly industrialized nations of the Pacific Rim.

As in Japan, U.S. officials and businesses began to complain about unfair trade practices and impenetrable markets in the four dragons. Asian leaders made the usual counterclaims about the United States' lack of competitiveness, poor management, high wages, and inflated dollar.

Exchange rates have played a major role in our worsening trade imbalance with the Pacific Rim nations. While the U.S.

dollar fell sharply against the yen and other currencies from 1985 to 1987, the NIC governments have held currencies artificially low in relation to the dollar to promote increased exports.

South Korea and Taiwan have also used a variety of quotas, tariffs, and other barriers to protect their domestic industries. Hong Kong and Singapore, however, are models of free trade. Neither protects its domestic markets through import restrictions, and both are relatively open to foreign investments. They refrain from export subsidies or predatory financing to assist their industries in overseas markets.

Currently, the United States provides all four of the newly industrialized powerhouses with duty-free treatment for certain imports under the generalized system of preferences, which was enacted to help spur economic growth in the developing world. Given their enormous trade surpluses and high per capita incomes, it makes sense to "graduate" these countries out of special-duty preferences. In January 1988, the U.S. government decided to withdraw preferential treatment for the four dragons effective January 1989.

The question of duty treatment of imports from the newly industrialized countries illustrates the evolution of the Pacific Rim economy and a reappraisal of America's role in the region. For several decades after World War II, the United States ignored or tolerated unfair trade practices by these nations because of our political and security interests in the Pacific.

The political stakes are especially important in South Korea, where our nation waged a costly struggle to protect the region against communism. And it was anti-communism that prompted strong American support of the Nationalist government's assumption of power in Taiwan. In both cases, America perceived at the time that our security interests were best served by developing healthy Western-dependent economies and attempting to foster democratic institutions in key Asian countries. To our dismay, Taiwan and South Korea have not yet achieved fully democratic systems but have become fierce economic competitors with a major impact on workers and firms in America.

In the years ahead, the United States will be challenged to reconcile our traditional security-based policies in Asia with our own economic interests.

OTHER ASIAN NATIONS

Just behind the four dragons, five more Asian nations—Indonesia, Malaysia, the Philippines, Thailand, and Brunei —represent the next wave of export-led growth strategies in the region. Though economically diverse and underdeveloped, these countries are rapidly acquiring the technology and foreign investment to boost their economies. Still hindered by political unrest, their governments nonetheless are being run by very able, usually Western-trained finance and trade specialists.

Each nation emerged from colonial rule during the 1950s and early 1960s with a different economic outlook. Indonesia had suffered from Sukarno's misrule and possessed only minimal economic development. Malaysia gained independence in 1957 with an economy dependent on tin and rubber. The Philippines had developed a relatively more varied industrial sector by 1960.

Over the next twenty years, each nation's economy was reshaped to emphasize a diversified export sector. Tariff reductions on a broad range of industrial and agricultural goods during the 1964 Kennedy Round trade negotiations opened up new opportunities for Southeast Asian nations. The World Bank, Asian Development Bank, and the International Monetary Fund (IMF) helped to facilitate growth through generous and well-directed lending programs. Western-educated technocrats emerged during the 1960s to direct economic policy in these countries. Indonesia's "Berkeley Mafia" led the way, emphasizing the opportunities of private-market economies and the liberal trading system.

Like their Asian neighbors, these five nations became heavily dependent on the U.S. market during the 1980s. Their exports to the United States increased by 200 percent from 1977 to 1984, compared to a 70 percent increase from all developing countries. At the same time, U.S. high technology exports to these four countries have increased substantially during the 1980s.

While U.S. high-tech sales have kept our trade deficit with Southeast Asia relatively low for the short term, they have paved the way for extensive modernization and explosive economic growth in the future. With their huge, low-wage labor force, state-of-the-art capital equipment, and Western management techniques, the nations of Southeast Asia will be formidable economic competitors indeed.

Despite the relative trade balance, the United States and Southeast Asia face a number of serious trade disputes. All these countries rely on textile and apparel exports to the United States and are terrified by the threat of a textile import clampdown. They also criticize U.S. import restrictions on commodities like tin and sugar and government subsidies of rice, which affect their sales in third-country markets. The U.S. government has its own list of complaints, including tariff and nontariff barriers on American products, piracy, violations of intellectual property rights, and counterfeiting.

Any escalation of these trade disputes could undermine the political stability of the region, as well as U.S. security interests. The Philippines, Thailand, and Indonesia all look to the United States for military and economic assistance. In recent years, Indonesia, Thailand, Malaysia, and the Philippines have successfully battled serious Communist insurgencies. The guerrillas could gain ground if trade disputes lead to economic problems and social unrest.

CHINA

Still relatively undeveloped, the People's Republic of China is potentially the most awesome economic power in Asia. When you add political stability and economic reforms to China's enormous population, abundant resources, and industrious workers, it is only a matter of time before China becomes an economic giant in the region.

Already the world's seventh largest economy, China is on its way to becoming one of the world's largest trading nations. After more than a quarter century of political turmoil and inefficient Soviet-style central planning, China has buried Mao Zedong's Cultural Revolution and launched bold reforms to modernize its economy. The scope of these reforms is staggering. Deng Xiaoping laid the groundwork for limited private enterprises, encouraged decentralization and new management responsibilities, and invited investments and joint ventures from abroad.

While the results are still inconclusive, the initial signs are impressive. Agricultural output has increased by 50 percent. China's industrial growth accelerated to 18 percent in 1985,[39] then leveled off at 7 percent in 1986. Collectives and individually owned rural enterprises grew 19 percent, and capital construction and investment continue at a healthy rate.

The results of reform are clearly evident in its export ledgers. Just eight years ago, China's main industrial exports were lace tablecloths, silk blouses, plastic buckets, and herbal medicines. Today, the country is churning out some $13.5 billion worth of manufactured exports a year, up from $4 billion in 1978. In the near future, China will be exporting billions in telecommunications products, sophisticated testing and measuring equipment, and consumer electronics and home computers.[40]

But to achieve its modernization goals, China must have a technological base. The Cultural Revolution all but ignored the technology gains by other Asian countries in the 1960s and 1970s. As a result, China remains twenty years behind most industrialized economies.

The People's Republic has embarked on an ambitious program to catch up by acquiring not only the primary technological products from the United States and other suppliers but the know-how as well. The Chinese clearly aim to be self-sufficient in technology, just as they are in agriculture.

United States technology exports to China, however, have encountered political and security problems. U.S. export control laws flatly prohibit exports of dual-use technology — products with commercial and military applications — to Communist countries and even limit those goods which do not have military uses. Since China is still considered a Communist nation, special rules have been established to permit it to import certain classes of U.S. technology.

Still, Chinese leaders are miffed by the restrictions, licensing delays, and uncertainties that hamper their efforts to modernize. Chinese officials repeatedly voice their frustrations over technology transfers in meetings with U.S. officials. U.S. restrictions are largely self-defeating, since Europe, Japan, and other countries are only too happy to fill the gap if the United States restrains its own technology exports.

Once they acquire technological expertise, the Chinese will be a gigantic economic threat to their Asian neighbors and Western countries. Smaller nations in the region have clearly demonstrated that advanced technology combined with a low wage base spells success in the global market.

Factory workers in China earn $20 to $35 a month; their counterparts in Hong Kong and Taiwan earn at least $200 a month. This wage differential means that China can produce handbags retailing for $5 to $10, while Taiwan bags sell in the $10 to $20 range.[41] Western countries will soon be awash in Chinese consumer electronic products and other cheaply produced items, which could lead to severely depressed prices and trigger economic havoc among the world's manufacturing nations.

Another issue of staggering dimensions is agriculture. Any nation with one billion mouths to feed must necessarily be preoccupied with food production. The reopening of rural markets, the promotion of individual responsibility in agriculture, and the licensing of rural enterprises has increased productivity and improved living standards in the country's 800,000 towns and villages, where all but 20 percent of China's population lives.[42] Once a major importer of wheat, corn, and cotton from the United States, China is now self-sufficient and is exporting agricultural goods, adding to the global glut problems that threaten many producing countries.[43]

Where their economic path may lead, not even the Chinese know for sure. While the current Five-Year Plan (1986–1990) stresses more control over the economy, China is expected to grow at an average rate of 7.5 percent per year compared to only 2.5 percent each for Japan, the United States, and Europe.

The plan envisions a 40 percent increase in total volume of foreign trade, with imports increasing by 6 percent and exports growing by 8 percent annually. It stresses imports of advanced technology, equipment, and durable consumer goods, as well as improvement in the investment environment for foreign firms. Joint ventures in manufacturing have two objectives: acquiring foreign production skills and exporting at least 50 percent of the production, irrespective of domestic demand.[44]

Clearly, the Chinese realize the importance of exporting and foreign exchange, and they have the tenacity, control, and patience to fulfill their economic goals. While other countries see the mainland as an attractive market for the moment, they will in time see an enormous economic challenger that may dwarf other countries in the region and force a major economic realignment in the West.

Latin America: In Debt

Two volcanic events have drastically changed the landscape of Latin America in recent years. One, an enormous debt crisis, has put many Latin-American countries on a perilous economic course. The other, democratization, is one of the most positive political developments in the Western Hemisphere's history. Together, they are bound to shape the destiny of the continent and the entire Western world well into the twenty-first century.

For most of the twentieth century, the United States enjoyed a lopsided trade relationship with Latin America, exporting a wide array of manufactured goods and buying coffee, bananas, natural rubber, oil, and minerals. Western investment in South America helped to build railroads, tram lines, public utilities, and production facilities.

The Depression hit Latin America particularly hard as the industrial world's demand for raw materials plummeted. Dwindling foreign earnings forced these countries to turn inward, promoting domestic industrial growth and greater self-reliance within Latin America. During World War II, renewed demand for raw materials raised incomes and facilitated the accumulation of badly needed hard currency revenues.

Following the war, a number of Latin-American countries imposed trade barriers to restrict imports but encouraged construction of subsidiary manufacturing plants. Brazil, for example, demanded that foreign firms increase their percentage of domestic content in auto production. In other cases, U.S.-owned firms were required to export a percentage of their output (as a way of generating hard currency earnings) or to balance the cost of their imported parts with increased exports.

The military juntas, so prominent in the Western Hemisphere during the 1960s, were ill prepared to confront the crippling debt problems they created. The economic policies adopted by these military governments failed to take the necessary corrective measures after the oil shocks of 1973 and 1979. Instead, these debtor nations continued to borrow rapidly in the vain hope that they could grow faster than their debt was expanding. Their gamble did not pay off. The democratization that occurred throughout much of Latin America during the 1980s was, in part, a popular reaction to the failed economic policies of the generals.

The heavy borrowing of the 1970s had artificially improved the standard of living throughout much of Latin America, but the benefits of growth were shared unequally. When the bubble burst in the 1980s, the depression in Latin America eliminated many of the gains of the 1970s. Per capita income fell by 12 to 15 percent from 1981 to 1986. Overall, Latin America's standard of living was no higher in 1986 than it had been twenty years earlier.

The debt crisis of less developed countries (LDCs) is a time bomb ready to go off. "Never before in history have so many nations owed so much money with so little promise of repayment," warned *Time* magazine in 1983. Since then, the problem has worsened steadily. By late 1986, global debt exceeded one trillion dollars for the first time.[45]

While Latin-American countries account for only one-half the LDC debt, their red ink poses the greatest threat to the lending institutions involved. Between 1978 and 1982, Latin America's foreign debt jumped from $162 billion to $331 billion. The World Bank estimated Latin America's foreign debt to be $383.9 billion at the end of 1986.[46]

Overall LDC debt appeared to be stabilized at the close of 1986, but a resurgence of debt-related problems again threatened financial markets in the mid 1980s. Hard-pressed LDCs could not generate enough growth to meet their external obligations.

The debt crisis can be traced back to the oil price explosion in 1973–1974. Oil-importing developing countries, forced to borrow huge amounts to pay their fuel bills, got over their heads in debt. Oil-producing nations, like Venezuela and Mexico, also borrowed heavily against expected earnings to pay for large, new development projects. Western lending institutions — especially the big money-center banks in New York awash with new deposits from OPEC countries — eagerly extended the credit. The lending spree was encouraged both to recycle petrodollars and to help promote economic growth in Latin America.

In 1979, more oil price increases set off another round of borrowing. At the same time, the United States launched a restrictive monetary policy to combat domestic inflation, raising domestic and international interest rates and precipitating the appreciation of the dollar in foreign exchange markets. The global recession that followed cut demand for oil and other commodities, curtailing export revenues of key Latin-American countries. Faced with the rising cost of servicing dollar-denominated debts accumulated during the 1970s and declining export revenues, these countries were forced to borrow even more to meet their obligations. Alarmed over the runaway debt build-up, Western banks began to tie additional loans to newly negotiated IMF agreements.

It was becoming apparent that the debt problem was serious enough to threaten the international financial system and retard economic growth of the borrowers and the lenders. The risks, noted then Federal Reserve Board Chairman Paul Volcker, were "without precedent in the postwar world." British financier Lord Lever observed that "the banking system of the western world is now dangerously overexposed." He feared an avalanche of large-scale defaults that would "inflict damage on world trade and the economic and political stability of both borrowing and lending countries."[47]

In the mid 1980s a new round of economic troubles swept the Western Hemisphere: a lingering world recession; high interest rates, stagnant exports, increasing protectionism in the industrialized countries; and low commodity prices. These conditions posed lingering doubts that debt-ridden Latin-American countries would or could meet their external obligations. Moreover, new loans were essential for these countries to revive their economies in order to pay the interest and principal due Western banks.

The crisis erupted in August 1982, when Mexico's Finance secretary, Jesús Silva Herzog, flew to New York to request a postponement of loan repayments on his country's $86.1 billion debt. The news, according to one bank, was "like an atom bomb being dropped on the world financial system."[48] The Reagan administration moved swiftly to package a bailout for Mexico, which included $3 billion in credits and a short-term loan put up by the Bank for International Settlements. This was closely followed by an IMF announcement of an adjustment program for Mexico and an extension of $3.9 billion in new credit.

Before long, Brazil, once regarded as the most creditworthy nation in Latin America, informed foreign creditors that it could not meet the $446 million scheduled payment on its $87 billion debt. Once again the U.S. government, working closely with U.S. banks, provided a short-term loan.

Next came Argentina. It fell months behind in interest payments on its debt of more than $40 million, necessitating a $1.1 billion loan from international leaders.[49] The shock of such big borrowers' falling on hard times so quickly alarmed bank and government leaders.

International banks, already tormented by recurring defaults, worked overtime to prepare rescue packages for the defaulting nations. The script became familiar. A debtor nation would announce indefinite suspension of payments on medium- and long-term loans owed to commercial banks, followed by intense negotiations between the banks and the debtor nations, then intervention by the IMF to facilitate new loans and a repayment program. These efforts kept the debt bomb from going off, but the fuse was still burning.

Then, in late 1986, the international financial system was jolted by another round of defaults. Argentina, hit by triple-digit inflation and poor economic growth rates, once again held up meeting its debt installments, threatening to withhold payments unless even more favorable terms were forthcoming. After consenting to freeze wages and prices, the Argentines received a $1.8 billion IMF loan, and negotiations continued for a new loan of $2.3 billion from reluctant commercial banks.

Brazil suspended payments on its $68 billion debt in early 1987. Paradoxically, the problem arose not from too little growth but from a sudden burst in economic activity that boosted gross domestic product by more than 8 percent in one year. The boom increased the demand for imports and redirected exports back into the domestic economy, causing the foreign trade surplus to fall dramatically. Inflation soared to an annual rate of more than 500 percent.

Ecuador, an OPEC member, also canceled payment on its debt in early 1987 after a devastating earthquake disrupted its oil pipeline and caused a loss of $400 million in revenues. Peru's charismatic new president, Alan García, restricted his nation's debt repayment to 10 percent of export earnings. Bolivia and Chile joined the others on the debt-repayment sick list.

The new escalation in the debt crisis made headline news in the United States. A World Bank report complimented debtor countries for working on policy reform but noted that "the conditions for renewed growth were generally not met."

Throughout the 1980s, Latin-American countries teetered on financial chaos trying to meet IMF-mandated austerity goals while coping with economic and political pressures at home. The IMF's hard line forced LDCs to increase their trade surpluses in order to service outstanding debts. The shrinking market for U.S. exports, combined with a 35 percent surge in Latin-American imports, left the United States with a $17 billion trade deficit with Latin America in 1985.[50]

The trade swing was most startling among America's four top Latin trading partners, Brazil, Mexico, Argentina, and Venezuela. Between 1981 and 1983, U.S. exports to the four countries declined 48 percent, while imports from them rose 11 percent. The U.S. trade balances with these four countries alone went from a $4 billion surplus in 1983 to a $14 billion deficit in 1986.[51]

In 1985, the United States' deficit with Latin America represented 12 percent of the total U.S. trade deficit.[52] More than anything else, the debt crisis and the resultant economic adjustments caused sharp reversals in U.S. trade flows.

All this was bound to escalate tensions and present inescapable dilemmas for U.S. policymakers. On the one hand, the United States pushed Latin-American debtor countries to adopt austerity measures as a means of responsibly meeting their external obligations. On the other, such measures sharply curtailed U.S. exports to the region and only exacerbated our trade deficit.

U.S. industries, upset over the sharp reversals in trade flows, presented federal trade agencies with over one hundred cases alleging various forms of unfair trade practices, most involving dumping and subsidies of products coming into the U.S. markets. In addition, official U.S. complaints were filed concerning import restrictions, like Brazil's informatics policy, that kept U.S. exporters out of markets.

In response, Congress acted to strengthen the eligibility requirements for advanced developing countries to receive preferential tariff treatment under the generalized system of preferences. These changes were designed to deny duty-free admission to products from countries deemed to be highly competitive with domestic producers. Congress also threatened to limit imports of textile and footwear products and included protectionist language in a major trade bill that would single out certain Latin-American countries for maintaining excessive trade surpluses with the United States.

Mounting debt and economic problems were putting immense strain on Latin-American debtor countries at a precarious time in the hemisphere's political history. Of the thirteen countries in Latin America, all but two—Colombia and Venezuela —have been under various forms of military rule for the past twenty-five years. In the late 1970s, an extraordinary political transformation began to sweep the continent. Argentina, Brazil, Peru, Bolivia, Uruguay, and Ecuador all restored democratic government. Most had popularly elected presidents in office by 1986. Even in Central America, where political unrest was the greatest, elections were called and civilians took over in Guatemala, El Salvador, and Honduras. Today, only Paraguay, Panama, and Chile are under de facto military rule.

The generals used extravagant borrowing from abroad to fuel economic growth and fend off political discontent at home. As a result, newly elected democratic leaders were greeted with enormous financial obligations and tough decisions on restructuring their economies and stabilizing monetary policies. These goals required deep cuts in government spending and self-imposed sacrifices across the economic system.

The debt problem, once seen as a frightening but momentary crisis, is a chronic and complex problem that will test the international economic system for years to come. The financial crisis of the last fifteen years has left in its wake the near collapse of several major debtors, clashes between debtor nations and financial institutions, a sharp reversal in trade flows between the United States and her southern neighbors, and continuing fears that the debt problem could imperil the international financial system.

The belt tightening of the early 1980s has stunted economic growth in the area. Despite mild recovery in the mid 1980s, the region is still worse off than it was in the more robust times of the late 1970s. Indeed, without foreign investment and fresh capital, it is unlikely that Latin-American debtor nations will achieve significant growth in the foreseeable future.

American policymakers now accept the fact that debtor countries must run large trade surpluses to generate the dollars to pay their interest bills and purchase needed imports. This inevitably pits U.S. bank lenders against U.S. exporters in competing for scarce resources in the Latin-American economy. In July 1986, Brazil announced that it was imposing higher tariffs on more than twenty-five hundred import items to improve its trade position and meet its external obligations. Latin-American leaders claim they have few alternatives given their debt situation, which has been caused, in part, by high U.S. interest rates.

Latin America's economic and trade position and even the probability of its paying its debts depends primarily on outside forces. Sluggish world economic growth, especially a collapse of commodity prices, another upward surge in interest rates similar to that in 1982, or a round of protectionist actions by industrialized countries would cripple these nations' ability to repay the $400 billion they owe.

Without continued cooperation and forbearance from the international financial system, favorable global economic trends, and more than a little luck, the LDC debt bomb could still explode.

SEVEN

The Elusive Goal of Competitiveness

IN 1986, the notion of "competitiveness" suddenly burst upon the American political scene. New enough to create some excitement and broad enough to appeal to almost everybody, competitiveness quickly eclipsed more polarizing terms like "protectionism" and "free trade" and dominated the trade debate. Everybody agrees that radical changes are necessary so that America can meet the competitive challenge, but competitiveness has different meanings for different groups.

U.S. corporations see competitiveness as liberation from high-wage agreements or government restrictions that drive up costs. Labor unions see top-heavy corporate management and the current merger mania as the problem. Academics think more federal funds for research and development might be the answer.

In the political arena, Democrats see the new emphasis on competitiveness as affirming their call for more investment in education and a national industrial policy. Republicans looking to deflect the political blame for the Reagan administration's record trade deficits also embraced competitiveness in 1986.

In short, competitiveness is a term so comprehensive, and so vague, that it appeals to all sides of the American political and social spectrum.

For political or rhetorical purposes, such a vague notion of competitiveness is sufficient. If Americans are serious about improving our nation's competitiveness in order to reclaim our position in the world economy, however, we must be much more realistic and honest about what the term really means. We should first understand what competitiveness does *not* mean.

Competitiveness is not a panacea. We cannot wave a magic wand to make our trade and economic problems disappear.

Competitiveness is not a short-term solution. Our nation's trade woes have been decades in the making. It will take years for even an all-out effort to bear fruit.

Competitiveness is nothing new. Ever since men have struggled to build a better mousetrap — or to build the old mousetrap more cheaply and more efficiently — we have seen competitiveness at work.

Competitiveness does not mean replacing our traditional smokestack industries with exciting high-tech ventures and service industries. If America is to remain a dominant economic and strategic power, we must excel in *all* sectors, including heavy manufacturing.

Conventional wisdom holds that the decline of America's heavy manufacturing is part of a natural progression to a post-industrial society. Just as agriculture gave way to manufacturing in the nineteenth century, the argument goes, manufacturing is now giving way to service industries and high technology. But as a number of analysts have pointed out, the analogy to agriculture is badly flawed. America did not withdraw from agriculture during the past 150 years; we simply learned how to produce more with fewer and fewer farmers. In manufacturing, our nation is losing entire industries, and the jobs they provide, to foreign competition.[1]

Finally, competitiveness is not something that can be imposed by the President or legislated by Congress. True competitiveness will involve every American in a constant process of improving our job performance, updating our management skills, searching for innovations, and stretching our world view.

The best way to understand competitiveness is to consider every policy, every program, and every action that will make U.S. goods, services, and marketing better than any others worldwide.

When our government provides incentives for talented students to become teachers, that's an effort to improve U.S. trade competitiveness.

When the owners of a factory involve the workers in management and improving productivity, that improves U.S. trade competitiveness.

When our tax system encourages research, new product development, and capital modernization, it represents a direct incentive for U.S. competitiveness.

And when a college freshman decides to take an entry-level course in Japanese, Chinese, or any other foreign language, that student represents one more small step toward bringing America into the world marketplace.

Competitiveness is not some abstract policy contained in a bill before Congress. Competitiveness is a way of thinking, a way of structuring our institutions so that they reflect the global nature of today's economy and are able to respond to its unprecedented rate of change. While government alone cannot create this state of mind among its citizens and institutions, it can play a constructive role in a number of ways.

Conversely, shortsighted government policies can undermine a nation's competitiveness and sap its economic strength. Many of these mistakes are obvious—cutting funds for education and training, eliminating tax benefits for research, development, and investments in new machinery.

Other steps that bleed U.S. competitiveness are more subtle. Our nation's recent defense build-up has drained scientists, equipment, and funding away from commercial research and design. Our nation's tax code and legal system have encouraged speculation and corporate takeovers rather than genuine investment, which boosts productivity and increases manufacturing output.

The most important component of our nation's competitiveness—a factor often overlooked by those who argue over wage rates and corporate mismanagement—is an educated work force. Perhaps more than any other single factor, America's future as an economic superpower depends upon the quality of education and training our people receive.

EDUCATION

Since World War II, the United States has taken for granted its preeminence in the world economy and our ability to compete against any nation. Our high literacy rate and outstanding educational institutions kept our nation on the cutting edge of technology and a step ahead of our competitors. Then, in 1983, the National Commission on Excellence in Education exposed glaring weaknesses in our educational policies. Its report, "A Nation at Risk," dramatically linked our sagging position in today's fiercely competitive world to our nation's educational performance for the first time.

> Our once unchallenged preeminence in commerce, industry, science, and technological innovation is being overtaken by competitors throughout the world . . . What was unimaginable a generation ago has begun to occur—others are matching and surpassing our educational attainments.[2]

The report set off a wave of studies and reports by educators, business, and advocacy and political groups that drew similar conclusions. Most revealed that American students did not perform as well as they had in the past or as well as students in other countries. Most disturbing from an economic standpoint, study after study warned that American students lacked the preparation and training to enable the United States to regain its competitive position in the future.[3] Our national lack of commitment to quality education is shortchanging our students and our national destiny alike.

Dramatic comparisons with Japan pose troubling questions about our government's level of support for education, the quality of U.S. teaching, and the discipline and study habits of American students. Japan, with half our population, produces twice as many engineers. The United States, by contrast, graduates proportionally far more lawyers. These comparisons underscore the way education can determine the course of economic events. Japan's emphasis on marketable technical skills has kept its productivity high and enabled its economy to adapt quickly to changing economic forces. In the United States, the decline of technical training in favor of law or business has accompanied our transition from an unrivaled manufacturing power to an uncertain service-oriented economy. We face a host of educational challenges if we are to regain our competitive edge. Before we train engineers, secondary schools need to do a better job with the basics.

The United States is the wealthiest nation in the world, yet we possess one of the lowest literacy rates of any industrialized nation. According to the Business–Higher Education Council, 20 percent of American adults are functionally illiterate; the figure is a shocking 50 percent among minority and disadvantaged adults.[4] These potential workers have difficulty filling out job applications, tax forms, or insurance papers. They cannot read instructions on machinery and computer printouts or write a report. As manufacturing jobs disappear, functional illiterates end up as displaced workers or are reduced to low-paying unskilled positions.

Adult literacy training will not come easily. The stigma attached to illiteracy inhibits those who need the training. Both public and private sectors need to provide a supportive environment and proper incentives for literacy training. This is not a social welfare issue; it is an investment in our nation's economic security.

Beyond literacy training, our nation's industrial capabilities will depend in large measure on the development of a future pool of scientists and engineers. Given the low wages, large labor forces, and overt government support enjoyed by many of our trade competitors, America's ability to develop and employ new technology in our products and manufacturing processes will be vital to our future growth.

Americans have been amused by the emphasis on studying the classics in the famous universities of Great Britain while its empire declined. Today, the newly emerging nations focus on math and the sciences to drive their economic growth. In America, these badly needed disciplines are on the wane. In the 1960s, when the first International Mathematics Study was conducted, American educators were pleased. Our top eighth- and twelfth-grade mathematics students were comparable to the best students anywhere in the world. But the second international test, conducted in the early 1980s, revealed a startling decline. The upper 5 percent of U.S. students ranked near the bottom when compared with top students in other nations; American students planning to attend college scored lower than comparable groups in every other country.[5]

TRAINING

The U.S. work force is undergoing its most dramatic transformation since the industrial revolution. The manufacturing plants that once dotted much of this country's landscape are slowly disappearing. For nearly a century, familiar smokestack industries provided each generation with opportunities and job security. Thanks to organized labor, the work force had the disposable income and the fringe benefits to keep local communities and entire cities prosperous. For the high school graduate, the choice was generally narrowed to pursuing a college education or working at the local mill. Choosing the latter usually meant secure lifetime employment.

As U.S. companies adjust to economic change, they need a work force that can keep pace with technological advances or new competitive threats. The term "competitiveness" can also take on a harsh meaning—plant closures, automation, or moving production jobs overseas.

The challenge for America is twofold: we must retrain displaced workers to give them new skills and provide all workers with the ability to adapt to shifting economic conditions and new technological job demands.

Displaced workers face more than the loss of a regular paycheck. They lose vital health and retirement benefits and must cope with the despair that comes with the lack of marketable skills for future employment. For laid-off workers and their families, unemployment can lead to psychological and social problems that eventually spill over to local government agencies. Plant closures deprive future generations of the continuity of jobs that their parents and grandparents relied on. In one-industry towns, these forces of change can be devastating.

As comparative advantage moves to meet the demands of a global economy, there are bound to be dramatic shifts in the work force. While the proportion of our nation's gross national product generated by manufacturing has remained constant for forty years, the decline of America's traditional industry has profoundly altered the character of the U.S. work force. The 5 million blue-collar jobs lost since 1980 carried high wages and traditionally high job security. Although nearly 13 million new jobs have been generated during that time, these positions generally pay lower wages and are far less permanent. In addition, displaced workers cannot always move easily into sectors where new jobs are created.

When talking about industrial competitiveness, economists refer abstractly to capital-to-labor ratios, factor costs, and labor mobility, but the bottom line is workers losing their jobs. The real victims of the wrenching changes in today's economy are the workers who are displaced. It's important to recognize, however, that no amount of government policy can prevent job displacement. Even during periods of strong economic growth, workers in some sectors will lose their jobs as consumer demands shift or new competitors emerge overseas. The Congressional Office of Technology Assessment points out that economic adjustments are necessary in a growing economy.

> The economic recovery [of 1983] neither stopped nor even greatly reduced displacement. Displacement is an ongoing process, associated with technological and economic change, and the problems of displacement are not the same as those of general or cyclical unemployment . . . The need for services to displaced workers does not vanish during economic recovery or growth. There is a continuing need for displaced worker services in an economy that is changing as rapidly as that of the United States.[6]

A major challenge of the 1980s and 1990s is how to devise a system to remobilize America's work force to reach into the large pockets of unemployment to properly train, relocate, and employ an otherwise stagnant working population. In many ways, the social organization of production is just as important as investments in capital equipment.

Job retraining and relocation are such formidable tasks that government at all levels, the private sector, labor unions, and academia must join in the effort. Workers and policymakers alike must confront difficult questions. Since the available new jobs will require specialized training and pay less, the displaced workers must be convinced that such a course is in their best interest. Should workers train for existing jobs or those which may arise in the future? Should training programs encourage relocation? Should training programs treat older workers differently from younger workers? How closely should we tie income support to training programs?

Displaced worker programs are necessary to absorb the shocks of unemployment and the fear of an open trade policy. They provide a labor market that allows private employers considerable latitude in hiring and firing, much more than is possible in some other industrialized countries.

Congress set up a job-training program back in 1962 as a domestic buffer against job disruptions resulting from international trade negotiations during the Kennedy administration.[7] Because of narrow interpretation by government agencies of eligibility requirements, the program was scarcely implemented until 1974, when Congress liberalized worker eligibility and increased benefits.

Trade adjustment assistance was designed to help provide training and job placement services to workers who became unemployed due to plant relocations or competition from foreign products, but in practice the system has functioned primarily as an income maintenance program for displaced workers.

From 1975 to 1985, nearly 1.6 million laid-off workers received trade adjustment assistance, but the vast majority of them merely received extended unemployment benefits. Only 70,000 entered retraining courses, only 28,000 completed their training, and fewer than 4500 found jobs as the result of their training, according to Labor Department studies.

During the early years of the Reagan administration, the trade deficit ballooned, but benefits to displaced workers fell sharply. In 1980, when massive layoffs in the U.S. auto industry were traced in part to foreign competition, 585,000 workers received trade adjustment benefits. The following year, after the administration pressured Congress to make major changes in the program, only 33,000 workers received such benefits.[8] While our nation's trade deficit set a new record every year and millions of U.S. manufacturing jobs were lost to foreign competition, poor administration and a relentlessly hostile White House all but destroyed the program.

When President Reagan vetoed the textile bill in December

1986, he pledged an additional $100 million to retrain workers who lose their jobs because of the increase in imports, but instead of giving the money to trade adjustment he had in mind committing it to the Job Training Partnership Act. A Reagan administration initiative in 1982, it was intended to provide training to youths and unskilled adults entering the job market and to offer job training to low-income individuals who faced serious problems in finding work. The program provided federal funds to the states and required that private businesses greatly expand their role in local training programs.

Congressional Democrats gladly supported the President's plan but refused to give up on trade adjustment assistance, which was tied more directly to import-sensitive industries. They earmarked new money for programs in the 1987 trade bill passed by the House.

COMPETITIVENESS:
RESEARCH AND DEVELOPMENT

America's competitiveness lies in the ability of U.S. business to stay on the cutting edge of technology, devising new generations of products and new processes to manufacture them. Advances in science and technology are what spurred the growth of America's living standard since World War II. Little wonder that the current "competitiveness" debate surrounds the need to expand and improve U.S. research and development (R & D) capabilities.

The debate is rooted in the fear that the United States slipped badly in advanced and applied research during the 1970s and 1980s. The Business–Higher Education Council in its 1986 report on competitiveness issued this dire warning:

State-of-the-art research and development is indispensable to America's competitive future. Yet, there are disturbing signs that higher education's R & D infrastructure, which supports much of America's basic research, is deteriorating. At the same time, there are equally troublesome indicators that the United States is not as efficient as many of its foreign competitors in developing its scientific and technological ideas—that is, in taking inventions from the drawing boards to the marketplace.[9]

The problem is how the nation invests its R & D money. While the United States continues to outspend other Western nations in total research and development as a percentage of GNP, an enormous portion is expended on military research and development that has only limited commercial applications. Worse yet, the proportion of U.S. research and development that is commercially applicable is falling rapidly. In 1978, military R & D represented 2.6 percent of the federal budget, civilian R & D, 2.7 percent.[10] In the Reagan administration's fiscal year 1988 budget, civilian R & D comprised only 1.7 percent of outlays compared to 4.1 percent for defense R & D.[11]

Not only has direct federal support diminished, but shifting federal policies have gutted traditional incentives for research and development. The 1986 tax reform bill cut R & D tax credits, which, it is estimated, will reduce tax incentive for industrial investment by 25 percent between 1986 and 1988.

Another area in which America has lost its competitive edge is innovation and product development—taking scientific research from laboratory to engineer to factory to store. The United States ranks number one in Nobel Prizes in science, but it ranks at the bottom in applying discoveries to demands in the marketplace.[12] Regrettably, over the past several decades the Japanese and others have taken U.S. inventions like robots or ceramic engines and applied them in production and marketing, while U.S. business has been slow to adopt these new technologies.

The latest example is the so-called superconductor, conceived and pioneered in American laboratories, which promises quantum leaps in electrical and electronic technology. This

discovery could have applications ranging from superfast computers to trains that float on magnetic guideways, from less
costly power generation and transmission to fusion energy.

Shortly after the U.S. researchers announced their finding,
Japan's Ministry of International Trade and Industry moved to
assemble a consortium of government, industry, and university
researchers to capitalize on the new American superconductor
technology. The ability of the Japanese to organize their research into a program with strong commercial goals gives them
the edge in moving research out of the laboratory to the market.
In the United States, no one government agency coordinates
attempts to exploit new scientific discoveries.

Nothing guarantees that a scientific breakthrough will yield
a marketable product or an improved manufacturing process.
Market considerations alone cannot justify a basic research
strategy, so American firms and government agencies have been
reluctant to make full commitments. Long-term scientific progress depends on an ongoing commitment from public sources,
private universities, research organizations, and business. The
lack of long-term strategic thinking has contributed to America's competitive decline in recent years.

According to a *Fortune* survey of high-tech industries in
1986, the United States has fallen behind in the fast-growing
field of optoelectronics. America had produced major breakthroughs in fiber-optic telephone transmission systems and
computers and data storage but did not follow up to translate
them into a dominant market position.

> The lead slipped away not because the U.S. lacks theoretical
> knowledge in physics and optics . . . It is far ahead in fundamen-
> tal optics . . . What is missing in the U.S. are size, direction, and
> sustained effort . . . All told, the U.S. may have more researchers
> in optoelectronics than Japan does, but for the most part they
> are scattered in tiny groups doing defense-related work, with
> only secondary fallout for civilian industry.[13]

The United States has been reluctant to engage in industrial targeting, which is aggressively practiced by Japan and other developing countries, but we can do more to coordinate our nation's research and innovation. In the early 1960s the federal government pumped billions of dollars into research for the space program, which has spun off countless benefits to the private sector. The Pentagon has proposed sponsoring a consortium to help the United States regain its independence in semiconductor production. While it is being promoted for national security reasons, it obviously will have many spin-off benefits for manufacturing.

Further advances in productivity, so vital to maintaining America's standard of living, will come with development of high-tech manufacturing processes. To compete with countries that maintain low wages, the United States must keep one step ahead in productivity. For many goods, labor represents only 10 to 20 percent of the total cost of production.[14] As the labor component of a number of U.S. industries continues to decline, technology advances rather than wage differentials will be the determining factor of competitiveness.

New technological processes should also improve the quality of products. Automation will reduce the variation in fabrication and the number of rejected items. One extremely promising new innovation is the advent of flexible manufacturing systems, which will enable a manufacturer to produce items in small quantities economically, allowing more customized production.

Some flexible systems have been introduced in the United States, but they represent only a small fraction of current capital expenditures. This equipment is still far too expensive for most firms, and few managers have the experience to use it to its greatest advantage. Advanced manufacturing systems underscore the interdependence of personnel and technology —proper planning and worker training are critical to maximizing the potential of any manufacturing operation. Large-scale application of flexible systems may help to preserve many manufacturing industries, and considerable further research is needed in robotics, software, and management techniques to bring about this new industrial revolution.

We should also take a lesson from the Japanese, who consistently apply advances from research and development to improve the design and performance of traditional product lines. This sort of constant "incremental improvement" is vital to keep consumers loyal to familiar products and to prevent future generations of foreign products from engulfing our goods.

Ironic as it may appear, America has come up short where it once was the pacesetter—in industrial design. Through all our abstractions about the trade deficit, it is not hard to see that Americans buy many imported products because they are more attractive, more exciting, or better designed. American industry has a notorious reputation for disregarding aesthetic elements in industrial design. An American coffeemaker may make a cup of coffee that is just as good as that from an Italian espresso machine, but there is no question which one modern consumers want in their kitchens.

One wry illustration of what's wrong with U.S. competitiveness is an account of the first visit to the Ford Motor Company design studios of Donald Peterson, the company's new president.

He was shown the customary sketches of big, boring boxes. Ford designers, truth be told, hated their own designs. Often they had tried to propose interesting cars like the Europeans and Japanese were building. Top management always shot them down. There was only one kind of car headquarters wanted to hear about: A Car Just Like Last Year's.

After examining some sketches, Peterson looked up at the designers and asked, "Are you proud of these?" . . . "No, I'm embarrassed by them," Jack Telnack, Ford's chief of design answered.[15]

Thus began the journey that culminated with the introduction of Ford's successful Taurus model. Not surprisingly, many have credited the design studios at Ford's European divisions with the company's turnaround.

The surge of sophisticated imported goods in recent years has had a permanent impact on the American consumer. No longer will "functional" be enough. American industry must move back into the daring reaches of design, much as Raymond Loewy did decades ago.

Defense-related research and development has doubled in real terms since 1979, a fact with far-reaching consequences.[16] The closest America comes to an industrial policy is the cozy relationship the Pentagon has with the handful of industries that are its clients.

In the past, defense R & D produced many breakthroughs with commercial applications. As weapons systems become more and more exotic, however, these spin-offs have slowed to a trickle. A September 1986 *Dun's Business Month* article cast doubt on President Reagan's boasts of commercial applications to come from strategic defense initiative (SDI)—"Star Wars" —research, which totaled $3.6 billion in 1987. According to *Dun's,* only about 3 percent of the SDI budget goes to basic research that might have broad applications, with the bulk of funds going into weapons research. Industry sees little practical use for the high-powered lasers being developed.[17]

Another factor limiting spin-offs is the differing goals of civilian and defense technological development. While civilian research aims for a balance between technology and cost, defense research does not. The Pentagon writes up its wish list and issues a cost-plus contract to anyone who can make those wishes come true. This "gold plating" seriously detracts from the cost-conscious practical civilian application of military technology.

Hanging over this whole question is the heavy veil of secrecy that surrounds so much military research. Despite the zeal with which the Pentagon protects military technology, it is hard to believe that scientific breakthroughs associated with Star Wars or other major weapons systems will be released for commercial application.

If the boom in defense research were only a question of a diversion of funding, we could solve the problem by simply providing more funding for civilian R & D to boost our nation's commercial competitiveness. Unfortunately, the true limits of our R & D capacity are measured not in dollars but in talent. Our nation's most talented scientists and engineers are increasingly lured into defense work by attractive salaries and exotic research projects, resulting in a serious brain drain. *Dun's* quoted a former White House science adviser as saying, "Researchers are being drawn into aerospace and defense-related fields, and in the meantime our manufacturing technology is going to the dogs."[18]

Just as excessive export controls can, paradoxically, undermine our national security by strangling our economic opportunities, the current emphasis on ultra-high-technology military hardware threatens to strangle the research and innovation needed to keep American products a step ahead of foreign goods. As our best and brightest scientists and the research dollars needed to support them are sucked into defense work, our basic manufacturing capability is shortchanged. National security depends not only on sophisticated weaponry, but also on the ability to manufacture goods that are needed and competitive in the global economy.

As the United States enters the 1990s, we need to do more than increase market-oriented research and development. We must expand our entire concept of innovation to include the processes of manufacturing, packaging, shipping, and marketing. As the Joint Economic Committee observed in a 1986 report, "Increased funding for R & D does not necessarily result in increased innovation. In fact, research and development are not always necessary for innovation to occur; innovations may be the result of incremental changes in a product or process."

Basic research facilities at our nation's colleges and universities must be upgraded. Many research institutions are attempting to perform state-of-the-art research with antiquated equipment.[19] At a time of tight budgets and increasing competition, many schools simply cannot afford to make costly investments in new equipment. Government must play a major role.

The Business–Higher Education Council has suggested that all federal R & D grant programs include set-asides for capital investment. The 1986 House trade bill contained a provision establishing a $50 million grant program within the Department of Education to modernize university research facilities.[20]

Many of the recent recommendations on R & D policy are aimed at creating a more effective link between basic research and its market-oriented applications. Researchers must be able to respond to markets just as markets respond to new technologies. One positive development has been the growth of joint research efforts between business, government, and academia. Close links between academia and business have played a role in the success of Silicon Valley in California, the Route 128 high-tech belt around Boston, and the Research Triangle development in North Carolina.

Businesses need to cooperate more closely on research efforts, as well. The Microelectronic and Computer Technology Corporation, a consortium of twenty-one electronics companies, is a start in this direction.[21] These sorts of ventures demonstrate that U.S. firms can do a lot more to pool their research efforts without violating our nation's antitrust protections.

Since government controls such a vast proportion of the R & D resources in this country, it should be brought into cooperative ventures wherever possible. And this does not mean just the federal government. The economic development agencies of state governments can act as a catalyst for cooperative activity. The National Commission on Jobs and Small Business recommends a state-sponsored effort to encourage partnerships between the academic community and small businesses, where so much innovation takes place.[22]

Funding for new research efforts will be a contentious issue, particularly as Congress and the White House struggle to balance the federal budget. A dramatic increase in civilian R & D spending by the federal government is unlikely, but federal funding may not be the best way to go. Research and development funded by industry itself often makes a greater contribution to productivity and growth. Federal R & D funding usually is linked to specific federal government goals, which are often not closely tied to commercial possibilities. Industry-funded R & D, on the other hand, is conducted with an eye to the market and specific commercial applications.

The future of American business is tied closely to technological development, both in terms of product design and engineering and in manufacturing techniques. As other countries use low wages to keep their products competitive in world markets, the United States must keep one step ahead by using advanced technology and sensitive management to maximize our human and natural resources.

"THE DEPARTMENT OF TRADE DISORGANIZATION"

No nation can afford to carry out its international economic and trade policies as we do in the United States. The problem can be traced all the way back to the Constitution, which gives Congress the authority to regulate foreign commerce but empowers the Executive to conduct foreign affairs. When it comes to trade matters, nobody knows who really speaks for our government.

As Ronald Reagan chats amiably with Japanese Prime Ministers Yasuhiro Nakasone or Noboru Takeshita at the White House about trade matters, prominent members of Congress angrily denounce Japanese trade policies and call for retaliation. Foreign delegations visiting Washington, D.C., are careful to spend as much time on Capitol Hill as they do at the other end of Pennsylvania Avenue. Small wonder they and the U.S. public are perplexed when a free-trade President and a protectionist-minded Congress clash over trade policy.

The tension between Congress and the President is inherent in the system of checks and balances our Founding Fathers constructed when they wrote the Constitution. Though such conflicts are a necessary evil in our political system, they have generally served our nation well over the years.

But the Constitution's drafters never intended conflicts to exist *within* the Executive Branch. They would be appalled at the disorganization, contradiction, and pitched battles that characterize our international trade apparatus within that branch of our government.

Our government is ill equipped to handle the urgent problems that accompany the enormous trade deficit. There is no coherent trade policy, nor is there a single department that oversees trade programs. Whatever policies do exist have accumulated over time, the product of a Congress more concerned with issues of the moment than a long-term trade strategy. Federal trade departments, agencies, bureaus, and commissions are scattered all over our nation's capital. No one could possibly understand the complexity of America's trade policy without retaining a Washington, D.C., law firm that employs former ranking officials from the Executive. Despite occasional attempts at reform, there is no clear mandate to make trade and economic growth a prime national objective.

As Republican Senator William Roth of Delaware warned his colleagues in 1983, "U.S. trade policy is no policy at all. Instead, it is little more than a swamp of ineffective and conflicting ad hoc responses to an ever-growing list of foreign unfair trade practices."[23] It will not be possible to restore American competitiveness until the U.S. government gets its trade house in order by establishing a single federal department to coordinate and conduct our nation's international economic and trade policies.

How did our government get into such a mess? One explanation is that trade policy has never been considered very important, at least not in the last fifty years. Since World War II, international economic issues have been subservient to U.S. foreign policy and security interests. Most of the time, policy was left largely in the hands of two cabinet-level departments — State, which is preoccupied with loftier foreign policy matters, and Treasury, which presides over international monetary policy.

Successive presidents have shuffled agencies and bureaus and even set up interagency groups to coordinate national policy and establish America's leadership role in international economic matters. During the 1940s, 1950s, and 1960s, there was no U.S. Trade Representative (USTR) and the Department of Commerce played only a minor role. As frustration over the old procedures for trade negotiations grew during the early 1970s, Congress debated creating a central Trade Representative. Even then, congressional leaders were upset with foreign nations that were not playing by the rules. When U.S. negotiators returned from international meetings with an agreement, Congress usually found a way to upset the deal.

Actually, the 1973 Tokyo Round, which reduced tariffs and non-tariff barriers and reformed GATT, forced our government to "get its act together" for the first time. Congress and the Executive, business and labor, eager to avoid the fiascoes of the past, rallied behind the establishment of a new structure for making trade policy. The 1974 Trade Act created the office of the Special Trade Representative, of cabinet rank, to coordinate and preside over U.S. trade negotiations. On the negative side, our government trade apparatus became larger and more unwieldy than ever. Altogether, by 1983, twenty-five different federal agencies were involved in trade policy and export promotion programs.[24]

In 1983, private witnesses before the Senate Government Affairs Committee listed a multitude of problems associated with the existing trade structure.

Uncertain Focus: Trade interests at the Department of Commerce must compete for the secretary's attention with a multitude of other agency functions. Trade's "clout" within the department depends on the inclination of the secretary.

Uncertain Power: The USTR is devoted to the trade interest institutionally, but his clout with the President depends too much on the vagaries of personal relationships.

Limited Influence: Neither the USTR nor the secretary of Commerce has sufficient influence to assure that trade interests receive due consideration when major economic and foreign policies are being formulated. Trade officials have not been significantly involved in policies that resulted in the overvalued dollar. They are not regularly included in major economic summit meetings, even when trade is a principal agenda item.

Unclear Responsibility: No one knows where the trade buck stops at the Department of Commerce or USTR.

Weak Policy: Neither trade leader can act decisively without consultation with the other, and it is simply not feasible to consult on all issues in sufficient detail. As a former trade official notes, "The result is that each official, instead of acting authoritatively and emphatically, must hedge, act with caution, and look over his shoulder."

Policy Vacuums: In order to avoid friction and maintain cordial relations with each other, the two leaders may choose not to raise certain issues. Thus, problems fall through the cracks.

Reactive Rather Than Strategic Policy: Neither trade agency has a strong industry sector analytical capability. The structure does not exist for turning industry data into information that can aid in the development of trade and internal sectoral adjustment policies.

Inadequate Leadership: Our trade structure does not stimulate adequate public attention to the need for American businesses and individuals to adjust to the interdependent world economy. Businesses continue to produce for the American market, with only excess production, if any, shipped abroad. Individuals are slow to adjust to economic change.

Turf Battles: In the real world, as opposed to an organizational chart, policy coordination and trade negotiations handled by USTR cannot be easily separated from the implementation carried out by the Department of Commerce. The unnatural division between policymaking and implementation is an open invitation to wasteful competition between the agencies and an open invitation to foreign negotiators seeking to exploit the differences in position between the two agencies.

Inefficiency: Trade problems are time-consuming. A former undersecretary of Commerce indicated that resolution of turf problems created at the staff level by the organization took about 20 percent of his time.

Duplication: The lack of a clear dividing line between the work of each lead agency leads to the duplication of functions.

Dual Hierarchy: USTR staffers frequently call on Department of Commerce resources for more staff-intensive work. Commerce staffers must go through two hierarchies—the Commerce management and the USTR management — in order to respond. The cumbersome management structure stifles creativity.

Lack of Accountability: Though USTR draws on the resources of another agency for its staff-intensive work, it does not have the usual management tools for assuring the quality of the work product it receives, e.g., evaluations, promotions, or hiring.

Personnel Turnover: Our trade negotiators often lack the experience and detailed professional competence of their foreign counterparts, and the absence of a clear and attractive career path for international trade experts discourages many talented people from staying in the government. At the Commerce Department, in particular, it has been difficult to retain a sufficiently high proportion of the more able employees.[25]

This litany of complaints is directed at two agencies, the Department of Commerce and USTR. A more complete list would include the role of the secretary of State, who generally has the final say on international economic issues. At virtually every economic summit meeting involving the heads of states of the seven industrialized nations, it is the secretary of State, not his cabinet colleagues, who weighs in on high-level policy matters. The secretary of the Treasury also plays a central role, both in setting U.S. policy and complicating the decision-making apparatus.

With so many agencies involved in trade policy and so many competing voices, it's hard to identify true administration policy. Who should Congress, foreign interests, or even the American people view as the spokesman for the Executive Branch? The Treasury secretary, who heads the interagency council? The secretary of Commerce, who oversees the International Trade Administration at Commerce? Or the Special Trade Representative, whom Congress has identified as the principal trade official?

As widespread frustration increased with the trade deficit during early 1983, our government seemed ill equipped to take any action. Leaders in both branches were beginning to realize that our officials lacked a trade policy and long-term strategy and did not appear to have any influence with our trading partners.

That year, a flurry of trade reorganization bills were introduced in the Congress. Senator Roth led the way in the Senate.

On the House side, a number of similar proposals were put into the hopper. While these bills differed in some respects, they were all designed to consolidate the many nonagricultural trade functions of our government into a single agency in order to expand trade and boost U.S. competitiveness. Within the new agency, all trade-related functions like data collection, analysis, policymaking, export promotion, and trade negotiations would be more coherent and better focused.

All the reorganization proposals carefully eliminate agriculture from the new trade department, recognizing the political muscle of the farm community. Rightly or wrongly, many farmers fear that a new department of industry and trade would sell out agricultural producers when tradeoffs are made during negotiations and at GATT meetings. As a result, agricultural functions would remain within the Department of Agriculture under nearly every trade reorganization proposal before Congress.

Despite the overwhelming logic of reorganizing and streamlining our government trade apparatus and strong support from key public and private officials, the idea has never really gotten off the ground. It has never been a high priority for industry trade associations, whose members are ambivalent about what to do. The real problem, however, has been on Capitol Hill, where jurisdictional problems have reigned. One House bill was referred to nine different standing committees.[26] Committee chairmen were cool to the idea, fearing the loss of turf on future trade bills.

Trade reorganization is getting a fresh look as Congress debates competitiveness. Republicans and Democrats alike are coming to the realization that our trade policy apparatus simply must be more effective in the future. Since Republicans, as the minority party, have few jurisdictional qualms, they generally support a scaled down and more efficient Executive Branch. Democrats are cautiously interested, but many want the government to adopt a more active role in channeling resources to certain promising sectors, a policy Republicans and the business community oppose.

Major reorganization of the Executive Branch is more likely to occur when a new President takes office. Such a move would avoid dislodging sitting cabinet officials and other political appointees; everybody would be coming into newly created positions. Particularly if the issue is highlighted during a national campaign, a newly elected President could seize his brief mandate and reshape our government trade agencies in one dramatic stroke, as Jimmy Carter did when he created the Department of Education in 1977.

Taxing America's Competitiveness

The 1986 congressional scene was viewed with utter dismay by the United States trade community. The two dominant issues were tax reform and trade, but they were moving at cross-purposes. Indeed, White House and Capitol Hill leaders were considering them as separate issues, virtually ignoring the overlap of one on the other. Throughout the two-year debate on tax reform, scant attention was paid to how changes in the tax code would help or hurt America's competitive position.

Failure to enact trade legislation has left America another year behind in the competitiveness race, while passage of the 1986 tax package has brought further damage to our country's trade position. The 1986 Tax Reform Act turned our tax code upside down. Many provisions that were vital to America's competitiveness were slashed in the name of "tax reform" by a popular President and an eager Congress.

Congress seldom views tax policy in the trade context. It considers taxation on the ability to pay, equity, the benefit principle, neutrality, and, more recently, as a stimulus to economic growth. But with globalization of the American economy, the way our tax laws treat our manufacturers, farmers, and exporters, compared with other countries, can make the difference in international competitiveness.

One definition of competitiveness is the ability to sell goods and services in world markets compared with the ability of foreign firms to do the same. Taxation is not the only determinant in competitive pricing, but it affects both domestic and export markets. A tax increase, whatever its form, is generally passed on to consumers through higher prices in domestic and international markets. As a result, U.S. exporters have that much more difficulty selling their products abroad.

Taxation affects U.S. competitiveness most directly in the manufacturing sector. Since 1980, the United States has lost millions of manufacturing jobs, as the numbing trade deficits attested during that period. Any tax increase on manufacturing that results in higher-priced U.S. products is bound to add up to more lost jobs.

The 1986 Tax Reform Act exacerbates our trade deficit in two ways. First, it saddles U.S. business with $140 billion in new taxes, which will make U.S. products more expensive at home and in the export market. Second, it places $140 billion of additional income in the hands of American consumers, who will undoubtedly spend more of their disposable income on foreign imports.

Incredibly, the tax increases in the bill were disproportionately centered exactly where the U.S. must be more competitive —on the manufacturing sector.

The bill repealed the investment tax credit and sharply cut back accelerated depreciation of capital investments, two components of our tax code that were critical to U.S. competitiveness. Our nation cannot hope to compete in the trade of manufactured goods on the basis of wages. The bulk of our advantage rests with technological innovations that enhance productivity. Such innovations are embodied in the machinery and equipment used to produce manufactured goods and services. By increasing the cost of capital investment, the Tax Reform Act will have serious long-term implications on the ability of U.S. firms to modernize, increase productivity, and compete internationally.

Our tax code can also determine whether U.S. firms continue to operate in this country or shift their manufacturing overseas to take advantage of lower wages or more generous tax laws. In today's world economy, American companies increasingly can consider foreign production. The more expensive it becomes for U.S. business to produce at home, the greater the pressure to move plants, equipment, and jobs overseas.

Ironically, many of the same congressmen who condemn U.S. firms voted to remove the one major incentive that keeps manufacturing capacity and jobs at home. In testimony before a House subcommittee in October 1985, Former Treasury Undersecretary Charls E. Walker offered this grim illustration:

> Take the case of Canada. Suppose that a U.S. manufacturer decides to replace an outmoded production facility. Does it build in the U.S., where it will receive no investment credit and the machinery and equipment will, in large part, be written off over seven to eleven years? Or does the company build the new facility in Canada, where it would (under current Canadian law) receive an up-front investment tax credit of at least seven percent and can also write off its total investment in machinery and equipment within three years?[27]

Beyond the overall impact of increasing business taxes by $140 billion and eliminating incentives for new investment, the Tax Reform Act included a number of more specific provisions. While many of these issues are highly technical, the net effect of the new law appears to perpetuate tax disincentives that are sure to plague American exporters and multinational corporations in the future.

Changing the rules for determining whether income or expenses derive from a U.S. source or a foreign source will prove vexing for U.S. international firms. Such rules apply to the allocation of interest expenses, export sales income of U.S. multinationals, and certain research and development expenses. While the issues involved in these changes are highly technical and complex, their net impact would be exceedingly negative on the companies affected.

American companies competing abroad want their representatives to live where the markets are located. Since 1918, our tax code has allowed U.S. citizens living abroad to credit some or all of their foreign taxes against any U.S. tax obligations, to avoid double taxation. In the early 1980s, Congress allowed U.S. taxpayers who met specified foreign resident qualifications to exclude up to $80,000 of foreign-earned income from their U.S. tax obligations. The exclusion was designed to increase gradually, to a maximum of up to $95,000 by 1990. Given the often steep cost of living abroad and the lucrative employee incentives offered by other governments, this provision was critical to help U.S. companies match the overseas operations of their competitors. Unfortunately, the 1986 tax bill dropped the ceiling and denied pay exclusion from certain countries. This provision obviously raises the cost for most overseas assignments and creates yet another hurdle for American businesses trying to sell U.S. products in foreign markets.

While the Tax Reform Act of 1986 did little to advance American competitiveness, intense industry lobbying convinced the Senate-House conference to retain the R & D tax credit, which had been slated for elimination in both the President's proposal and the House Ways and Means bill. Further, the corporate tax rate was dropped to 33 percent, down significantly from the previous 46 percent level. Overall, it appears that older, capital-intensive industries came out losers under the act, while newer, high-technology firms fared better.

The ultimate test of taxation on competitiveness is how the United States compares with other countries. While any report card on the international competitiveness of the U.S. tax system is bound to be complicated, prior to 1986 our code generally compared favorably in terms of investment incentives to upgrade and modernize our industrial plant. Unfortunately, these incentives were removed in the 1986 bill.

American firms also have the unique distinction of enduring double taxation; dividends are taxed at both the corporate and shareholder levels, which hampers the ability of firms to raise equity. Only the United States offers no relief from the double taxation of corporate dividends. Japan, Canada, and the United Kingdom offer partial relief for dividends paid to shareholders either at the individual or corporate level. Our Tax Reform Act of 1986 did nothing to clean up this problem.

Finally, no analysis is complete without considering the ways our trading partners, notably Western Europe, give their exporters special tax breaks. The value-added tax (VAT) is imposed and paid on the increase in value of products at each stage of production and distribution. Japan imposes a commodity tax that factories pay at the final stage of production. However, these taxes are rebated if the products are exported. For imports, these taxes are imposed at the port of entry and are usually assessed on the value of the import, including shipping costs and customs duty.

U.S. firms have no similar tax benefit. They cannot "rebate" their corporate income tax when exporting. GATT rules permit adjustments for such "indirect" taxes as the value-added tax but not for such direct taxes as income taxes. To address this inequity, Congress set up the Domestic International Sales Corporation in 1971. This allowed U.S. exporters to create "paper" companies to purchase goods from their domestic parent companies, thus permitting a portion of the export-related income to be deferred indefinitely. Our trading partners objected to this arrangement, however, so Congress had to rewrite the law in 1984. Now U.S. corporations must establish offices in foreign countries in order to qualify for a tax rebate. The new law allows 65 percent of the taxable foreign trade income to be exempted from U.S. taxation. This is not a problem for large multinationals, but many small exporters find it difficult to set up offices overseas.

As U.S. policymakers confront the riddle of competitiveness, one fact is clear: we cannot ignore the tax aspects of our trade posture. Congress may look at a value-added method of taxation, both to increase revenues for deficit reduction and to give U.S. exporters a better chance to compete overseas. Whatever the final answer, we must heed the lessons of the 1986 Tax Reform Act and recognize the interdependence of our tax and trade policies.

America's Hollow Corporations

America's gaping trade deficit can be blamed on many factors —the overvalued dollar, sagging growth rates in other countries, unfair trade practices, U.S. government–imposed impediments—but corporate America holds the key to our nation's competitive future.

Competitiveness involves a number of elements, ranging from price and quality to meeting a customer's specific needs, but it adds up to a bottom line—the ability to outproduce and outsell the other guy or the other country.

Over the last twenty years, U.S. industries have jogged along, watching the trading world go by. In what has become a global marathon, America's corporate runners have been overtaken by foreign sprinters who are fresh, quick, and in the race to the finish. Many U.S. companies lag far behind; others have dropped out altogether. The distance lost may be impossible to make up, despite recent efforts by the United States to recapture our position at the front of the pack.

No one disputes that the fundamentals have changed. The U.S. economy is undergoing one of the most challenging periods in its history. America's entrepreneurship is being challenged as never before. A central question in the entire competitiveness debate is whether corporate America has the strength and determination to recapture a dominant position in the world economy.

Many experts say U.S. industry is fatigued and lacks the spirit and fortitude to compete anymore.

> Some important industries are being left in the dust, and since the current business expansion began in late 1982, the manufacturing sector has generated few new jobs.[28]

> Wrung out by recession, restructuring, and the inroads of foreign rivals, large parts of U.S. industry are only tentatively emerging from five years of turmoil.[29]

> You're seeing a substantial deindustrialization of the U.S. and I don't imagine any country maintaining its position in the world without an industrial base.[30]

> The U.S. is abandoning its status as an industrial power.[31]

Tom Peters, coauthor of *In Search of Excellence* and a critic of America's Fortune 500 companies, says today's corporate system is unwieldy. "Its managements are ensnarled in hopelessly cumbersome structures. Sometimes it seems that the only animation or boldness on the part of management is in selling things off, belatedly responding to raiders or designing even more parachutes for themselves."[32]

A stinging report on America's industrial retreat was dramatically portrayed on the front cover of *Business Week* for 3 March 1986. Its feature article, "The Hollow Corporation," predicted that the United States "will continue to lose markets and see its industrial base shrink if business persists in the process of hollowing its own manufacturing capability and focusing only on short-term returns. This is an economic gratification, an abdication of responsibility to future investors, workers and consumers."[33]

That article shattered any remaining illusions about America's industrial greatness. The special report openly acknowledged that legions of U.S. manufacturers were closing up shop and opting to become "marketing organizations for other producers, mostly foreign." It told of traditional industries that do less and less manufacturing and more and more service functions. Today's rising businesses "perform a host of profit-making functions—from design to distribution—but lack their own production base." Thus, according to *Business Week,* they are "hollow corporations."[34]

America's industrial retreat involves a number of related trends: companies abandoning manufacturing to boost profits; the exodus of manufacturing, and with it America's know-how, to other nations; the false paradise of a service economy that lacks industrial jobs; the absence of government programs to ease the transition to a more complex and competitive global economy.

The 1980s have been marked by the biggest reshuffling of corporate assets in U.S. history. The enormous number of acquisitions, mergers, leveraged buyouts, spin-offs, sell-offs, buybacks, layoffs, and recapitalizations have sapped the vitality and diverted the talents of our nation's industrial sector. Corporate managers preoccupied with fighting off raiders have little time for strategic planning. Companies that used to concentrate on long-term growth, return on investment, and earnings per share are more worried about surviving raiders who attack at any sign of vulnerability.

Freelance takeover artists like Sir James Goldsmith, T. Boone Pickens, Carl C. Icahn, and Irwin L. Jacobs have terrorized corporate America by launching one assault after another. With the help of junk bonds and the ingenuity of investment houses, these raiders have acquired immense leverage to intimidate and control some of our nation's largest companies. These takeovers involve billions in corporate debt but do little to produce jobs or improve our nation's competitive position.

The acquisition binge of the 1980s has been like an all-night party; our nation will deal with the economic hangover in the years ahead. American firms now owe creditors nearly $2 trillion, a massive debt that will cripple future efforts to expand or modernize.

"While we in America devote a major part of our material and human resources to promoting and fighting mergers and hostile takeovers, we are becoming less and less competitive with Japan and all the new Japans," says Peter Jones, former senior vice president of Levi Strauss.

In the last decade, the U.S. economy has undergone a startling transformation. Two million blue-collar workers have been dropped from our nation's payrolls. During the same period, white-collar employment in management and service industries has risen by 10 million.[35] The numbers don't tell the whole story. White-collar service jobs don't necessarily contribute to the country's productivity. In fact, dismal white-collar productivity has dragged down respectable productivity increases by blue-collar workers.

These findings, first presented by MIT's Lester Thurow, were supported by economist Stephen Roach of Morgan Stanley, who calculates that blue-collar productivity rose by 13 percent between 1978 and 1984, while white-collar productivity declined by nearly 10 percent.[36]

As the United States adjusts to the world economy, we will have to iron out such wrinkles. American productivity stayed flat from 1900 to the mid 1920s even as industry reorganized itself to take advantage of the assembly line.[37] Only then did rising American productivity help to advance our industries into world markets. But will we find it so easy to increase exports of services sixty years later? Today's service exports will face barriers of language, culture, and customs, areas where our nation is admittedly weak.

As foreign manufacturers overwhelm the U.S. market,

threatened domestic industries appear to have few choices: go overseas for cheaper production, plead for government protection, or close up business altogether. But there is another choice —to rise to the competitive challenge. Some businesses simply defy the odds and stay in competition. These are the survivors.

Despite the setbacks of the 1980s, America's entrepreneurial genius is still at work in a number of firms. The forces of competition are driving companies back to the drawing board. Examples in every sector of the economy, no matter how beaten and battered, demonstrate that we can innovate with the best and offer better quality and services.

Yesterday's big conglomerates are giving way to today's leaner, more focused, and better managed enterprises. The giants of the postwar era proved too top heavy, complex, and bureaucratic to meet the competitive forces of the 1970s and 1980s. Corporate arteriosclerosis crippled American industry for years, while trimmer foreign companies ran rings around us in the world marketplace. According to the CEO of Gulf and Western, "Big is no longer a sign of strength. In fact, just the opposite is true."[38]

Tom Peters describes the successful firm of the future as one which offers "superior quality, superior service, and . . . a high rate of innovation and does all this through newly flattened, non-bureaucratic organizations whose every person becomes a full-scale participant and owner of the operation where people finally count more than capital, where ingenuity supplants mass."[39]

Today's successful firms may be restructured versions of familiar corporate giants, spin-offs from divestitures, or new capital formation ventures. Whatever their origins, the emphasis is on innovation, efficiency, and finding a "niche" in the marketplace.

By carefully tailoring their strategies, reducing costs, improving productivity and marketing techniques, and sheer hard work, U.S. firms can stay ahead of the pack and restore their reputation for Yankee ingenuity throughout the world's marketplaces.

High on the altar of American capitalism is the tenet that free-market forces are sufficient to direct the manifest economic destiny of a great nation. Free-market apostles believe that the pursuit of opportunity and profit, unimpeded by government and social obligation, is the way to create wealth and spread benefits to every person in a society. They reject any government intrusion in industrial and marketing decisions and believe that any inequities will be resolved in the long run.

As with any dominant dogma, periods of dislocation and distress give rise to heretical challenges. During the past decade of American industrial decline, free-market theory has been under attack from a number of quarters. Critics point to our nation's declining position in international trade, our rapidly eroding industrial base, the loss of jobs, the growing number of distressed communities, the threat to our national security, and question whether some government economic direction might not be preferable to the "invisible hand" of the free market.

In the past, pressure for increased government activism spawned talk of socialism. Today, it leads respected economic theorists to advocate an overarching national industrial policy. Industrial policy is by far the most controversial aspect of the current normally amiable competitiveness debate. Any mention of central planning or government intervention to protect failing industries, help distressed areas, or support promising new sectors sparks emotional discussions.

"What our federal government cannot do is make hard and objective choices among individual industries, firms, and localities, determining which shall live and which shall die, which shall receive help and which shall not," argues Charles Schultze, economic adviser to Presidents Lyndon Johnson and Jimmy Carter and author of several books.[40]

Usually the question is whether the United States needs or

should have an industrial policy. But some, like Lester Thurow, argue that our nation already has one. According to Thurow, "Every tariff on imported motorcycles and cheese, every trigger price protecting steel, every corporate bailout for Chrysler and Lockheed, every import quota on autos and textiles, and any government allocation of private credit is an implicit industrial policy."[41] Thurow's list could also include our nation's huge defense expenditures, our enormous farm support programs, and our entire tax code, which favors some industries over others.

To be sure, the Pentagon's $300 billion budget and sizable contracts to private sector firms make the Department of Defense (DOD) a major player in our nation's economy. Some even compare DOD to Japan's Ministry of International Trade and Industry because of its financing of fifth-generation computers and large-scale integrated semiconductor projects.

The Defense Department is the principal underwriter of research and development in the United States, the biggest buyer of scrap metal, and the largest employer of scientists and engineers. Pentagon contracts provide corporations with a steady income while they seek out new commercial markets. Military spending often is pivotal in developing new U.S. technological advances. Industry experts estimate that 70 percent of such advances in aviation since 1925 have arisen from military-sponsored research. Little wonder that many of America's most competitive firms are also defense contractors, particularly aircraft firms like Boeing, Lockheed, and McDonnell Douglas.

When the semiconductor industry wanted government backing for a state-of-the-art manufacturing center, it went not to Congress but across the Potomac to the Pentagon. After industry sounded the alarm that America's decline in high technology posed grave risks to U.S. national security, the Defense Department embarked on a half-billion-dollar assistance program. The result: a Semiconductor Manufacturing Technology

Institute, funded by government and private sources to develop advanced manufacturing processes and equipment for the private sector.

Agriculture, another major sector of the economy, has also been the recipient of generous government spending. Our early homestead and land-grant programs, heavy federal investments in basic research at agricultural colleges, experimental state farms, and county extension agents all provided financial or technical assistance to farmers. Investments in infrastructure brought irrigation and electricity to every farm in America. A number of public institutions have provided low-interest loans to the farming community. More recently, government price supports, acreage controls, and export subsidy programs have attempted to prop up farm income and increase U.S. sales overseas. All these programs fly in the face of our nation's free-market ideology. They represent, in fact, a comprehensive industrial policy tilted heavily toward agriculture.

Professors Barry Bluestone and Bennett Harrison support Thurow's view that we have a de facto industrial policy and take his argument a step further. They advocate a planning process at all levels of public life to help ease the pain of economic transition, replace the jobs that are lost, and choose the shape of our economic future.[42]

According to Bluestone and Harrison, industrial policy is not solely the province of Washington, D.C., but of all levels of government. At the local level, industrial policy can take a variety of forms — a neighborhood development corporation, a city council trying to promote health care in a depressed community, a state-funded economic revitalization program that allocates tax revenue to start new businesses, retool old ones, or repair deteriorated roads and bridges.

The heated debate over industrial policy seems to miss another critical point — all of our trading partners maintain some form of industrial policy. Korea's trade barriers, Europe's subsidy of Airbus, Japan's predatory targeting programs, and a host of other unfair trade practices worldwide are all designed to protect or advance a given industrial sector.

In most countries, it is not unusual to ask the components of an ailing industry—the firms, unions, suppliers, creditors, and even whole communities—to work together on a revival strategy. That is exactly what happened in the case of Chrysler Corporation. Our government put its support behind an ambitious package in a gamble to make one of the Big Three competitive again. It worked, and today Chrysler is one of the nation's best-run industries and the U.S. government is $350 million richer for its $1.2 billion in loan guarantees.

Governments today are playing an increasingly greater role in determining the terms of trade in world markets. If our government doesn't learn to play by the same rules, our producers won't be in the game. So the question is not whether our nation should or should not have an industrial policy. The real question is whether we will have a front-door industrial policy that openly advocates the building of a world-class economy or continue our back-door industrial policy of ad hoc, case-by-case policies directed more by political pressure than a realistic assessment of the world economy.

The case of the U.S. steel industry is a useful example of our back-door industrial policy. Since 1968, the United States has attempted to protect the steel industry through a variety of tariffs and quotas, but the industry is weaker than ever. Even with government relief, several big steel companies have chosen to invest in other enterprises rather than meet the competitive challenge head-on. Our nation's industrial policy should be aimed at strengthening or restructuring industries into world-class competitors, not indefinitely sustaining noncompetitive industries or financing the movement of firms into more profitable ventures.

Another long-standing U.S. practice that smacks of industrial policy is the section of our trade laws allowing domestic industries to petition for up to five years' protection from a surge of imports, even those which are being manufactured and marketed fairly. The intent of this procedure is to give U.S. firms a relatively short period in which to restructure and modernize. Once the temporary protections are lifted, the domestic industry must succeed or fail on the basis of its own competitiveness. Unfortunately, the track record in making U.S. industries more competitive as a result of this procedure has been spotty at best. We should require firms to file a detailed modernization plan in order to qualify for import relief.

Assisting troubled firms may be the least controversial aspect of any explicit industrial policy adopted by our government. Congress will have to grapple with some extremely difficult questions in the years ahead. How should our government allocate scarce resources between promising new industrial sectors? Does our government have the will to terminate support to distressed sectors that can no longer be competitive? Are we willing to commit the massive sums necessary to retrain millions of displaced workers and retool our entire economic base?

Congress will also have to exercise a great deal of self-restraint. Congress cannot insist that R & D or capital investment funds be spent equally in each district, as it did with the model cities program, the Economic Development Administration, and Urban Development Action Grants. If individual congressmen simply go to bat for their constituents, industrial policy will turn into a 1990s version of the old-fashioned pork barrel.

The competitiveness magnet draws disparate groups together. It is more positive than protectionism and takes a more comprehensive approach to our nation's trade problems. A long-term strategy, involving government and the private sector, could restore American preeminence, provide millions of jobs, and bring our trade deficit under control. But as *Washington Post* reporter Peter Behr notes, "At this early stage, competitiveness is still more slogan than substance. The common goal papers over some deep, unresolved differences on specifics."[43]

Whether a competitiveness strategy will ever achieve the political backing necessary for a sweeping national program remains to be seen. Robert Keefe, a Washington, D.C., consultant, argues that competitiveness is too distant and complex an issue to expect concrete action in the short term.

> The simple problem of competitiveness in political terms is that it's a hot, sexy thing to talk about in generalities and damn tough to develop into specifics. Most of the specifics get into very long-range kinds of things—education, capital investment —which have very little in the way of popular appeal and public understanding.[44]

Furthermore, despite the recent proclamations by administration officials, it is unlikely that the Reagan White House will support any substantive recommendations, for the same reasons they shunned the Young Commission report on competitiveness in 1985. Any competitiveness program will cost money —big money.

Improving U.S. competitiveness will require increased funding for education, training and trade adjustment assistance, easing of restrictions on technology transfers, reorganization of Executive Branch departments, more export promotion, and other ideas that are anathema to this administration.

Regardless of which party claims the White House in 1988, new leadership in the Oval Office may be required before our nation can expect a fresh blueprint to restore America's competitiveness.

EIGHT

Exporting in a Cutthroat Global Economy

A U.S. TRADE DELEGATION visiting Buenos Aires, Argentina, in 1986 encountered what has become a familiar tale in the world of international commerce—someone else beat us to the punch. This time it was the Swedes, though in other instances it has been the Japanese, the Germans, or the French.

The trade mission was made up of wood product and heavy construction specialists who were invited by the Argentine government to explore the business possibilities associated with its plan to relocate the country's capital city from Buenos Aires to Viedma, 500 miles south.

It was a massive order—the Argentines wanted to build a major new city, including housing for 300,000 new residents, by 1995. They needed materials and technology, plus the credit to get the effort under way during President Raúl Alfonsín's tenure in office, which would end in 1989.

The difficulty of assembling the trade mission says a great deal about our nation's shortcomings in the area of export promotion. Recognizing the limited export assistance resources of the various federal agencies, the firms, needing a member of Congress to give the mission added stature and clout in the eyes of both the Argentine government and U.S. personnel in Argentina, invited me to accompany them. Each participating company had to foot the entire bill for its portion of the four-day mission, a risky investment for a market still largely on the drawing board.

When we arrived in Argentina, we learned for the first time that a major housing exhibition was being held that very week in Buenos Aires. We were shocked to find that the United States housing industry was not represented. Our foreign commercial officers at the U.S. embassy were not even aware of the exhibition. Ironically, our officials' first inkling of the housing conference came when our trade mission showed up for a meeting with the minister of Housing. The walls and tables throughout the ministry lobby were covered with slick, attractive promotional materials in Spanish. After scurrying to find a proper translation, our commercial attaché learned that the Swedish government had sent a well-prepared, high-level delegation to advance the marketing of their wood and housing products in Argentina.

This is not an isolated incident. Every American working abroad can relate horror stories about losing business because foreign governments go all out to help their firms in today's fiercely competitive world marketplace. While the U.S. government makes a limited effort to help our exporters, Japan, Germany, France, and other trading nations are masters at trade shows, marketing, market analysis, research, and other export promotion efforts. American export promotion is often poorly funded and fragmented in comparison with the efforts of our major competitors.

The most dramatic contrast, not surprisingly, is between the United States and Japan. In 1985, Japan outspent us on export promotion by half a billion dollars and employed more than five times as many overseas promoters as we have working for American interests.[1]

But the Japanese aren't the only ones beating us. America

falls far short of other countries in these figures as well. In 1985, the United Kingdom and France each had twice as many overseas trade representatives as the United States, and Italy's personnel numbers nearly tied ours despite dramatic differences in export volumes.[2] In its home offices, Japan employed more than eight times as many export specialists in 1985 as we did in the United States. Italy had three times our home export staff, and West Germany beat us by half.[3]

The United States government has been naive in what has become a cutthroat global marketplace. While our "hands off" government policies seek to let the market forces prevail, foreign governments are pouring billions into programs to fuel their competitive drive. Americans discuss and theorize about economic policy while foreign nations actively pursue and fight for markets. Political conservatives blindly embrace government noninterference to keep the marketplace pure; liberals react instinctively against the idea of government's assisting business in any form.

These attitudes color our approach to domestic economic policies. With a few notable exceptions such as the Small Business Administration, farm price supports, and huge government contracts to defense contractors, most federal laws are intended to protect consumers and promote competition. Over the last fifty years, the government has been viewed as an adversary, not a promoter, of business. The Carter and Reagan administrations were committed to deregulating private industry and privatizing government services. The fashionable attitude is that most government policies are impediments to business and economic progress.

But how do such efforts square in an international economy when other nations aren't playing by the same rules? How can U.S. businesses compete with foreign governments that set up programs to give their firms an advantage? How should the U.S. government respond when our trade deficit is caused in part by foreign countries' boosting their export industries?

For years, American businesses have enjoyed an expanding domestic market and been slow to seek foreign sales. As a result, our firms have been outpaced by foreign companies, which have always had to seek potential markets outside their own countries.

Because international trade involves long distances, special language skills, and potential risks, most commercial ventures are left to large corporations and a few globe-trotting entrepreneurs. Just 20 percent of the total number of American companies account for more than 80 percent of the goods leaving U.S. ports.[4]

The era of U.S. multinational dominance is fading. The new corporate giants have names like Hitachi, Mitsui, and Mitsubishi. As America's multinationals begin to lose their grip on foreign markets, smaller U.S.-based companies must pick up the slack. Convincing small and medium-size businesses to be active players in world trade and helping them overcome their fear of competing in foreign markets are tremendous challenges.

The bottom line is clear: if we are to get back into the competition, we have to match the efforts of our competitors. Time is running out. We must increase our exports dramatically to bring down the trade deficit or succumb to inevitable protectionist pressures. Left with the bitter alternatives of checking our trade imbalance by exporting more or importing less, government must dramatically change its policies and spending priorities.

To restore American competitiveness, Congress and the President must set aside their abstract dreams about a fully liberalized trading system and adopt policies that will encourage more U.S. firms to get into foreign markets. We must set up programs to match other governments' efforts to help their exporting industries. Government and private leaders must cooperate in developing marketing strategies, conducting trade missions, and ensuring that our industries are as well equipped as any other nation's to fight in the world marketplace.

CASE I: CREATING A NEW MARKET — HOUSING FOR LATIN AMERICA

The Pacific Northwest timber industry, once a dominant economic force, suffered through a number of bad years in the early 1980s. From 1979 to 1984, dozens of sawmills closed their gates. Wood product employment in Washington State dropped from 55,000 to 37,500, a loss of nearly 30 percent in just five years.[5]

Even the robust growth of housing starts in 1984 did not bring the customary surge in demand for Northwest lumber. For a variety of reasons, wood product mills in Oregon and Washington were losing their competitive hold on the domestic market and would have to look elsewhere or close their doors forever.

But were there potential markets abroad? Japan, Korea, and China all need softwood timber from the western United States, but they buy raw logs almost exclusively so they can keep the jobs and economic benefits in their own countries. These nations maintain steep tariffs, discriminatory inspection standards, and other barriers designed to frustrate U.S. lumber exporters and protect their own mills.

As a result, Japan purchases nearly two thirds of its wood in the form of raw logs, Korea buys 83 percent in logs, and China imports a staggering 95 percent in logs and almost no finished products.[6] While U.S. wood product companies continue to press for sales in these traditional Asian markets, the message is clear: to achieve dramatic expansion of our markets, we must look elsewhere.

In the early 1980s, public and private sector studies pointed to Latin America, with an estimated housing need of 15 to 20 million new units, as a possible market.[7] There were serious obstacles. To most of the population, wood housing conjured up images of *casas de pobres*— flimsy-looking shantytowns of the poor. Latin-American officials had to be convinced that wood housing was affordable and could be protected against fire, termites, and other hazards.

U.S. builders compared their costs with those of traditional Latin-American building techniques and discovered that they could produce wood housing 20 percent cheaper, even after import duties, transportation costs, and factoring in the exchange rate. The use of quicker, more efficient U.S. building technologies also would keep interest and labor costs down.[8] By using structural lumber precut in the United States instead of masonry, a builder in Chile could reduce the time it takes to build a home from twenty-one weeks to three.[9]

Recognizing both the market potential and the obstacles facing U.S. firms, the late secretary of Commerce, Malcolm Baldrige, and I teamed up in 1984 to develop a strategy that would break the barriers and open up new markets in Latin America. Again, given the absence of U.S. export promotion efforts on the scale of other nations', Secretary Baldrige and I strongly believed that direct participation by top administration and congressional officials was necessary to offset our competitors' advantage.

The objectives of the strategy were straightforward but ambitious. First, we needed to identify the housing needs in Latin America and the Caribbean. Then we would introduce U.S. wood housing products and technology. In time, we would establish the basis for a continuing cooperative effort, resulting in expanded housing for the region. Ultimately, we hoped to establish a pattern for the expansion of trade in other areas.

We selected twenty-one Latin-American countries that faced immediate housing needs. At a Commerce Department luncheon we made our pitch to the ambassadors of those countries, telling them that we recognized their critical housing needs and felt we had the products and technology to help them achieve their housing goals. We then invited the ambassadors to send their Housing ministers to a major Inter-American Housing Conference in Seattle, Washington, later that year. The high-level U.S. support and the offer of housing assistance made this a rare offer for the ambassadors. Most could not resist. Fifty-nine officials from nineteen Latin-American nations participated in the conference, along with one hundred U.S. government and industry leaders.

Beyond the technical sessions designed to demonstrate the advantages of wood products and U.S. housing technology, we had a graphic surprise for our foreign guests. During the three-day conference, a crew of untrained workers built an all-wood, 400-square-foot home in the hotel lobby. The construction began the first evening, as the participants gathered amid the lumber stacked on the lobby floor. Three days later, the visitors marveled at an attractive two-bedroom, stucco-finished home that would have taken months to complete using traditional materials.

The Inter-American Housing Conference generated a great deal of interest among the Latin-American nations, but we had to prove our case on their own turf. We devised demonstration housing projects in six key Latin-American and Caribbean countries. Several government agencies put up $350,000 to finance the program, and the U.S. timber companies, led by the American Plywood Association, provided materials at or below cost. Under the plan, more than fifty prefabricated houses were built in Chile, Peru, Ecuador, Barbados, the Dominican Republic, and Jamaica.

In nearly every case, these demonstration projects excited tremendous interest among the local people. In Peru, nearly twenty-five hundred families applied for the right to buy the fifteen demonstration units.[10] Clearly, we were making some headway against the image of shantytowns, the fear of insect and fire damage, and other traditional biases against wood housing.

Marketing opportunities have to be pursued, however. Sponsoring a conference and funding demonstration projects are necessary steps, but they do not cinch a deal or create an entire new market. To keep up the momentum for U.S. wood housing, we formed a government–private sector trade mission to visit several of the countries where the model houses were being built.

Less than one year after we had first contacted the Latin-American ambassadors, I led a delegation of housing and wood product specialists to Chile, Peru, and Ecuador. We arrived as the model units were being finished and met with housing officials and builders in each country. The trip was an eye opener. In Chile, government and construction industry officials marveled that wood housing had held up better than concrete during a major earthquake six months earlier.

In Peru, President Fernando Belaunde was so excited about the model homes that he offered to send a naval vessel to the United States to pick up the material. President Belaunde, an architect by profession, personally escorted the trade mission to the demonstration units and proudly showed us a number of other projects his government had on the drawing board. We felt the idea of wood housing had truly taken hold in Peru.

We found quite a different story in Ecuador. There, the U.S. government was involved in an $18 million program to build low-income housing, the largest project of its kind ever financed. The fifty-two-hundred-unit Solanda housing project was intended to be a model of U.S. planning, materials, and know-how. Unfortunately, it was a nightmare that raised serious questions about the appropriateness of traditional U.S. foreign aid. The project was substantially completed, but when we visited, no residents had moved in because water and utilities were not available. The core units were extremely small, even by local standards for the poorest families. The project carried 18 percent interest rates while 13 percent government housing loans were available for middle- and upper-income housing.

While the results varied from nation to nation, the export

promotion effort—from the conference to the model units to the trade missions—laid the groundwork for American firms to begin to compete in a previously nonexistent foreign market.

CASE 2: CRACKING AN EXISTING MARKET— TELECOMMUNICATIONS IN ASIA

Although the United States has fallen from the number one spot in many industries, we still boast the giants in the telecommunications industry, where global competition is especially stiff. IBM, AT&T, and the Boeing Company still dominate in vital areas. In the growing service sectors, U.S. banks, credit card companies, airlines, and others have managed to stay on top of markets worldwide. According to one observer, "The Americans are light years ahead of everyone."

We are still on top, but other nations are closing in rapidly. The economic superpowers are jockeying for an enormous prize. Huge markets for high-tech and telecommunication products are opening up in the emerging industrialized nations. Their leaders recognize that a technological base is essential to achieving their economic goals. Countries like the People's Republic of China, Indonesia, and India are greatly expanding their telecommunication systems and service. These three nations alone represent half the world's population, with virtually unlimited telecommunication needs in the future. The stakes are high. Because these nations have government telecommunication monopolies, any firm that captures a contract today will have a foothold in a massive future market.

U.S. companies got a late start in the global telecommunication market. AT&T, the world's largest producer of telecommunication equipment, was prohibited from seeking market opportunities abroad until deregulation in 1982. By that time, former colonial powers like Great Britain and France already had installed systems in many developing nations, giving them a decisive edge on new contracts.

Nations like China and India not only want telecommunication equipment, they want to make it themselves. Furthermore, they have every intention of exporting once they acquire the manufacturing expertise. Thus, technology trade is a double-edged sword. Cooperative arrangements and joint ventures that win contracts may also create future fierce competitors.

Considering the limited finances of developing nations, the costs of major telecommunication systems pose another problem for U.S. exporters. Many nations base their buying decisions not on quality or even price, but the financing arrangements. France, Japan, and other industrialized nations often mix foreign aid with traditional financing to sweeten the deal. To date, the United States has been very reluctant to match this concessionary financing.

The difference can be startling. On a $1 billion loan over twenty-five years, a difference of 2 to 3 percent in interest rates can add up to hundreds of millions of dollars. Without comparable financing, even superior U.S. products cannot compete. To overcome these hurdles would require a comprehensive government-industry export promotion effort. I set to work with industry leaders and other federal officials. We started with an in-depth survey to determine telecommunication policies and U.S. export potential in ten major countries.[11]

Armed with this information, I worked with several other West Coast members of Congress to sponsor a major international high-tech trade conference aimed at the most promising markets identified in the study.

To demonstrate the importance of the conference, Republican Congressman Rodney Chandler of Washington and I led a delegation of telecommunication firms to the Pacific Rim to extend a personal invitation to the top officials of each targeted nation to the November 1985 conference. The industry-government mission paid off. Seven countries, including the People's Republic of China, Hong Kong, India, Indonesia, the Republic of Korea, Malaysia, and the Republic of Singapore, sent high-level delegates to the conference in Seattle and California. The three-day meeting, jointly funded by government agencies and participating firms, enabled U.S. companies to show their wares, make contacts, and take foreign buyers on tours of their manufacturing facilities.

Based on the market potential identified at the conference, we decided to focus our export efforts on India and Indonesia. In January 1987, Chandler and I again led a top-level group of telecommunication manufacturers on a ten-day trade mission to India and Indonesia. Traveling with congressmen opened many doors for our businesspeople, both with foreign officials and our own embassy personnel. Instead of beating their heads against a maze of low-level bureaucracy, the company officials on the trip met with the heads of state, top cabinet ministers, and key businesspeople in each nation.

Our first stop was Indonesia, a nation of 169 million people and over one thousand islands, covering an area as large as the continental United States. Telecommunications is the modern bridge that connects the islands. The Indonesian government plans to spend $5 billion over the next five years to double its communications capacity. With such a huge potential market, foreign governments are working behind the scenes to give their telecommunication companies every advantage in securing the business.

The story of Indonesian telecommunications mirrors America's predicament worldwide. A U.S. firm, the Hughes Company, built the original Indonesian satellite systems in the mid 1970s to early 1980s. At that time, America's technological edge overshadowed all foreign competition. Government financing helped each sale by providing near-commercial rates.

During the bidding for the third-generation system, a French team knocked out the American consortium. The French system did not win because of its superior quality or lower price;

it won by offering its consulting and design work to the Indonesian government free of charge. The French took the risk and then the market.

Our trade delegation had a secret weapon to counteract several years of losing out on Indonesian telecommunication contracts caused by lack of competitive financing. Two weeks before our trip, the Export-Import Bank made a surprise announcement of a $100 million line of credit targeted for telecommunication purchases in Indonesia and Thailand. Eximbank's announcement was a desperate response to a $1 billion line of credit offered by Japan at extremely generous terms. The Eximbank pledge made a difference on our trade mission. At last, in at least one market, the United States was on roughly equal footing.

From Djakarta, we flew to New Delhi, India. With 780 million people and an aggressive modernization schedule, India may hold the potential for the largest telecommunication system in the world.[12] The Gandhi government has earmarked $5.6 billion for communication equipment in its 1985–1990 Five-Year Plan, nearly five times the amount allocated in the previous plan. Indian leaders told us that government outlays could go as high as $35 billion in future five-year plans.

India's telecommunications goals are truly ambitious—a fully automated local telephone exchange network by 1990, self-sufficiency in telecommunication equipment and services, more telephones—twenty for each thousand people instead of four. Paradoxically, India needs to import a greater amount of technology in the short term in order to achieve these goals.

Both the French and English have major footholds in the Indian market, but the American firms represented by the delegation feel they can compete. The biggest obstacle facing U.S. manufacturers is technical—Indian specifications are vastly different from those for American systems.

Unlike Indonesia and most developing countries, India does not consider financing a major issue. Indian officials have negotiated a long-term World Bank loan, so favorable credit terms are available for telecommunication purchases regardless of the source. Without the World Bank, U.S. companies would again have to deal with foreign credit financing.

The Lessons of Export Promotion

These cases are only two examples of aggressive, creative export promotion efforts. While they differ in many ways, they provide several valuable lessons.

LESSON 1: COOPERATION

The Latin-American housing strategy attempted to open new markets for U.S. lumber producers, but it also broke new ground for U.S. export promotion policy. The housing effort was a rare display of mobilizing America's resources. At least five federal agencies joined forces with members of Congress and dozens of private firms to create a market where none had existed. In Baldrige and me, we had a Republican cabinet official and a Democratic congressman plotting together to get U.S. timber into foreign markets!

To meet the challenge of trade competitiveness, business, labor, education, the Congress, and the administration must all work together. Our competitors in Japan and Europe have already recognized this imperative. The longer we delay, the further we fall behind.

LESSON 2: CLOUT

Working alone in overseas markets, American exporters often have tremendous difficulty gaining access to foreign decision makers. U.S. business agents can spend months, or even years, trying to see the right person. But when a U.S. congressman or top agency official leads a trade mission, industry representatives enjoy unheard-of access to decision makers and potential buyers.

In India, Indonesia, and Latin America, our embassies had set up dozens of meetings with key foreign officials long before the trade mission arrived. The reason is obvious. Members of Congress and top agency officials are in a position to influence decisions and legislation of critical importance to foreign governments and businesses. Foreign officials are also starved for in-depth information about bills and issues under consideration by the U.S. government.

In India, for example, government officials wanted to talk to us about sales of highly sophisticated electronic and nuclear technology. In Latin America, debt rescheduling and foreign aid were major topics of discussion.

U.S. actions are still felt all around the globe. As a result, key U.S. decision makers can open doors for U.S. exporters. The presence of a congressman or top federal official also ensures that our overseas State Department or Commerce Department personnel go the extra mile for the business delegation. They know they'll hear about any lax performance.

Even governors, mayors, and other state and local officials can help smooth the way for U.S. firms. While these officials generally do not influence foreign policy decisions or other national policies that affect our trading partners, their official stature and influence over certain local economic issues can often improve the access for our exporters.

LESSON 3: CATCHING UP

American exporters sometimes complain that our Foreign Commercial officers are uninformed or disinterested, compared with foreign government export promotion personnel. What they forget is that ten years ago, the Foreign Commercial Service did not exist! Before then, the only assistance available to

U.S. business came from the economic division in each embassy. While some did an excellent job, most focused on abstract fiscal and monetary analysis and turned up their noses at commercial activities.

Jimmy Carter created the Foreign Commercial Service by Executive Order in January 1980. Many of its officers were drawn from the ranks of the State Department's embassy economic personnel. Today, the program has offices in sixty-three countries, and its forty-eight district offices around the United States conduct a wide range of export promotion services. Many of its specialists are recruited from private business, so they know firsthand the problems our exporters encounter overseas.

The Foreign Commercial Service is patterned after a highly successful farm export promotion program, the Foreign Agricultural Service, which administers a wide variety of market research, trade promotion, and export financing programs and maintains a network of trade specialists in seventy embassies around the world.

Despite this highly effective export promotion program and $5 billion in government loans and loan guarantees, U.S. farm exports dropped from $44 billion in 1981 to only $26 billion in 1986. In this case, however, the culprit is not lack of U.S. export promotion and financing but falling world demand because of the growing worldwide surplus of grains and other commodities.

America has also lagged behind our competitors in the use of export trading companies to facilitate exports. An export trading company is a specialized firm with the contacts, expertise, and financial backing to market the products of a number of small manufacturing firms in difficult overseas markets. Other nations have employed export trading companies for years. At last count, Japan had 6000 of them pursuing world markets and bringing export opportunities to the doorstep of its local firms.

The Department of Commerce estimates that the creation of U.S. export trading companies would enable up to 25,000 American firms to export for the first time, creating 300,000 or more jobs.

Unfortunately, U.S. banking and antitrust laws made the formation of trading companies difficult, if not impossible. In the early 1980s, I, with several other Democratic congressmen, proposed loosening these restrictions, an effort that quickly became bipartisan. In October 1982, President Reagan signed into law the Export Trading Company Act.

To date, trading companies have not revolutionized U.S. trade, as many had predicted they would. Banks and businesses have been slow to embrace the concept, some restrictions still apply, and the overvalued U.S. dollar has hampered any trade innovations. With more rational exchange rates and further tinkering with the regulations, however, export trading companies may play a significant role.

One of the most exciting federal export initiatives is the Trade and Development Program (TDP). This little-known agency finances relatively low-cost feasibility studies on major overseas infrastructure projects or other export opportunities. As the French demonstrated in the Indonesian telecommunications market, feasibility studies and design work are often the key to winning huge contracts in developing markets.

Since its formation in 1980, TDP has spent $75 million on feasibility studies and other export promotion work. These efforts have generated $605 million in exports, with a staggering $7 billion in follow-on sales expected in the next five to twenty years. If even half these sales materialize, every dollar spent by TDP will have leveraged $40 in U.S. exports.[13] TDP is one of the real success stories in U.S. export promotion. While other agencies occasionally funded feasibility studies, it has greatly expanded and institutionalized this program, with spectacular results.

Another little-known recent addition to the U.S. export promotion arsenal is the Overseas Private Investment Corporation. Established in 1971, OPIC is designed to assist U.S. investment in Third World nations to promote economic development in the recipient nations and generate export opportunities for U.S. firms.

Studies show that nearly one third of all U.S. exports go to American subsidiaries overseas, so OPIC's work can be a major shot in the arm to our trade balance. From 1982 to 1984, OPIC insured or financed 395 projects. In addition to the economic and financial benefits to the developing nations, these projects will generate $5.5 billion in exports of U.S. equipment and supplies and an estimated 71,000 jobs for American workers.[14]

Despite these advances in export promotion activities, the United States still ranks dead last among the major industrialized nations in export promotion activities. In 1985, the U.S. government spent only $0.56 per capita to assist the nation's exporters. By contrast, Japan spent $5.22, Great Britain, $4.07, and Canada, $7.52.[15]

LESSON 4: COMPETITIVE FINANCING

Export promotion efforts like the Inter-American Housing Conference or the trade mission to Argentina can help open doors for U.S. exporters. But all the marketing shows and trade missions in the world won't accomplish anything if foreign nations can't afford to buy our products.

American goods are still number one when it comes to quality worldwide. Our products are often very competitive when it comes to price. But as we have seen, many nations, particularly in the Third World, make their purchasing decisions on the basis of financing rather than quality or price.

On the telecommunications trade mission to India and Indonesia, we heard again and again from foreign trade ministers,

"Our number one consideration is financing. If you don't offer competitive terms, you won't get the deal." Unless our firms can offer financing equal to that of the Japanese, the French, the Germans, and our other competitors, we're going to be shut out of foreign markets.

Unfortunately, the United States does not measure up when it comes to export financing. In 1986, our government assisted only 5 percent of American non-farm exports, compared to 28 percent in Japan, 30 percent in France, and 34 percent in Great Britain.[16]

In the area of housing exports, for example, several U.S. government agencies offer financing programs, but these are mainly empty promises. Congress created a Housing Guarantee Program within the State Department and authorized $1.74 billion for loans and loan guarantees in 1984, but little or no money has ever gone to assist commercial ventures. Instead, the State Department has used the program to support traditional housing projects in developing countries by financing land, sewers, or other infrastructure, leaving our homebuilders and manufacturers out in the cold.

The Agriculture Department's Commodity Credit program could also provide significant financing for housing exports. Under the program, the federal government guarantees private bank loans for periods up to ten years, allowing greater security and lower interest rates. Unfortunately, the Reagan administration refuses to make lumber, plywood, and other wood products fully eligible for the program. Without this financing, U.S. wood products are simply not competitive with Scandinavian or Canadian products.

From November 1986 to February 1987 alone, $21 million in U.S. wood exports were lost through lack of financing.[17] Sadly, these lost revenues represent just a small part of the potential business. Once U.S. products gain a foothold in a given market, consumers tend to continue to "buy American." The lack of government financing may have cost our economy hundreds of millions in future sales.

These are the grim realities of international commerce. Most foreign governments, trying to carve out a larger piece of the world economic pie, have adopted aggressive export promotion programs. Today's international rules deal mainly with import barriers; government export promotion efforts go virtually unchecked.

Export promotion offers hope and a warning. By improving U.S. efforts to compete in international markets, we can help pull our country out of its trade tailspin and get our farms and factories humming again.

But if America fails to match our trading partners in the export promotion arena, we face only higher trade deficits, deeper unemployment, a reduced standard of living, and intense pressure to take protectionist steps that could undermine the international trading system and precipitate another worldwide depression.

——————

NINE

Updating the World Trading System

THE MOOD was tense on 21 May 1986, as the House of Representatives debated the sweeping trade package assembled by the Democratic leadership. The galleries and hallways around the House chamber were filled with nervous White House officials, high-priced lobbyists, and harried staffers.

On the floor, the members were debating a Republican amendment to strip out some of the central provisions of the bill. The Reagan administration was fighting hard, but it looked as though the Democrats had the votes.

Finally, Sam Gibbons, the chairman of the House Ways and Means Trade Subcommittee and a Florida gentleman from the old school, had had enough. He seized the floor and began talking in a slow, deliberate voice that commanded respect:

> Mr. Chairman, the problem with the Crane amendment is that it takes us back to the status quo, and the status quo is not sufficient for the conditions today.
>
> Through [this bill] we serve notice on the world that we stick to the high principles of free and open and competitive trade. But we have changed our tactics. The tactics that we used in the

1940s were sufficient for the conditions of the 1940s but the tactics of the 1940s are not sufficient to the condition today.

When these tactics were promulgated, the world was far different than today. There was not a surplus of consumer goods on the world market. There was not a surplus of high-technology goods available to the world. There was not a surplus of any kind of goods available to the world.

I can remember when I tried to buy a car and they were not available unless you had a certificate of necessity. I tried to buy a business suit to start my practice of law and what I got was really disreputable because there were not any consumer goods available. Clothing was still being rationed. Tires were still being rationed.

Consequently, there was no dumping of consumer goods on the world market in the 1940s. There was no subsidization of goods on the world market in the 1940s. We could have a rather relaxed attitude toward those practices.

Today, the world is awash with consumer goods, agricultural products, high-technology goods, and all kinds of capital products. Governments now are subsidizing into our market unfairly, targeting our market to take it away from us by unfair business practices and dumping their goods in here in conspiracies to take our market.

These are the kinds of problems we have got to face. We cannot have free trade, we cannot have competitive trade, unless we are willing to fight, with the tools of our trade law, those unfair business practices and unfair governmental practices that dominate today's market.[1]

Moments later the amendment was defeated by a more than two-to-one margin.

Gibbons's history lesson illustrates a critical point often overlooked by analysts of America's current trade situation. The problems facing our nation have grown and changed dramatically over time, but our laws have often not kept pace with these new developments. Even more important, many of the international trade and monetary institutions that govern today's complex trade and financial activities were established over forty years ago to address a radically different set of circumstances. Confronting today's trade problems with these outdated laws and institutions is like trying to play a compact disc on an old 78 rpm phonograph.

Today's international transactions have virtually no rules, and those that do exist are often honored only in the breach. The governing body for world trade, the General Agreement on Tariffs and Trade (GATT), was originally conceived in 1945 as a temporary trade policy panel while a far more sweeping trade organization was being assembled. Forty years later, GATT is still the closest thing to a world trade dispute resolution mechanism, but its authority covers less than 10 percent of world trade, excluding such vital sectors as agriculture and services. When disputes arise, GATT is slow to move, slow to decide, and its rulings are often ignored or derided. Demands for broader GATT coverage of trade issues are, more often than not, politely ignored by member nations.

It is not only trade that lacks rules and guidelines. International finance has been on a roller coaster for the past twenty years, and no one seems to know how to get off. Billions in international capital move around the world with a single telephone call. Financial markets have become worldwide, twenty-four-hour-a-day institutions. Rumors of trouble at Illinois's Continental Bank in May 1984 caused foreign investors to withdraw billions in capital, which could have led to widespread bank closures if the Federal Reserve Board had not stepped in with a bailout plan. Meanwhile, much of the developing world is staggering under a trillion-dollar debt burden, with hundreds of billions owed to American banks. Big banks, already weakened by energy, agriculture, and real estate loans that have turned sour, are terrified by default threats on long-standing debts. The United States itself has an external debt that depends on foreign borrowing. The need for credit is immense, but the global capability for extending it is rapidly shrinking.

In the 1930s and 1940s, the dominant international economic concerns were avoiding a recurrence of the Great Depression and rebuilding the war-torn economies of Europe. As a result, the major economic institutions created in the 1940s — the Marshall Plan, the Bretton Woods exchange rate system, the International Monetary Fund, the World Bank, and GATT — reflect these concerns. The architects of the economic system of the 1940s could not possibly anticipate the staggering economic problems of the 1980s — huge bilateral trade imbalances, enormous debt in developing and developed nations alike, the possibility of default by debtor nations. While national leaders and the managers of our economic institutions have tried to keep pace with shifting economic problems, the rate of change in the world economy has far outstripped the ability of our institutions to adapt. One of the great tasks confronting U.S. and foreign leaders in the next few years is the overhaul and expansion of our international economic system to cope with these complex emerging problems.

Restoring a Global Finance System

To restore the world trading system after the Depression, a new financial system was necessary. The economic planners of the late 1930s and the 1940s were determined to avoid the chaos and competitive devaluations of the Depression years.

In 1944, the major Allies met in Bretton Woods, New Hampshire, to map out a new international economic order. While most countries favored the stability of the gold standard, they feared a system that invited competitive devaluations as a means of gaining trade advantages. Nor did they want a system that could push a country into a recession as a response to a temporary trade deficit. There was even skepticism about tying world liquidity to the supply of gold.

The conference was a landmark in economic and political

affairs. Nations agreed, for the first time, on a method for regulating the international financial system. Even though some of the rules have changed since 1944, many of the principles and institutions outlined at Bretton Woods still form the basis of financial and trade transactions.

The conference set up a framework for managing exchange rates, which eventually became known as the Bretton Woods exchange rate system. The idea was to "tie" currencies, establishing their value in relation to one another and to a universally accepted gold standard. Under the Bretton Woods system, exchange rates were to be fixed but could be adjusted as necessary. Currencies were to be devalued or revalued (raised in value) only in cases of a "fundamental disequilibrium" — another way of saying that big changes could come only if things were really out of kilter. The exchange rates were to be worked out cooperatively between countries, allowing for adjustments of relative prices between nations to cushion the painful deflation and unemployment that occurred under the gold standard. For much of the 1950s and 1960s, exchange rates proved to be very stable. The comparative evaluation of the U.S. dollar and the British pound, for example, remained constant from 1948 to 1967.[2]

Despite the success of the Bretton Woods system in the early years, a fixed rate proved unsustainable against the spectacular growth of Japan and the countries of Europe in the 1960s. The stresses on the U.S. economy were increasing — mounting balance-of-payments deficits, a growing run on American gold reserves by other nations eager to convert their U.S. dollars, and inflationary pressures that began when President Lyndon Johnson tried to fight both Vietnam and poverty without raising taxes.

Then in August 1971, President Richard Nixon closed the American gold window, thus ending the Bretton Woods system of fixed exchange rates. Nixon's action was probably inevitable. The world had crossed a threshold — nations could no longer maintain fixed exchange rates while huge quantities of financial capital changed hands so rapidly around the globe.

A number of international meetings were held in the 1970s to seek consensus on a new system to replace Bretton Woods, but the United States, with the concurrence of Germany and several other large powers, resisted going back to a regime of rigidly pegged exchange rates.

In the absence of a new agreement, the world has moved to a de facto "managed" floating exchange rate system. Today, only the United States and a few other countries allow their currencies to float freely. Most other countries, including Japan, Canada, and the European Community, manage their exchange rates by buying or selling domestic or foreign currencies to raise or lower the worth of their currency when they believe it is improperly valued. Many countries still peg their monetary value to a major currency, usually the U.S. dollar. Finally, some countries group together in currency blocs in order to stabilize exchange rates among themselves, the most notable example being the European Community.

The floating exchange rate system has not been kind to the dollar. By 1978, the dollar had dropped to a low of 79 percent of its 1970 value. The combination of President Carter's "dollar rescue package," followed by President Reagan's tight money policy and higher interest rates, drove the dollar's value up by 60 percent between 1979 and late 1984. Indeed, by mid 1985, the dollar had risen to levels above those attained just before the collapse of the Bretton Woods system. By the end of 1987, it plunged to its lowest level since World War II, creating near panic in financial markets around the world. Where it will go next is uncertain.[3]

Exchange rate volatility has also led to severe dislocations in the global economy. High U.S. interest rates increased debt-service burdens on poorer countries and reduced investment and real GNP growth in other industrialized countries. Extreme fluctuations in currency values also made it impossible for merchandise traders to adjust the prices of their products in international markets.

The high value of the dollar was responsible for a large share of America's record trade deficits and caused severe economic dislocations in domestic industries that depend on export sales or are vulnerable to foreign imports. This decline in the automobile, steel, textile, chemical, and agricultural industries resulted in millions of lost job opportunities, heightened concern about America's competitiveness, and sparked calls for protectionist action.

Such fears prompted the Reagan administration to abandon its firmly held position of abstaining from exchange rate intervention. Treasury Secretary James Baker's secret meeting with the finance ministers of other industrialized nations in New York on 22 September 1985 marked a turning point for the United States' policy toward exchange rates. From then on, these governments agreed to monitor exchange rates and even to intervene to ensure stability against a higher dollar.

Would the United States be better off with a rigid fixed rate or the current floating rate, which some say is excessively volatile? One critic asked, "Do we want our countries to be at the mercy of every whim of the gnomes of Zurich or the Federal Governors of Washington?"[4] Is it possible to avoid the extremes of fixed-rate and free-floating exchange systems, or are other untried methods worth pursuing?

Under the fixed gold standard, a country was strictly bound by the system. If domestic prices rose and a balance-of-payments deficit occurred, gold would leave the country, causing a monetary contraction, recession, or worse. Yet under a floating system, countries are free to determine their own domestic price levels without collectively imposed restraints. The system lacks the discipline so necessary in the coordination of currency values.

Without institutional rules and built-in constraints on the movement of international currencies, global traders will be at the mercy of the financiers and government policymakers. The state of a nation's economy, the political mood back home, or the election of national leaders with new agendas could possibly undermine, if not destroy, any exchange rate system.

The Bretton Woods conference set up the International Monetary Fund (IMF), in part to administer the exchange rate system. The IMF was also designed to function as an international bank, loaning money to countries that were experiencing temporary balance-of-payments difficulties. Instead of moving toward recession to lower the price level and make its products more competitive in international markets, a country could secure a loan from the fund. Small loans could be negotiated as a matter of right, just as if the country had a checking account at a corner bank. The more a country sought to borrow, however, the more the fund would seek assurances that it would adopt the economic policies necessary to balance its international accounts.

If gold supplies or national treasuries were unable to supply the world with enough liquidity to conduct world business, the fund could create a limited amount of a world currency called Special Drawing Rights. Also known as paper gold, the SDRs were to be held by the fund or by governments, not by individuals.

When first established, the IMF was expected to deal with short-term balance-of-payments problems and infrequent adjustments to essentially fixed exchange rates. But, as we have seen, fixed exchange rates floundered in the late 1960s and finally broke down in 1971 because of inflationary pressures in the United States, severe balance-of-payments disparities, and the enormous stresses on world currency markets.

As balance-of-payment problems shifted from the industrial to the developing world in the 1960s and 1970s, the IMF suddenly found itself dealing with an unfamiliar set of economic problems. Instead of short-term economic adjustments for highly developed countries, the IMF was dealing with structural poverty in the world's most desperate nations. The IMF worked to help agriculture-dependent developing countries cope with severe climatic conditions and wide fluctuations in world commodity prices. A similar program was developed for oil-importing countries that were hit with sharply higher oil prices in 1973 and again in 1979.

But the IMF was equipped with only one set of tools, and these policies created serious problems for many developing countries. The budget cutting and tighter monetary policies that worked fairly quickly to correct imbalances in an industrial country often meant severe pain to a country with millions living on the edge of poverty or starvation. Where cutting budget deficits meant increasing the price of foodstuffs for urban populations, riots in the streets could follow.

Much of the IMF's advice was sound on technical grounds. Countries had to get their key economic rates in line—the exchange rate to reflect world market conditions and the interest rate to encourage long-term investment. Where a country had agricultural potential, it needed to set agricultural prices at a level that would encourage long-term production rather than provide a short-term subsidy to industrial workers. But the IMF was not well suited to look at the longer-term needs of many developing countries.

During the 1970s, a number of developing countries accumulated sizable external debts that threatened the world financial system. After some prodding by the United States, the IMF played a central role in negotiating and approving agreements between commercial banks and less developed debtor countries to stave off defaults and serious ruptures in the world financial system.

The Bretton Woods conferees realized that more than the IMF was needed to rebuild the economies of the Allied nations. So the International Bank for Reconstruction and Development, the World Bank, was formed as part of a broader effort to restore the industrial strength of Europe and Japan. The bank's first loan of $250 million went to France in 1947.

At the outset, the bank had been dedicated to helping Europe recover its prewar economic position, but in the 1950s, it turned to the challenge of long-term growth in the developing world. The initial focus of the bank was on infrastructure projects such as dams, roads, and electric transmission lines. In the bank's view, adequate physical infrastructure was a prerequisite for economic growth and development. Manufacturing and services could be left to private initiative or, in some cases, to the initiative of a developing country's government.

To encourage the growth of private, indigenous business, the members of the bank created a separate affiliate, the International Finance Corporation (IFC), which served as a source of hard currency for individual firms or groups of businesses. Loans went directly to businesses rather than passing through a government department. The bank raised most of its funds on capital markets, but it relied on the promises of the United States and others if the World Bank portfolio should not perform adequately.

Development loans were often risky, so the backing of the major industrial nations was essential to raise capital at low rates, relative to world financial conditions. But the bank still had to earn enough to cover its own expenses and pay interest on its own borrowings. And even the bank's more favorable terms proved to be too steep for many of the poorest countries, so in 1960 steps were taken to form another affiliate, the International Development Association (IDA).

Instead of medium-term loans at essentially market rates, the IDA made long-term loans—thirty years and more—at highly concessional interest rates. The terms were so generous that many of the loans were virtual grants. To keep IDA funding distinct from the operations of the bank itself, members of the bank agreed to make separate allocations to the IDA.

The 1960s brought more than the IDA's willingness to help foster growth in the poorest of the developing countries. The World Bank began to move beyond its earlier emphasis on physical infrastructure to fund projects in education, health care, and small-scale agriculture.

Like the IMF, the mandate of the bank has shifted over the years, and the bank has proved remarkably adaptable to changing world conditions. It has moved from reconstruction for war-torn Europe to broad-based development throughout the Third World, from physical infrastructure to human capital; from individual project loans to structural adjustment loans that target an entire economy.

Flexibility, however, is no substitute for money. The needs of the developing world have rapidly outpaced the resources of the bank. Many projects in the poorer countries cannot meet the payback criteria of regular bank loans. Funds for the IDA are limited and are not likely to grow rapidly in an era of budget stringency. The trillion dollars owed by developing nations to the developed world are far beyond the bank's resources. The problems of debt and development have proved awesome, even for the World Bank.

Managing World Trade

In 1945, the leaders of the West were eager to distance themselves from the Smoot-Hawley legacy by erecting a set of rules and institutions to govern international trade. Their goals were to prohibit international cartels, reduce tariffs to manageable levels, eliminate the national licensing requirements that impeded foreign trade, and curb discrimination in trade regulations. Clearly, such steps would help to create a free and open international trading system.

These objectives formed the basis of a draft charter for the International Trade Organization (ITO), which was to set tariff reductions and establish broad rules for international trade. The goals of the ITO proved too ambitious, however, and the draft charter was shelved. Many of the fifty-two nations that participated in drafting the ITO charter, including the United States, balked at the idea of an international organization that might challenge or inhibit their national sovereignty.

The General Agreement on Tariffs and Trade was originally intended to be a stopgap agency—a framework for trade liberalization efforts while ITO was being redrafted. As such, it was ill equipped to handle contentious trade disputes from the start, and certainly lacks the authority to deal with the complex trade pressures that have emerged over the last forty years.

Not having the mandate to regulate trade, the staff resources to deal with ongoing trade problems, or the clout to enforce its decisions, GATT quickly became more a referee than a judge. Ultimately it had to rely on the enlightened self-interest of the participating nations and the still vivid memories of the political and economic calamity of earlier times.

Despite its limitations, GATT worked as a shock absorber that enabled competing nations to get through some bumpy economic times. The rules and the spirit of GATT have helped keep markets open, especially among the industrialized countries, and discouraged the imposition of new trade barriers. It proved to be an important instrument in molding U.S. and world trade policy during the three decades following World War II. And it also made clear, among leaders in business, labor, and government circles, that the United States had to take a leadership role in shaping the postwar economy.

U.S. efforts to deal with the problems of increased competition, especially with the newly created European Economic Community in 1957, led to negotiations that produced steady, if rarely dramatic, progress toward the goal of trade liberalization. For a decade, the United States negotiated bilateral agreements to reduce tariffs on a reciprocal basis. The first GATT-sponsored multilateral trade negotiations (MTN) convened in

1947, with four more rounds held over the next fifteen years. Progress was slow because of political pressures in the United States and uncertainty on how to integrate the European Community in the world trading system.

The Kennedy Round, which lasted from 1964 to 1967, produced the first significant results for a GATT-sponsored MTN. Tariffs were cut an average of 36 percent on almost all dutiable items, and for the first time an agreement was reached to resolve conflicts over some non-tariff barriers.

At the next round of multilateral trade talks — the Tokyo Round, beginning in 1971 — the U.S. mood was increasingly somber. The previous decade had produced high inflation, a deteriorating trade position, and a breakdown in the exchange rate system. Europe and Japan's advancing competitiveness had caused U.S. producers to lose markets at home and abroad. Congress linked new authority for the President to lower tariffs with efforts to negotiate an end to non-tariff barriers. The two rounds succeeded in lowering tariffs from 20–30 percent to roughly 5 percent.

Despite the success in reducing tariff rates, by the 1970s the United States was becoming dissatisfied with GATT and the world trading system. Increasingly, Americans were piqued by what they perceived to be the asymmetrical impact of GATT's provisions. Many of the competitive newly industrialized countries enjoyed grandfathered tariffs and protection for domestic producers. This had been tolerable so long as the United States was the preeminent economic power, but its favorable trade position had begun to erode by the 1970s.

American policymakers were also taken aback when other countries replaced their tariffs with extensive non-tariff barriers designed to protect their domestic industries. The United States could rightfully claim credit for pressing GATT to deal with high tariffs and quotas in the Kennedy and Tokyo rounds, but GATT had little authority to break down more subtle non-tariff barriers.

In 1974, Congress demanded that the President reduce trade barriers and granted him authority to take retaliatory measures against countries that maintained "unjustifiable or unreasonable" import restrictions. Congress wanted more results from GATT whenever it granted the administration new authority to negotiate lower tariff agreements.

For the world trading system to survive — and for the American public to maintain confidence in the equity of international trade — the "rules of the game" must be expanded to include the new problem areas that have emerged or intensified during the last four decades. These new flashpoints — trade in services, non-tariff barriers, agricultural trade, and others — are currently outside GATT's jurisdiction. When the eighth round of GATT-sponsored trade negotiations convened in Punta de Este, Uruguay, in September 1986, the administration's negotiating team had one objective: to get these items on the table for in-depth negotiations.

The significance of the Uruguay Round lay in its very location — far from Europe or Japan or North America, the traditional centers of world economic power. Punta del Este was a vivid symbol of how much the world economy had changed. Where once developing countries were merely observers of multilateral trade negotiations, they were now considered major players in international trade and finance matters. Several were among the world's biggest exporters. Brazil had become an important supplier of arms to the developing world, and its commuter aircraft industry was a formidable competitor to Gulfstream and other U.S. companies. Japan's high-quality, low-priced autos had to compete with lower-priced Korean cars. India and other developing countries were acquiring the technical knowledge to advance their production capabilities. The older industrialized nations could no longer ignore the developing nations' trade distorting practices, such as dumping, subsidies, and tariffs, that were creating trade imbalances.

Over the years, America had often treated GATT deferentially, making economic concessions or ignoring trade practices that violated the rules and spirit of the agency. But in the 1980s, the economic climate changed and so did the United States' attitude and bargaining position at GATT. The United States posted a staggering $156 billion trade deficit in 1986, a figure that represents several million lost job opportunities. The political climate across the country was less tolerant of multilateral solutions. Increasing numbers of labor and business leaders denounced GATT with calls to "get tough" with our trading partners on a "level playing field." Little wonder that as the U.S. delegation prepared for the Uruguay meeting, it intended to take unusually tough stands. This time U.S. negotiators were prepared to confront the issues and wrest concessions from the rest of the world.

The U.S. agenda was packed with tough and controversial issues. While the emphasis at the Uruguay Round was to be on liberalizing trade policies, especially non-tariff barriers, the American delegation had a large list of grievances and objectives, including trade in services, intellectual property rights, agriculture, and a new dispute settlement mechanism. Both the agenda and tone signaled that the U.S. team was ready to do battle at Punta del Este. U.S. Trade Representative Clayton Yeutter warned that if GATT did not accept key issues for discussion, the U.S. delegation would walk out of the session. Such drastic action by the ranking economic power would end any hope of another GATT round and would threaten the agency's very existence.

Other industrial countries were staking out their own positions. Some backed the American proposal to bring agricultural subsidies under the scrutiny of GATT, but France spearheaded Common Market opposition to even placing the item on the agenda.

India and Brazil, the two giant developing nations, formed a bloc to resist U.S.-led efforts to include services, investment, or intellectual property as sectors to be covered by GATT. The United States let it be known that these sectors could no longer be ignored, because U.S. firms were being denied potential markets. U.S. negotiators argue that restricting trade in services and violating intellectual property rights clearly breached the principles of free trade and the spirit of GATT. The U.S. delegation pointed to Brazil, which had built much of its industrial base through a variety of protectionist measures, including an informatics policy that restricted technology imports and subsidized domestic manufacturers.

Trade ministers from other countries quickly realized that the United States had come to play hard ball. They feared that a failure at Punta del Este would undermine GATT and possibly jeopardize their own trade relations with the United States. Yet there was little progress throughout the strained week. As the U.S. negotiators were preparing to leave, a last-minute accord was reached. The United States got most of what it wanted on services, after conceding to Brazilian demands for separate negotiations before future GATT consideration. And it agreed to language that broke a deadlock on agriculture issues.

The U.S. delegation returned home triumphantly boasting of their accomplishments in press releases and testimony before congressional committees.[5] Punta del Este eluded failure, but the U.S. "victory" only means that these contentious issues will be on the agenda for multilateral talks that could last years.

Despite all its flaws, GATT remains the only international organization that can preside over trade disputes. Without GATT there would be little hope for resolution of the inevitable trade problems that arise in an international economy.

The time has come, however, to deal with GATT's shortcomings. At a time when serious trade tensions threaten to ignite an all-out trade war at any moment, the world cannot afford a dispute-resolution body that presides over only 10 percent of all world trade. For starters, GATT should be expanded to cover agricultural products, commodities, and trade in services.

While it was decided at Punta del Este to put those issues on the table, there is no guarantee that these problems will be remedied.

Textiles and apparel are another area not covered by GATT. These controversial items are negotiated under the Multi-Fiber Arrangement (MFA). In general, agreements dealing with textile and clothing trade violate at least two of the cardinal principles of GATT: that tariffs are preferable to quotas and that trade barriers should come down over time. The MFA provides a valuable framework for bilateral negotiations between importing and exporting nations, but we should be moving toward including textiles and clothing within the overall GATT structure.

GATT has evolved as a set of rules built for market-oriented systems but it is not well equipped to deal with centrally planned economies such as those in the Soviet Union, Eastern Europe, and the People's Republic of China. Nor has GATT proved particularly well suited to deal with economies in which governmental guidance or industrial targeting are widely practiced. All these problems must be addressed before GATT can be considered a truly effective trade organization.

GATT was not the only postwar effort to coordinate economic policy and deal with trade problems. The Organization for European Economic Cooperation was created to carry out the Marshall Plan and successfully removed many economic controls and restrictions imposed by the war. By 1960, the Europeans had grown prosperous and the Americans wanted a forum where they could sit down together with the Europeans and other industrialized democracies. The Organization for Economic Cooperation and Development (OECD) is a result of those efforts.

Macroeconomic policy was to be central to the OECD's work, but it has long since been eclipsed by the IMF and the GATT. Despite its relative homogeneity, OECD is not a heavy hitter on economic and trade policy. It made one effort to

discredit protectionism with a 1985 study on its costs and benefits, confirming that import restrictions aggravate the problems
of developing countries that rely on expanding their sales to
OECD countries in order to service their debt.

One observer, Nicholas Bayne, offered this description of
OECD:

> It is something of a Cinderella among international organiza-
> tions. That does not mean it is waiting for a fairy godmother;
> but rather that it works away quietly and efficiently in the
> service of its member governments. It does not always go to the
> balls like its grander sister organizations, though it often runs
> up their dresses and sometimes clears up the mess after the
> party.[6]

As GATT and OECD were working to restore economic
order and trade among industrialized nations, the less developed countries (LDCs) often felt left on the sidelines. Their
frustration led to the establishment of the U.N. Conference on
Trade and Development (UNCTAD) in 1964. It was designed
to address the unique trade needs of the developing countries,
but it has since been pushed aside by the operational roles of
other organizations, especially GATT.

UNCTAD is primarily a forum at which LDCs make their
needs known and pass resolutions. Lacking enforcement powers, UNCTAD is most important as a rallying point for LDCs
to air frustrations over economic policies they can do little to
alter.

The problem with GATT, OECD, IMF, and other international entities is that they cannot speak or act with the authority
of world leaders. Meetings are held at ministerial levels and
resident bureaucracies must weigh in on every decision. The
process involves lengthy negotiations, usually a consensus is
required, and no enforcement power exists to ensure that rulings are carried out.

As the world economy becomes more integrated and strained, there is a growing need for strong leadership and a viable means to set direction for better management of trade and financial movements.

When Valéry Giscard d'Estaing invited world leaders to his residence for a weekend of unstructured talks about economic and trade matters in 1975, he realized that heads of state need to meet face to face to deal collectively with economic problems. However ideal the notion at the time, the thirteen summits to date have produced far more press criticism than concrete results.[7]

The 1983 Williamsburg summit stands out for its lack of action in the face of such formidable global problems as recession, volatile exchange rates, threats of protectionism, higher LDC debt problems, and growth differentials among trading nations. This was clearly the time for another Bretton Woods, or at the minimum an effort to confront the issues before they worsened or reached crisis proportions.

The seven heads of state, however, did not come prepared to solve economic problems or give new directions for the world community. They appeared more concerned about saving their own political scalps. For example:

Margaret Thatcher, busy running for reelection, cut short her visit.

France's François Mitterrand, humiliated by economic deterioration in his country, was uncustomarily subdued.

Prime Minister Yasuhiro Nakasone, embarrassed by Japan's mounting trade surpluses and trade barriers, was clearly on the defensive.

Ronald Reagan, still unsure about the effects of his economic policies, concentrated on playing host.

Economic summits offer a rare occasion for industrialized nations to shape international economic policy and solve trade problems. They provide the heads of state a unique opportunity to address, collectively, the problems that threaten the world economy.

But at Williamsburg, as at most of the previous summits and those since, pageantry and symbolism were more in evidence than courageous action. There was little interest in airing differences and confronting problems. Instead the participants confronted the cameras, and Williamsburg became known as a photo summit.

At week's end a bland ten-point program, consisting largely of platitudes and self-congratulations prepared well in advance of the summit, was adopted. Then everyone, including two thousand journalists, photographers, and the entourages of ministers and aides, went home.

One of the most unfortunate developments in economic summits is that in recent years, largely at the insistence of the Reagan administration, more and more noneconomic issues have been jammed into the allocated forty-eight hours.

In 1980, the summit was dominated by discussions of how to respond to Russia's invasion of Afghanistan.

The 1982 Versailles summit had to deal with the Falkland Islands crisis involving Great Britain and the Israeli invasion of Lebanon.

The top photo opportunity at the London summit of 1984 was Ronald Reagan's side trip to France, where he delivered an emotional tribute to the American soldiers killed in the Normandy D-Day invasion.

The 1985 Bonn event was even more of a spectacle, with President Reagan's visit to a West German war cemetery at Bitberg, where members of Hitler's SS troops were buried.

At the Tokyo summit in 1986, President Reagan lobbied his fellow chiefs of state into signing a short statement against international terrorism.

The most pressworthy event surrounding the 1987 Venice summit was President Reagan's side trip to Berlin, where he challenged General Secretary Gorbachev to tear down the Berlin wall.

The United States is no longer the preeminent economic power, nor can it unilaterally dictate policies for the rest of the world. Other nations' trade barriers, fiscal policies, or actions can dramatically affect our social and economic well-being.

Economic order requires collective action among countries, and meaningful institutions to manage and enforce the world economic system.

With steady economic growth and relative world prosperity, fundamental problems have been swept under the rug. Unless world leaders take immediate action to shore up our beleaguered trade and financial institutions, the day of reckoning will come when recession hits the industrialized world, an LDC country pulls the plug on debt repayment, the U.S. Congress turns toward protectionism, Japanese investors recall their sizable investments in the United States, or sectoral disputes flare into an uncontrollable trade war.

━━━

TEN

Trouble Ahead for the World Economy

AS NATIONS STRUGGLE to keep the world trading system afloat, new problems are posing even greater risks ahead. America's high-powered growth rates of the 1970s and 1980s, which fueled consumption at home and kept factories humming abroad, were bound to end, as *The Economist* editorialized in November 1987.

> For 15 years politicians have run economies like jugglers at a fairground, trying to dazzle their audience with spectacular stunts and a stream of jolly promises. One Monday last month the audience booed and stock markets crashed.[1]

The 1987 Black Monday collapse served as a grim warning that there were limits. National economies, being so inextricably linked by finance and trade, were most heavily dependent on one another. The failure of one could imperil the well-being of another.

Indeed, a single economic event could bring down the whole system. The mere reporting of America's monthly trade figures caused stock and bond markets to tumble and brought instant panic to financial houses all over the world. The stock market, after a fretful week, regained its composure but not the confidence it once enjoyed.

What else could go wrong? Would higher interest rates hasten a serious default by Brazil or Peru? Would a rapidly plunging dollar torpedo financial and trade markets worldwide? Would overproduction and shrinking markets precipitate recession in industrialized countries? What would be the effect if Japan hastily withdrew its substantial investments in the United States? Would staggering trade deficits prompt a testy U.S. Congress to enact protectionist measures? Who would possess the resources to provide economic leadership in the years ahead?

It all adds up to trouble for the world economy. If today's political leaders are responsible for the high-spending, high-borrowing policies that created such problems, how can we expect future leaders to initiate bold steps, especially belt-tightening sacrifices, to put things back on track?

Another Year Older and Deeper in Debt

In just six years the United States has performed an extraordinary feat, making an uncharted 180-degree turnaround from being the world's largest creditor nation to being the world's largest debtor nation. Our external debt, which will rise to $700 billion by the end of this decade, is expected to reach $1 trillion in the early 1990s.[2] Incredibly, the U.S. foreign debt has surpassed the combined Third World debts that gravely threaten the world's financial system.

Is it possible that the United States, given its new status as a debtor nation, will end up in the same predicament as a Mexico or Peru? What does it mean for a nation like ours to owe hundreds of billions to foreign investors? How threatening are the U.S. and worldwide debts to a stable global economy?

What will it cost Americans to get back on the road to financial responsibility? If America's capital reserves have underwritten the world trading system these past forty years, who will pick up the tab in the future? If Japan and other capital surplus nations refuse to assume some responsibility, who will bail out what has become a debt-ridden world of borrowers?

The figures are hard to believe. Only five years ago, foreigners owed the United States $147 billion more than we owed them; in 1986, the United States owed foreign investors a cool $250 billion.[3] Economists say that the trade deficit—the balance on the books for trade and financial transactions—is the source of our foreign debt. Net earnings on overseas holdings helped to offset trade deficits in the past, but beginning with the 1981–1982 recession the United States' insatiable demand was much greater than what the nation was producing.

Imported goods filled the gap. Each year, our nation's trade deficit set a new record. The total deficit from 1981 to 1987 was a staggering $762.8 billion.[4] Domestic savings were lagging far behind consumer, business, and government borrowing. With the federal budget deficit rising and personal savings falling, interest rates went higher to lure foreign capital. Foreign portfolios of U.S. corporate and government securities increased sevenfold from 1981 to 1985.[5]

With low savings and heavy consumption at home, Americans are forced to obtain capital from abroad. Such a huge foreign debt will place a heavy burden on the U.S. economy for decades to come. Put another way, future generations will have to pay back the borrowed money that keeps today's standard of living higher but inevitably means less affluent times ahead. One New York investment house estimated that the bill for this extravagance may be "perhaps as much as $400 per person by 1990."[6] It is like today's parents' taking out a huge loan to maintain an affluent lifestyle, only to have their children pay it back with interest—to foreigners!

Capital imports in 1986 amounted to $150 billion, or 3 percent of GNP, which precisely matches the U.S. savings shortfall.[7] A nation cannot borrow and consume more than it saves and produces without paying a heavy price later on.

According to *Business Week,* "America's $250 billion IOU will be hell to pay."[8] The magazine's startling analysis of October 1986 offered these unpopular choices for the American public: "[They] will have to consume less and save more, pay higher taxes for less government and face higher prices for fewer imports but it is no longer a question of whether Americans will eventually pay their credit binge. It is only a matter of when."[9]

Whether America intends to inflate its way out of the debt crises, endure a recession that will trigger a lower standard of living, or commit itself anew to stiff deficit reduction efforts remains to be seen. One painful consequence is certain, however. The United States has unwittingly put its economic fate in the hands of foreign investors, which could compromise its political and security interests in a troubled world.

Is it possible that the United States, the giant creditor nation for decades, is going the way of other debtor countries that are addicted to foreign borrowing just to pay interest on their existing debts? When the debt crisis hit with Mexico's near default in 1982, there was panic that the international banking system would collapse. The United States bailed out Mexico. Who will bail out the United States in the 1990s?

The huge payment of interest and dividends to non–U.S. residents will most certainly be a drag on America's relative affluence in the global economy. When the nation's negative net investment position reaches $750 billion in 1990, a return of 7 percent means outflow payments of $50 billion per year.

Foreign investors, worried about the dollar's depreciation, are demanding higher interest on long-term loans to the United States. Without foreign lending, the U.S. government and other megaborrowers will have to compete for scarce dollars at home, thus adding inflationary pressures on the domestic economy. Faced with the continued expansion of an inflationary debt, the

Federal Reserve Board has alternated between pumping up and cooling off the economy, thus keeping the business community perplexed about the future.

During the 1980s, our consumption binge was far beyond what we produced. A combination of consumer and government and business spending outstripped production by 3 percent. Economist Robert J. Gordon predicts that, like the wage earner who works three months out of the year to pay his taxes, "our export industries will be working January to March to work off this splurge."[10] Stating the obvious before a congressional committee, former Federal Reserve Chairman Paul Volcker worried that "the implications for growth on America's living standards are adverse."[11]

As U.S. citizens adjust to the new economic realities—lower net income and consumption, higher production—policymakers must ponder the ominous ways out of the foreign debt crisis. Our choices are clear: reduce domestic public and private debt and/or turn around the trade deficit and export more than is being imported. Both will involve unpleasant choices.

How can the United States meet its foreign debt obligations if it is plagued by heavy debt burdens at home? The political debate has been centered on federal budget deficits, thanks in part to Ronald Reagan's rhetorical attacks on federal spending over the years. As President, he doubled the public debt in just six years, far surpassing all his predecessors combined. His policies will leave a wake of deficits for years to come, owing primarily to the strategic defense initiative and other costly military projects that are secure in multiyear authorizing bills.

Currently, 14 percent of the budget deficit goes for interest on the $2 trillion public debt. When you exclude the free-standing Social Security Trust Fund to get a more accurate view of the federal budget, interest on the debt actually counts for nearly one-fifth of all federal spending. It is conceivable that in 1988–1990, one-half the entire federal budget will be concentrated in two categories: interest and defense.

Despite the Gramm-Rudman-Hollings deficit reduction targets, there is little prospect that Congress will severely reduce spending, and President Reagan's adamant opposition to tax increases means no improvement on the revenue side. The government can no longer depend on optimistic projections to improve the economic picture.

The major fiscal achievement in 1986 was enactment of the Tax Reform Act. Not only did it damage America's competitive position by increasing consumption—mostly of foreign-made goods—and make U.S. products more expensive in world markets, but it effectively closed the door to major tax increases. Congressmen cannot go back to their constituents and reclaim the tax cuts they passed one year before. Nor do they dare raise taxes on business after having imposed a $140 billion increase. The President and Congress are frantically searching for new revenues—a cigarette tax hike here, new user fees there—but the inescapable fact is that they have painted themselves into a corner.

So much for the public debt. Many economists are more worried about the nation's staggering private debt. The federal government can always print the money it needs, but private borrowers have no such luxury. "Defaults could soar," predicted economist A. Gilbert Heebner of Corestale's Financial Corporation in Philadelphia, who added that "we may pay an especially high price for the debt binge within the private sector."[12]

The problem is so grave that the nation's leading economists gathered at Jackson Hole, Wyoming, in September 1986 to warn that an economic disaster could lie ahead. They estimated the total U.S. debt owed by government, businesses, or households to be $8 or $9 trillion dollars, nearly double what it was in 1981. One participant, L. Wilson Seidman, chairman of the Federal Deposit Insurance Corporation, noted the link between rising corporate debt burdens and bank failures: "Over the 40 year period from 1941 to 1980, only 262 banks failed. Since 1980, over

400 banks have failed. Last year's record of 120 bank failures will soon be eclipsed . . . this year. Next year it will likely be as bad or worse."[13]

John Berry reported in the *Washington Post* that the recent debt increases have "shattered what had been a quite stable relationship between debt and the size of the American economy."[14]

Most of the recent loan defaults, bankruptcies, bank failures, and savings and loan closures have occurred during relatively good economic times. The fear is what will happen if and when a recession hits. The surge in debt vis-à-vis general economic growth is now higher than it was during the worst years of the Depression, when the nation's output of goods and services nose-dived and bankruptcies soared.

At a time when we ought to be saving, our household debt burden is mounting. It jumped from 25 percent of disposable income in 1981 to 31 percent in 1986. The ratio of household debt to America's net worth, now at a post–World War II high of 19 percent, is the result of easy credit and widely used credit cards.[15] A slowdown in the economy often increases indebtedness just when people ought to be saving more.

Corporate borrowing is yet another dimension of the nation's debt load. The total outstanding debt of U.S. corporations has risen spectacularly during 1983–1986, up to $483 billion in various kinds of borrowing, while equity financing fell $226.1 billion. A Federal Reserve Board study cautioned that many firms, already highly leveraged, would be "vulnerable to adverse economic or financial developments."[16] As Mark Potts reported in the *Washington Post* in January 1987, the "rapidly escalating amount of corporate debt is a ticking time bomb waiting to go off if interest rates jump or the economy slumps, which could drive scores of debt-laden companies into bankruptcy and put considerable pressure on the financial institutions that lent them the money."[17]

Worse yet, the quality of debt is crumbling. The number of

AAA-rated industrial and utility corporations has dwindled from 56 to 27 in the past decade, as speculation has swelled.[18] John Kenneth Galbraith, noting the current rash of mergers, acquisitions, takeovers, leveraged buyouts, and junk bonds (in 1985, some $139 billion worth of mergers and acquisitions was financed with new borrowing, including some $100 billion in perilous junk bonds) concludes that one day a "fall in earnings will render the debt burden insupportable. A minor literature will marvel at the earlier retreat from reality as is now the case with the Penn Square fiasco and the loans to Latin America."[19]

These debts are overloading the American economy and they must be dealt with, sooner rather than later, or the nation's entire financial infrastructure will be imperiled. The choices are painful ones requiring courageous actions by the Congress and sacrifice by the American public.

Debt reduction is the solution. When the stock market crash hit in October 1987, Wall Street spokesmen pointed with a vengeance to Washington, D.C., chiding the President and Congress for not getting tough with deficit reduction. A high-level budget summit was hastily convened to come up with a bold budget package to ease fears in financial markets. But with over one half of budget outlays in untouchables — Social Security, programs for the poor, interest on the debt — and another one-fourth in defense, the prospects were dim on the spending side. The revenue picture was no brighter. President Reagan's pathological resistance to tax increases dashed any hopes of improving revenues.

It is unlikely that the nation's other debts — corporate, consumer, and foreign — will be seriously addressed, if for no other reason than lack of incentives. U.S. fiscal policies, if anything, encourage borrowing rather than savings. Tax provisions that reward credit purchasing, writing off bad debts, or using junk bonds for mergers and hostile takeovers do not assure fiscal responsibility.

Another answer is to improve the nation's crumbling savings rate. How little we save, especially compared to other countries, is a clue to why the nation has debt problems and needs to borrow heavily from abroad. The nation's savings rate—of individuals, corporations, and government—was just over 2 percent in 1986 and has averaged less than 3 percent over the past five years. Our skimpy savings rate is a shocking one fifth of Japan's and lags way behind that of Great Britain and most other industrialized nations.

Our failure to save substantial amounts reduces the available capital so vital for investments and improved productivity. It means high cost of capital, which leads to sporadic short-term corporate planning. With no domestic savings, the U.S. government and companies must borrow from abroad, which drives up the dollar and sets the stage for importing more than we export.

To improve the nation's savings rate requires the tough choices already mentioned: reduce current levels of consumption, scale back federal and corporate borrowing, especially to finance takeovers, and implement fiscal policies to encourage savings rather than reward borrowing.

If the United States does not tackle its debt problems through deficit reduction and increase its savings rate, only one alternative remains: take the advice economists offer other debt-ridden countries—consume less and produce more for export. This is unlikely, considering the nation's annual $150 billion–plus trade deficits, with merchandise imports running about 80 percent higher than exports.

Not only must American consumers buy fewer foreign imports, but the nation's GNP needs to grow faster than domestic demand. Even the dollar decline in recent years—making imports more expensive and U.S. products cheaper abroad—has barely dented the trade deficit. The 1986 tax reform law, ironically, hurt the U.S. trade position by giving consumers more disposable income to purchase more imported goods and placing an additional $140 billion tax burden on U.S. manufacturers, boosting the cost of their products overseas.

An increase in exports presumes that our trading partners will buy more goods and services, which is utterly contrary to what has been happening since 1980. The industrial nations have steadfastly refused to adopt fiscal policies that would spur growth. Reagan officials have pleaded, jawboned, and threatened Japan and West Germany to lower taxes and interest rates to boost their economies, but to no avail. Since domestic demand has been growing three times faster in the United States than in Japan and Europe since 1983, those countries would have to embark on radical growth policies to turn things around.

Nor can the United States expect developing countries to help. If anything, their debt obligations and International Monetary Fund (IMF) austerity requirements compel them to maintain trade surpluses. The only way less developed countries can purchase more U.S. products is to increase net capital flows to finance an increase in their deficits. It is a Catch-22 that has all debtor nations in the same net.

Regaining control of our economy will require sacrifices not to be taken lightly by a consuming and prosperous public. It calls for unthinkable actions by political leaders who are struggling to reduce a trillion-dollar budget by a mere $23 billion. The only alternative left is to continue what we've been doing for the past six years—borrow more from abroad.

But putting our nation in hock to foreigners is also risky. The $400 billion the United States has borrowed from Japan and Europe must be paid back with interest. In 1987 alone, that interest, along with dividends and rent, amounted to $17 billion. It will soar to an estimated $27 billion for 1988 and $50 billion for 1990. Today's youth will have to pick up the future tab for our generation's rollicking good times.

The U.S. government, once the world's largest creditor nation, now asks foreigners to finance its deficits. In 1987, nearly all of the budget deficit was financed by foreign central banks, making our mighty nation perilously dependent on others to keep its economy afloat.

Bad choices, yes. But to do nothing may be the worst option of all, as the October 1987 stock market crash clearly demonstrated. The markets did not wait for the policymakers but went ahead with their own austerity plan. A debt load of this magnitude is not sustainable, and short of a bold national austerity program to spur savings, curb unnecessary consumption, and reinvigorate our industries, it could prove terminal to the world economy.

Coping with Global Glut

At no time in recent memory have the experts been so brazenly wrong as they were in their agricultural forecasts in the mid 1970s. At that time, the Club of Rome proclaimed that desperate shortages for all raw materials were an absolute certainty by the year 1985. In 1980, the Carter administration's *Global 2000 Report to the President: Entering the Twenty-first Century* warned that world demand for food would increase steadily for at least twenty years, that worldwide food production would fall except in developed nations, and that real food prices would double.[20]

These grim forecasts were woefully exaggerated. Indeed, just the opposite occurred. Global agricultural output has increased by one-third since the prophetic warnings of a decade ago. Terrible malnutrition and hunger still exist in many areas but, paradoxically, overproduction of agricultural goods has become a bitter trade problem.

The world is awash with more food than ever was believed possible. Many countries that were recently tragic symbols of starvation have achieved miraculous self-sufficiency. While such news is an answer to prayer for countless millions around the world, it has hurt American farmers who rely heavily on world markets.

Even more worrisome is the startling fact that agricultural growth rates, if anything, will move upward despite today's surpluses and bring a furthur decline in food and commodity prices. Some economists have predicted that agricultural output will rise at an almost exponential rate of growth in the years ahead.

The International Monetary Fund, in its 1986 World Economic Report, projected increased agricultural output and depressed prices of most food items, with commodity output averaging 3 percent growth per annum through 1991.[21]

Statistics bear out the unease that is spreading across the American heartland. From a historic peak of $43.8 billion in 1981, overseas farm sales plunged to $26.3 billion five years later. The shocking news on the trade front in 1986 was that the United States registered its first monthly agricultural trade deficit in twenty-seven years.[22]

In 1980, U.S. farm exports were running double the level of imports; in 1988 we are struggling to break even on the trade ledger. Not only is the United States losing its grip on export markets, it is racking up sizable imports—up 40 percent in the 1980s!

The sharp curtailment of U.S. export shipments has added to a growing backlog of unsold stocks. This means lower prices for dismayed farmers bent on producing for markets that no longer exist. The figures are dry, their effect devastating. Since 1980, corn exports dropped a startling 46 percent as the U.S. share of the world market sank from 71 percent to 58 percent. Meanwhile, the number of U.S. corn suppliers quadrupled. The picture was the same for wheat: U.S. exports went down 40 percent as the U.S. share of export markets fell from 45 percent to 29 percent. Wheat farmers had to double their storage space. The same story could be told of rice, soybeans, and other foodstuffs.

Put another way, in 1980 two out of three bushels of wheat American farmers produced went overseas; today only one half of U.S. wheat production is exported. American grain elevators are bulging as overseas markets dry up and global competition for sales intensifies. U.S. farmers stand helplessly by as crop prices drop sharply. For many it means trying to survive under intolerable circumstances; for others foreclosure is inevitable.

It is not difficult to understand the forces that influence overproduction. They can be traced back to the nineteenth century, when Thomas Malthus theorized that world population would outstrip the available food supplies. In recent years, successive administrations have urged farmers to expand and plant more to meet a seemingly insatiable world market. Politicians, farm leaders, bankers, and academicians all called for greater farm output in an era of worldwide scarcity. Without any budgetary restraints, powerful corporations and farm lobbyists collaborated and Congress went along with costly federal programs to enhance production of grain, corn, sugar, soybeans, rice, dairy products, and even tobacco. Agricultural interests usually wrote their own tickets when Congress considered farm legislation.

Spurred by overly optimistic reports, government support programs, and the 1970s inflationary spiral, U.S. farmers took advantage of low interest rates to invest more heavily in farmland and equipment. When interest rates rose in the late 1970s, grain demand and prices fell. The sharp reversal crushed producers who had banked on low interest rates and rising prices to sustain their heavy investments.

The humanitarian desire to feed the hungry masses in India, East Africa, and other remote areas struck by drought conditions also fueled overproduction. Congress repeatedly authorized PL-480 food-aid and other programs that subsidized exports to needy countries. Resolutions, like Food for Peace and

Bread for the World, were routinely introduced in the House and Senate to commit a large percentage of foreign aid to food giveaway programs.

The United States was also displaying its technological superiority during this period through bilateral and multilateral aid programs. The incredible advances in agricultural science by U.S. public and private enterprises over the years was passed on to other nations, which have since become significant competitors. The United States, the World Bank, the United Nations, and regional development banks have spread this knowledge to virtually every country that wanted it.

One example of multilateral efforts to improve food production is the Consultative Group on International Agricultural Research. This global network of thirteen strategically located centers is pioneering work in developing countries to increase the cultivation and yield for corn, rice, potatoes, wheat, and other staples.

Today's developing nations, no longer content with mere self-sufficiency, have applied new irrigation techniques, creating vast, fertile land to increase their exports, often at the expense of the United States. Dennis T. Avery, a State Department agricultural analyst, made a startling observation before the National Grain Council: "Sitting where I do, with an overview of world agriculture, I have one basic comment to offer about the increases in agricultural productivity: we ain't seen nothing yet."[23]

In another speech Avery made the following points:

· European wheat yields were up 23 percent in 1985.
· Indonesia has gone from being a major food importer to self-sufficiency.
· Japan and Taiwan, which pay their rice producers well above world prices, are trying to cope with rice surpluses.
· New hybrid seeds are pushing the corn belt 250 miles north —a development of major importance to farmers in Europe,

the Orient, and the Soviet Union, not to mention the United States.[24]

Even some African countries are enjoying bumper harvests, thanks to heavy rains. U.S. agricultural sales to Africa have fallen 34 percent. Other countries are emerging as major producers; many, like Australia, Argentina, and Brazil are doing it without subsidizing their exporters. All have become highly mechanized overproducers aggressively competing for diminishing world markets.

The People's Republic of China, with its one billion population, has increased farm production over 40 percent in just five years. Not long ago a net importer of corn, in 1986 China exported five million tons a year—roughly the production of Iowa. The world's second most populous country, India, has doubled its wheat production since 1970 and is exporting its surpluses. Even Bangladesh, while still importing rice and wheat to feed its 100 million people, has been doubling the world's agricultural growth rate for the last fifteen years to reach its goal of self-sufficiency.

The Soviet Union is one of the largest potential markets for the export-hungry nations in the West. In 1972, experiencing severe crop failures, the USSR began to purchase massive quantities of grain on the world market. That year it imported a total of 39.4 million metric tons of wheat and corn, half supplied by the United States. Senator Henry M. ("Scoop") Jackson, a Democrat from Washington, and others called the megasale the "Great Russian Grain Robbery." It was former President Richard Nixon's backdoor way of helping farmers in a presidential election year.

The large, sudden, and secret Soviet purchase of grain depleted domestic stocks, increased food prices at home, and skewed world market prices radically. Pressure developed for an agreement to stabilize and regularize Soviet purchases, which was reached in October 1976. It was a windfall for U.S.

grain and corn producers until President Jimmy Carter imposed a grain embargo on the USSR as punishment for its 1979 invasion of Afghanistan.

In 1978–1979 the United States enjoyed a 57 percent share of the Soviet wheat market, but it fell to 9 percent after the embargo and has recovered to only about 20 percent since 1982. What was worse, the sixteen-month embargo did not have the intended effect on the Soviets. They simply turned to willing supplier nations like Canada and Argentina to fill the gap.

A second agreement, negotiated in 1983, called for more generous terms. The Russians pledged to purchase at least 9 million metric tons of corn, wheat, and soybeans annually. But the soaring dollar, coupled with the United States' reputation as an unreliable supplier, could not convince the Soviets—even with subsidies of $13 to $15 per ton under the Export Enhancement Program—to buy from the American farmer. In fact, by August 1986 the Soviet Union had purchased only some 152,000 tons of its 4 million metric ton quota of wheat in that year.

The global glut problem was the basis of a new episode involving the USSR in September 1986. Soviet officials, shopping around for new agreements to purchase millions of tons of grain, found plenty of willing suppliers. The United States, having claimed that the Soviets reneged on their bilateral agreement, realized it was in a fiercely competitive match with other nations. In a last-ditch effort, President Reagan made a controversial offer to sell 3.85 million tons of subsidized wheat under the recently enacted Export Enhancement Program. The USSR ignored the offer and proceeded to sign with Canada for guaranteed sales of 25 million tons over the next five years.

The 1986 Soviet grain deal sparked worldwide debate about agriculture subsidies. In the same week that President Reagan offered a bonus on wheat sales to the USSR, he denounced the "mutually destructive practice of subsidizing agricultural exports." He was referring to the sizable amount in restitution that the European Community (EC) was paying its wheat exporters. Reagan's original subsidy offer had been a response to these European subsidies. In turn, Canada had matched U.S. and EC prices to get the grain agreement with the USSR. Left out, and complaining loudly, were Australia and other nonsubsidizing nations.

"A monstrous absurdity" is how a chagrined Australian Prime Minister Robert Hawke described it. "What those two major trading blocs have to understand is not only are they hurting Australia . . . but they are ruining their own economic prospects."[25]

U.S. economic prospects have been fading under the pressures of mounting surpluses and shrinking world markets. Former and present policies to increase production have been painfully successful. The bilateral and multilateral programs we introduced in our desire to help others have proved so effective that many beneficiary countries no longer need our subsidized agricultural goods.

In recent years, U.S. policymakers have turned their attention to export promotion. The Reagan administration has attempted to steer the farm bill away from support prices of major commodities to export marketing programs. But a subsidy is a subsidy in the eyes of the world.

The 1985 farm bill created a new $2 billion export bonus program. In signing the bill, President Reagan warned that the program threatened to "precipitate an agricultural commodity trade war with our allies." The program is in addition to existing programs which help, some would claim unfairly, U.S. exporters compete in world markets. These include the so-called Payment in Kind program, subsidized loan rates and credit guarantees, PL-480 food assistance, targeted export assistance to combat competing country subsidies, and specific programs for red meat and dairy producers.[26]

The two largest agricultural exporters, the United States and Western Europe, pour about $20 billion each into subsidy programs that give them a huge advantage over nonsubsidized and less developed nations, many of which depend on farm income for their economic viability.[27]

According to the World Bank's 1986 World Development Report, farm subsidy programs cost taxpayers and consumers of the United States, Europe, and Japan $104 billion—almost twice the $55.6 billion that the farmers of those countries receive. These programs shield 2.25 million U.S. farmers and 11 million EC farmers from world market conditions.

The report, examining the impact of these subsidies on developing countries, said: "Industrial countries' agricultural policies may be aimed at solving domestic problems, but their effects spill over onto the rest of the world."[28]

The Philippines, the Dominican Republic, and a host of Central American and Caribbean countries angrily denounce what is happening but are helpless to do anything about it. A group of ambassadors told the House Ways and Means Committee that U.S. and EC unfair trade policies undercut Reagan administration efforts to improve the economies of countries in the region through the Caribbean Basin Initiative. Developing countries themselves impose discriminatory policies on their farm sectors in order to keep domestic food prices low and pacify politically volatile urban consumers. The fear of street riots and other disturbances prevents governments from raising food prices to realistic levels. In Zambia, fifteen people were killed in a protest over government policies to double prices of cornmeal.

But it is the accelerating political pressures among major producers that threatens the world trading system. The United States and Europe were on the brink of a trade war over agricultural policies twice in 1986. The entry of Spain and Portugal into the Common Market in particular had both sides poised for battle. Only after the United States threatened imposition of a 200 percent tariff increase on certain EC wines and specialty cheeses did the two sides resolve the matter.

The prize for the most restrictive market goes to Japan. While that country has been the United States' largest single market for agricultural goods, the Japanese obsession with food security has resulted in a government policy to erect high tariffs and quotas on a range of agricultural imports, including rice, wheat, barley, on meat, dairy products, high-value crops, and processed foods. It's more than tariffs and quotas. Food products are subject to a gauntlet of tariffs, taxes, certification and distribution barriers, labeling regulations, and additive restrictions.

Congressional delegations visiting Tokyo angrily confront Japanese officials about import restrictions only to receive the familiar pledges to look into the problem or pursue negotiations.

In foreign capitals, farm interests are among the most influential politically. And national political pressures are rising along with the surpluses, making it even more difficult to negotiate agreements. Without binding agreements, nations will look inward to shielding themselves by resorting to protectionism or boosting export subsidies.

The political drama being played out back home is suggested by this episode, described by Robert J. Samuelson:

> Senator Edward Zorinsky of Nebraska may have fired the first shot in the global grain wars. When the White House needed the Democratic lawmaker's support last year on a crucial budget vote, he exacted a price: a commitment to subsidize overseas grain sales to help America's beleaguered farmers. What Zorinsky started has turned into a bitter trade brawl. While the United States and the European Community—which has subsidized grain sales for years—claw each other, the other major grain exporters (Argentina, Australia and Canada) scream loudly that they're being mauled in the process.[29]

Politicians eagerly support government programs to subsidize their growers while self-righteously denouncing unfair trade practices in other countries. Farm producers aggressively pursue what they believe are their fair market shares overseas. Newspapers display warlike headlines when reporting on trade conflicts over agricultural issues. Europe and the United States are intent on continuing their taxpayer support programs, making it difficult for nonsubsidized nations to compete. Less developed countries are at the mercy of the rich megaproducers and are falling further behind. No one yields as global problems intensify and bilateral trade talks break down.

There are no international rules to check governments that protect their farm producers and use subsidies to increase output and unfairly target foreign markets. Except for the General Agreement on Tariffs and Trade, which handles disputes but seldom resolves them, there is no international forum to address this troubling issue.

If anything, GATT has condoned the practices that are considered unfair. The organization's rules even permit a wide range of non-tariff barriers in agricultural trade, especially import quotas and export subsidies, that are not allowed for trade in manufactured products.

The big agricultural players (United States, EC, and Japan) have more or less sanctioned market-sharing through GATT agreements over the years, so long as the subsidized products do not gain "more than an equitable share of world trade." It was a convenient arrangement until the U.S. position in agricultural trade went sour in the mid 1980s.

When the so-called Uruguay Round of trade talks convened in Punta del Este in September 1986, the United States insisted that agriculture be on the agenda for future negotiations. U.S. officials claimed it a victory just to have the issue discussed, but meaningful action would take decades. In November 1987, Japan strongly resisted a unanimous GATT ruling against its protective action on rice. It was another blatant example of a government's yielding to farm-belt pressures.

GATT is a long process. It may take years before there is any dismantling of government support programs. Meanwhile, tensions could easily escalate into a full-scale trade war in agriculture and possibly other sectors.

Any international agreement to reduce agricultural support programs is likely to face stiff opposition from agricultural groups, which represent a major political force in every nation. In Japan, Prime Minister Noboru Takeshita's Liberal Democratic Party, in power for three-three years, is beholden to the agrarian community. In the United States, the farm lobby heavily influences both political parties and is fully capable of tipping the balance in a close national election. The European Community unabashedly commits 80 percent of its budget to farm subsidies and other agricultural programs.

Part of the farm lobby's clout is emotionally based; farming has always exemplified the values of hard work, thrift, and family values. On a more concrete level, the strength of the farm lobby is rooted in good organization, clearly defined goals, and a thorough understanding of how to get things done in the political process.

Allowing market conditions to guide farm prices and output would benefit consumers and ease the financial strain on many governments that currently maintain costly agricultural support programs, but many farmers would be made worse off in the near term. Without government assistance, more families would lose their farms, and farm communities could suffer irreparable damage.

In an ideal world, all nations would remove their agricultural subsidies and market barriers, so that market conditions could guide farm prices and output. Few farmers in this country like the current system of price supports, production controls, and export subsidies. But until every major nation agrees to dismantle its trade-distorting programs, the United States cannot afford to send American farmers into the international marketplace unarmed.

In July 1987, when President Ronald Reagan announced a

sweeping plan to end all subsidies and allow free trade in agriculture, it was met with deafening silence in the U.S. Congress and Europe. The "most ambitious proposal for world agricultural trade reform ever offered," if carried out, would eliminate all of the $30 billion–a-year U.S. farm support programs and the $26 billion Europeans spend to protect their farmers. Japan would also be forced to dismantle barriers to food imports. The President of the United States, who formally offered his proposal to the multilateral trade talks in Geneva, called for a ten-year comprehensive phaseout of all farm programs, including water resource policies and research and advisory services, by the major producer countries.

European leaders rejected the idea, saying it would force 11 million of their farmers off the land. Japan soon joined European opposition, labeling the plan "impractical and undesirable."

Reagan's plan also met with stiff resistance at home. Only Argentina, Australia, Canada, and a few other agricultural "free traders" welcomed the bold U.S. move, labeling it "courageous, ambitious, innovative, revolutionary, and historic."

The National Farmers Union feared it would throw American farmers back to the pre-Depression boom-and-bust cycles; the American Farm Bureau conditioned its approval on EC and Japanese agreement to move forward with the plan. "U.S. farmers," the Farm Bureau stated, "are eager to compete against our foreign counterparts, but not with treasuries of their government."[30]

Any major reform of farm policy, especially one that involves binding multilateral agreements, must first have a national consensus among the countries involved. That is unlikely, given the economic and political realities in most agricultural communities in the world. The Reagan proposal has been called "visionary" and "bold," but it will probably end up in the GATT archives rather than on the negotiating table.

The situation is perilously close to the economic conditions and political climate of the 1928–1930 era that led to Smoot-Hawley and collapse of the world trading system. Then as now, global overproduction, especially of wheat, sugar, and coffee, left an unbalanced situation. Then as now, most countries tried to deal with the problem by various restrictive schemes, which proved unworkable but resulted in stocks going up and commodity prices coming down.

World War I had stimulated the expansion of wheat crops in Argentina, Australia, Canada, and the United States. Europe was especially noted during the postwar era for its bulging surpluses and protective import duties, which contributed to depressed world prices.

Then as now, the lower prices brought havoc to farm communities and aroused political action to save the farmers. In 1928, a Republican candidate for President traveled around America promising farmers that, if elected, he would convene a special session of Congress to enact a "limited" tariff bill to save their farms. Herbert Hoover fulfilled his promise and, as President, signed the Smoot-Hawley Tariff Act. The rest is history. The question today is whether world leaders can avoid repeating the mistakes of the past.

Not only are farmers overproducing for declining international markets, but the world's manufacturers may be producing goods far beyond consumers' capacity to absorb them. The 1990s may be remembered as the decade of unwanted surpluses in both agricultural and manufactured goods. With so many industrialized countries producing so many goods, the supply will far outpace demand in the years to come, precipitating depressed prices, lower wages, plant closures, and crushing unemployment. The parallels to a saturated market in the late 1920s are frighteningly evident.

P. T. Ellsworth, in his study of the economic conditions that led to enactment of the Smoot-Hawley Tariff Act of 1930, cites overproduction as one of the principal factors responsible for the onset of the Depression: "It was simply that major fields of investment, whose activity primed that of the whole economy, had become saturated." He cites examples of automobiles, vacuum cleaners, and other major manufactured goods at production levels far beyond what the market could absorb.[31]

National Journal reporter Bruce Stokes recently described the 1980s with a statement reminiscent of sixty years ago:

> Nearly every major industry and sector of the world economy is now or soon will be awash in excess production capacity . . . the result of a global glut of automobiles, computer chips, petrochemicals, steel and a host of other products. Producers are quite simply producing far more than the consumers are consuming.[32]

In the 1920s, overcapacity led to Smoot-Hawley and collapse of the global trading system. In the 1980s, overcapacity is straining the American economy and bringing the world economy once again to the brink. The United States not only has to absorb its own surplus production, but our vast and largely open market has historically accommodated the excess capacity of other nations.

Without more capital to spur more consumption, all nations are left with the grim alternatives of cutting excess capacity or securing overseas markets at any cost. Such action could heighten national and international tensions, ignite political reaction, and inflame the already hot rhetoric between trading states.

Traditionally, manufacturing capacity has been driven by the ups and downs of the marketplace. But government policies and corporate excesses have put production at excessive levels that defy the market forces. Overproduction and artificially low prices set by foreign companies caused a record number of U.S. companies to lose money in 1985 and 1986. Aftertax profits of U.S. corporations dropped by 6.6 percent, precipitating a round of wage freezes, operations curtailments, and plant closures.

By pursuing agendas of overproduction for the export market and tight controls on domestic demand, our trading partners succeed in postponing unemployment and other economic pain. In the long term, however, these strategies will distort and undermine the economies of our trading partners. These malevolent attitudes also court a protectionist backlash from the U.S. Congress.

Economists speculate that oversupply could eventually trigger the wholesale dumping of products on the international market, causing a worldwide deflationary spiral followed by a wave of bankruptcies, massive unemployment, and a catastrophic protectionist outburst. The governments of the world may have to intervene to avoid such a calamity. Currently, however, governments are acting more as villains than saviors.

There is room for responsible government action through efforts to curb overproduction or agreements to increase growth and consumption in nations like Japan and Germany. But political leaders generally do not act altruistically or even rationally during times of economic distress, as evidenced by the actions taken in 1929. Unless world leaders can agree on such measures, the future is bleak. Overcapacity is the most imminent threat to the world trading system, and time is running out to avert the coming trade crisis.

The U.S. Economy in Pain

Given the inaccurate predictions of commodity shortages in the mid 1970s, will the experts be any more accurate about what the world will look like in the year 2000?

In another preposterous forecast two decades ago, French writer Jean Jacques Servan-Schreiber, in *The American Challenge,* ventured that the United States would be so economically advanced by 1980 that it would "stand alone in its futuristic world—holding a monopoly of power, dominating Western

Europe in every basic area where power matters: culture, politics, the military, and economics."[33]

Today's experts are more subdued. Professor Peter F. Drucker of the Claremont Graduate School claims that the world is "not changing; it has changed—in its foundations and its structure."[34] If that is so, the transformed world economy poses some troubling questions about America's future.

· What will America's economy look like in the year 2000 if present trends continue?
· Is it possible for the United States to sustain our current standard of living, or are we moving toward an irreversible decline?
· What will be the ultimate effects of U.S. companies' locating their manufacturing abroad to take advantage of cheaper capital and labor costs?
· Is there any reason to fear heavy foreign investment, both portfolio and manufacturing, in the United States?
· Are we approaching a world that is overly saturated with merchandise?
· If small Southeast Asian countries—Taiwan, Hong Kong, Singapore—have revolutionized trade and commerce in just twenty years, what will happen when China (with a billion people) and India (750 million people) fully develop their economies?
· If high tech is the promise of the future, how can the United States compete against Pacific Rim nations that combine cheap labor and advanced technology?

Many economic storms are brewing, but one of the most imminent is the problem of global overproduction. Recurring waves of Asian products are battering America's Pacific shores. The first and most devastating surge, from Japan, was soon followed by waves from Hong Kong and Singapore. Today, America's economy is being pounded by low-cost Taiwanese and Korean products, and tomorrow's trade storms are already brewing in Indonesia and China.

The new economic forces in Asia pose the greatest threat to America's industrial base and high standard of living. A congressional delegation touring a modern aircraft manufacturing plant in Bandung, Indonesia, was struck by its sophistication and state-of-the-art technology. "Just like Boeing," gasped Seattle Congressman Rod Chandler.[35] And indeed, a Boeing Company joint venture had gotten the plant started.

The Indonesian company, with over thirty thousand workers at its spacious plant, produces Bell-type helicopters and sixty-passenger airplanes suitable for the commercial market. Boeing, along with Messerschmitt of Germany and Fokker of Holland, has contracted with the Indonesians to produce an eighty-five-passenger plane, the advanced technology regional aircraft. The Indonesians have also arranged with General Electric to establish an aircraft engine repair and maintenance facility. These joint ventures allow Indonesians to combine modern technology with a low-wage work force, making them awesome competitors in the years to come.

The Indonesian minister of State for Research and Technology, B. J. Habibie, is the embodiment of Indonesia's aggressive trade future; he is an energetic, visionary leader with a degree from MIT, work experience with Germany's top engineering company, and a close association with Indonesian President Suharto. Habibie informed the stunned delegation that his two thousand resident engineers earn an average of only $300 per month—one-tenth their American counterparts' compensation.

How can American aerospace companies like Boeing, McDonnell Douglas, or Martin Marietta compete with countries that combine technological advances with a minimally paid work force? Fortunately, wages and salaries represent only 10 to 20 percent of a modern firm's costs, but in this era of rapid technology transfer, how long can American firms afford to pay engineers monthly salaries of $3000 while Asian Western-trained engineers are paid a fraction of that amount?[36]

For the past 150 years, the most frequent complaint about the industrial powers was their exploitation of less developed countries. By siphoning raw materials from LDCs, developed nations were able to hoard the economic benefits of manufacturing and marketing the finished goods. Today it is arguably the less developed nations that are turning the developed world's technology against them, using low wages and aggressive marketing to peddle low-cost manufactured goods to the high-wage Western nations.

Manufacturing jobs are clearly shifting from the United States to the Orient. In 1986 alone, U.S. imports from these nations grew by 10 percent while American exports remained stagnant. As a percentage of GNP, Asian exports to the United States were three times greater than European exports. Manufactured goods make up a much higher percentage of U.S. imports than exports, and the difference is magnified by the much smaller level of U.S. exports.

Korea represents a classic example of Asia's prodigious economic advances at U.S. expense over the past twenty-five years. Since 1960, Korea has catapulted its overseas sales from a meager $52 million to about $30 billion in 1986, with 90 percent in manufactured products.[37] It followed a familiar pattern, beginning with textiles and apparel and culminating in light electronics, shipbuilding, engineering, steel, automobiles, television sets, and videocassette recorders. Korean products are a concern not only to American and European nations but even to neighboring Japan.

Today's global market carries both benefits and liabilities for the United States. To be sure, fierce competition from abroad provides American consumers with a great variety of inexpensive products. But foreign competition also means lost manufacturing jobs and lower wages. The pressure of foreign imports has already required wage freezes or rollbacks in some industries.

Joseph A. Boyd, chairman of Harris Corporation, encountered this problem firsthand in 1981 when he discovered that his company could buy small computer terminals in Taiwan and ship them to Dallas for 40 percent less than the cost of building the terminals. As a corporate manager, he had few choices. To keep manufacturing in the United States, he needed to cut wages across the board by 35 percent and automate production. For his workers that meant fewer jobs and lower earnings. The same is true in other industries.[38]

Certainly, the increasing globalization of our economy does not mean that wages will be standardized worldwide in the near future. The United States enjoys a number of advantages over even low-wage, technically advanced nations like South Korea or Indonesia. Particularly in complicated manufacturing industries, workers' wages account for a smaller and smaller share of a product's total cost. Our technological superiority, highly developed financial institutions, access to capital, and better educated work force can all help to offset wage disparities.

On the other hand, the increasingly rapid diffusion of technology, comparatively low wage costs, and steep trade barriers employed by Japan, Korea, Taiwan, and other nations will doggedly challenge America's once vaunted position in the world economy.

Another threat to jobs and economic growth in the United States is the phenomenon of "outsourcing"—firms' locating their production facilities abroad. Over the last two decades, U.S. companies in record numbers have moved their entire operations overseas or purchased their parts and components from foreign sources.

While such moves may make good sense for individual companies, outsourcing steadily erodes vital manufacturing jobs and capital investments that help keep the American economy sturdy. "The Hollow Corporation" represents a new kind of company that has little to do with manufacturing. "Instead, they import components or products from low-wage countries, slap their own names on them, and sell them in America. Left unchecked, this trend will hurt our economy, retard U.S. productivity, slow innovation and reduce our standard of living."[39]

Familiar U.S. enterprises like Caterpillar, General Electric, Eastman Kodak, Honeywell Bull, and hundreds more have all gone elsewhere for production, taking advantage of lower wages and other generous benefits offered by host countries eager to obtain U.S. investments.[40] Often these companies search the globe for plant sites that offer the best financial breaks. They then ship products back to the United States and other markets. For years American companies transferred blue-collar jobs to low-wage countries, but today firms are locating abroad their fundamental technology, management functions, and even the design and engineering skills that are crucial for innovation.

The most absurd display of government-promoted outsourcing came in 1986, when the Department of Commerce sponsored a conference in Acapulco to advise U.S. companies how to locate manufacturing plants in Mexico. Called Expo-Maquita 1986, it focused on transferring manufacturing facilities to Mexico and shipping finished products back to the United States for final assembly, thus avoiding the tariff on finished goods. Not amused, Congress quickly passed a resolution prohibiting the use of public funds for conferences and trade shows that promote foreign assembly line locations for U.S. firms.[41]

Mexico has long been a target of American organized labor's ire. Nonskilled Mexican workers earn only one-sixth what their counterparts in Japan receive and only half the average wage in Taiwan, South Korea, and Singapore. Over the past twenty years, Mexico has offered tax breaks, tariff exemptions, and other benefits to encourage foreign firms to establish manufacturing plants along our two-thousand-mile-long border. The new plants are called maquila d'oros, "golden mills." Hundreds of U.S. companies have responded, seeking their "gold" in the form of greater profits generated by the subsidies and low wages. Today, nearly a thousand, mostly U.S.-owned, maquila d'oros employ nearly a quarter million Mexican workers to make products for export to the United States.[42]

U.S. government promotion of manufacturing in other countries will only hasten the materialization of *Business Week's* prediction that "U.S. manufacturers will wind up simply licking the labels and sticking them on products that are made abroad . . . [and] looking forward to a lower standard of living."[43]

While many firms shift production to foreign sites in order to exploit cheap foreign labor and boost profits, other factors can lead to outsourcing. Many developing nations have imposed foreign performance standards on firms seeking access to their markets. Under this entirely legal form of blackmail, firms must agree to locate production facilities in a given nation before they can sell products there.

In addition, today's rapidly shifting world economy places special demands on multinational firms. Many have been forced to locate production facilities on several continents as a hedge against rapid exchange rate fluctuations. Pat Choate, director of policy for TRW and a top expert on competitiveness, notes that Ford Motor Company might have been driven into bankruptcy by the overvalued dollar in the early 1980s had the firm not had European operations to fall back on.[44]

While these motivations are understandable, they are little solace for millions of U.S. workers who have lost their jobs as firms shut down domestic plants or choose to locate new facilities overseas. Ironically, as American companies relocate their manufacturing facilities abroad, foreign firms have invested $250 billion in U.S. manufacturing and assembly plants. In addition, foreign entities have purchased more than $200 billion in Treasury bills, $450 billion in banking assets, and more than $200 billion in land and real estate.[45]

The influx of foreign capital cuts both ways in its effect on the American economy. Martin Tolchin, a *New York Times* reporter who has coauthored a book on the subject,[46] says such investments revitalize local economies, help finance the national debt, buoy the stock market, and heighten real estate values. But they also erode the nation's economic and political independence, siphon profits out of the United States, and involve states and cities in a destructive bidding war aimed at landing foreign investment. The foreign firms then use the grants and tax breaks to compete against U.S. companies.[47]

The new jobs that accompany foreign plant investments generally pay less than the manufacturing jobs lost through outsourcing by American firms. And while Nissan, Honda, and other foreign companies are setting up manufacturing plants in the United States, most of their components are produced elsewhere. Often the U.S. production role is basically final assembly. American workers will have to adjust to a different management style, strange cultural habits, and, since most of these jobs are nonunion, lower wages and fewer benefits.

Interestingly, the advent of Japanese-American joint ventures in automobiles and other products may provide ammunition for U.S. negotiators seeking to open the Japanese market to our products. For years, Japanese negotiators have maintained that our poor performance in the Japanese market is due to the shoddy quality of American workmanship. This charge has taken hold in the American psyche, to the point where most Americans would probably agree that U.S. craftsmanship is inherently inferior to the precision of Japanese workers.

This argument loses some of its integrity, however, when one realizes that Honda and other Japanese firms intend to ship a portion of their American-made goods back into the Japanese market. If the Japanese can import American goods with a

Japanese brand name, they can import American goods with an American brand name.

The United States is in the midst of a fundamental, if not painful, transition. Traditionally, we have relied strongly on agriculture and heavy manufacturing for our employment. In the 1920s, one of three Americans in the work force held a blue-collar job; in the 1950s the figure dropped to one in four. Today, only one in every six jobs in the United States is in manufacturing.

Any comparison of today's crisis in manufacturing and the decline in farm employment in the last century has to allow for one crucial difference: while farm employment dropped, America's agricultural output remained constant or increased. Today we are witnessing not the mechanization of American manufacturing but the loss of both jobs and production. We are conceding entire industrial sectors to foreign competition.

The prospects for the future are even grimmer. While nearly 18 million people are employed in blue-collar jobs today, it is projected that the figure will decline to 12 million by 2010. Even if American production increases, the odds are that manufacturing jobs will be lost to foreign competition and plant automation.

Indeed, many analysts argue that a cut in blue-collar employment is a prerequisite for increased productivity. In *Frontiers of Management,* Drucker points out that when Henry Ford introduced the assembly line in 1909, he cut the number of man-hours required to produce a motor car by 80 percent in two or three years.[48] While the example is extreme, many of today's manufacturing sectors realize that innovation means lower labor costs and greater efficiency.

As Americans leave the farms and factories to compete for highly specialized and lower-paying jobs, the political debate on the state of the economy has turned to employment. President

Reagan, who rightly takes credit for keeping the nation's civilian unemployment rate under 8 percent, rarely fails to remind Americans that 9 million new jobs have been created since he arrived at the White House. When the figures were released in late December 1986, White House spokesmen talked glowingly of "more American workers, creating more goods," while a less sanguine commissioner of the Bureau of Labor Statistics told Congress the figures "show weakness in manufacturing, but strength elsewhere in the economy."

What Ronald Reagan fails to point out about his 9 million new jobs is that most are low-wage, marginally skilled positions. According to a report to the Joint Economic Committee by economists Barry Bluestone and Bennett Harrison, during the 1980s nearly 45 percent of the net new jobs created paid poverty-level wages, more than double the level of such jobs during the 1960s and 1970s.[49]

Their study dispels the myth that the poor-paying jobs went only to minorities and young people. Since 1979, three quarters of the net jobs gained by white men have been at the low end of the scale, showing the highest percentage of any demographic group.[50] Bluestone and Harrison claim that "manufacturing has not added a single new job to the economy since 1979. Virtually all the employment growth has been in service and trade—industries with twice the proportion of low-wage jobs as the manufacturing sector."[51]

While some have challenged the accuracy of Harrison and Bluestone's figures, their basic argument is irrefutable. Unless our policymakers and business leaders recognize the forces reshaping our economy, America's future holds deindustrialization, lower wages, and a declining standard of living.

Nearly every congressman can relate horror stories about plant closures, displaced workers, economic and social stress, even entire communities folding. In my district in Washington State, the major industries have either shut down or curtailed operations during the 1980s. When the Alcoa smelter in Vancouver—an aluminum plant that once employed two thousand workers—closed in late 1986, it quickly became a crisis in the community.

Lost manufacturing jobs can paralyze local communities —no bankers and creditors, erosion of the local base, and spiraling economic problems that affect the entire area. In the Alcoa shutdown, company officials cited foreign competition as a contributing factor. As a result, the Department of Labor certified the displaced workers as eligible for trade adjustment assistance, which is available only if the industry has been severely injured by imports.

Despite government training and relocation programs, displaced workers often must scale down their future expectations. Alcoa's unemployed workers qualified for unemployment benefits and training assistance, but these are usually a ticket to a lower-paying job at best and a six-month extension of unemployment benefits at worst. In the case of the Alcoa shutdown, the best that a worker earning $16 to $18 per hour could expect was a $6 to $8 per hour job in one of the local Japanese-owned electronics plants.

Unfortunately, these diminished expectations may be signs of the times. American workers in certain sectors like autos, steel, or aluminum were able to negotiate ever increasing wage and benefit packages over the past twenty years because U.S. firms enjoyed hegemony in the market for those products. With the rise of highly competitive foreign sources for nearly every manufactured item, these wage and benefit levels may no longer be possible.

Median real income peaked in 1973 and has declined ever since, leading some economists to predict the demise of America's middle class.[52] The median pay for jobs created during the Reagan administration is 30 percent lower than previous levels. Average real weekly earnings were lower in 1985 than they were thirteen years earlier.[53] Researchers at Chase Econometrics reckon that even the most conspicuously well-off group of

Americans—the baby boomers of 1946–1964—are worse off than their parents or their counterparts of ten years ago.[54] A lower wage base contributes to a downward spiral of less disposable income, reduced consumption of goods and services, less demand for manufactured goods, fewer manufacturing jobs, and further erosion of the wage base.

Another indicator of our deteriorating competitiveness is the growth in part-time employment—jobs offering less than a thirty-five-hour work week. In 1954, 15 percent of all jobs were part time; today, that figure is 20 percent. The surge will continue. Between 1974 and 1985, part-time jobs grew twice as fast as full-time jobs, accounting for 80 percent of the total net employment growth. The average 1984 wage of part-time workers was $4.50 an hour, compared with $7.80 for full-time workers. A part-time employee would have to work nearly seventy hours per week just to keep pace with his or her full-time counterpart.

Robert Kuttner describes whole regional subeconomies being rebuilt around low-wage, part-time, back-office work. He tells of displaced factory workers who are working two and three part-time jobs to earn less than their former full-time paycheck provided.[55]

The quality of our work force, as well as our standard of living, is in jeopardy. The newly created service jobs are often low-skill clerical and retail sales positions. Everyone agrees that America needs a high-quality work force to meet the competitive challenges ahead. Our economy, however, is heading in the opposite direction. The blue-collar, semiskilled, well-paid workers of the past are being replaced by the part-time, unskilled, poorly paid, highly transient, nonunion workers of the future.

To achieve the goal of a highly trained work force will take more than government programs to improve our schools, vocational centers, and workers' training programs. It will require a radical change in how management views its "human capital" and how labor and management view each other.

Currently, many employers and employees view one another with indifference at best and distrust or friction at worst. Rarely is there a sense of loyalty, commitment, or shared endeavor. In our footloose, highly transient economy, managers are reluctant to invest too much training in their workers for fear that the employees will be gone tomorrow or apply their newly acquired skills elsewhere. Workers have little incentive to upgrade their skills when they have no confidence that a plant will be around the following year to reward their investment.

Left unchecked, these downward trends in America's work force will also affect our trade ledger. In theory, as American wages drop, American products ought to be more price competitive in both the domestic and world markets. When workers have less disposable income, they will buy fewer foreign-produced goods. But how far would American wages need to drop before American products could undercut the state-of-the-art sweatshops of Asia, South America, or Africa?

Even if America could reduce wages enough to compete with Indonesia or Mexico, the loss of national income would have ominous consequences for our nation as a whole. Declining personal income will require either a reduction in government services or a drastic increase in taxes. In an era of lower wages and falling national income, how could the United States afford vital programs like national defense, health care, or Social Security with a shrinking tax base? How could we meet the annual $150 million interest charge on our $2 billion national debt?

The key to solving our competitiveness problem does not lie in surrendering the wage, safety, and environmental gains of the last century. The challenge for policymakers, managers, and workers alike is to forge a comprehensive competitiveness strategy based on realistic wage rates, continued technological superiority, flexible institutions and management styles, better financing and marketing techniques, and a highly trained and committed work force. The alternative is a steady decline of America's economic influence, a narrowing of our national agenda, and a steady erosion of our standard of living.

World Economic Leadership: Is Pax Americana Enough?

Since World War II, the United States has provided the leadership that sustained the institutions and shaped the trends that account for today's global economic success. America has been the nucleus of the world's financial system, with our dollar universally accepted as the primary currency. U.S. savings and farsightedness hastened the economic recoveries of Western Europe and Japan, and U.S. foreign aid underwrote much of the development in Third World countries.

America has shouldered the cost of Eastern security, spending up to two thirds of its annual military budget on defense abroad, making it possible for our allies to enjoy economic success in a relatively safe and secure world.

Since 1980, America's fiscal policies and robust consumer spending have kept many of the world's factories humming. The United States may not be able to sustain this leadership role much longer. The magnanimous policy of the past forty years could well undermine America's present and future economic leadership.

After World War I, England no longer had the patience and political will to carry a war-shattered world through the twentieth century despite its vast colonial investments and heavy dependence on trade. At first America shunned the opportunity to be the world's economic leader, and only after the collapse of the world trading system in 1930 did the United States, under President Franklin D. Roosevelt's leadership, assert its economic might and political influence in restoring trade relations and keeping the rest of the world safe for democracy and capitalism.

But if today's America can no longer afford to carry this responsibility, what nation is prepared to do so in the years ahead? Japan? West Germany? Or will we see the emergence of collective leadership, involving several industrialized nations? Perhaps one of the dominant economic blocs, like the European Community or Association of Southeast Asian Nations, will yield a new system of finance and trade in the world.

The leadership will most likely fall to nations that possess the financial muscle to do the job. Hobart Rowen posits that "as was true for Britain in the 19th Century and the United States after World War II, the nation that is chief supplier of capital to the world acquires enormous power and influence."[56]

If that is the case, the burden may go by default to West Germany or Japan, since they are today's capital surplus countries. As America's economic power recedes, theirs is on the rise. In 1990, when the United States will carry close to one trillion dollars in external debt, owed mostly to foreign investors, the Japanese will have accumulated a capital surplus in excess of $500 billion.

Traditionally, the world's economic leaders have also been the dominant political and military powers. The combined strength of wealth and might thrust a nation into a leadership position. That was the case with Britain in the nineteenth century and the United States throughout most of this century. Since World War II, our nation especially has been so preoccupied with its geopolitical and security responsibilities that it has let its economic position slip. As America's economic preeminence fades, our political and military responsibilities seem to get more burdensome. Under Democratic and Republican administrations, America has steadfastly assumed the costly role of maintaining the peace, deploying half a million troops—more than one-third its armed forces—on foreign soil, from Korea's demilitarized zone to the Berlin wall.

The United States' troop commitment in the mid 1980s included 48,104 military personnel in Japan and 43,133 in Korea. Our Pacific air and naval forces probably total another 50,000. That adds up to 141,237 people at a cost of roughly $30,000 per person, which comes to an annual budget expenditure of over $4 billion. In Europe and the Mediterranean, U.S. troops in England, Germany, Greece, Turkey, Italy, Spain, Portugal, and Belgium represent a total of 357,598 armed service personnel, at a cost of $10.7 billion. To this we must add the enormous expense of the nuclear shield, which is difficult to calculate but takes a large percentage of our $300 billion annual defense budget.[57]

World leadership comes at a high cost, which explains the reluctance of other nations to take on the task. Everything purchased by the Pentagon amounts to a tax expenditure, much of it used in protecting the countries that are invading our markets at home and beating our businessmen abroad. America's heavy spending for defense—a major factor in the budget deficit—takes 6.7 percent of gross national product, while our allies commit only 3.4 percent of their GNP to defense. Foreign aid, a key element in projecting U.S. power abroad, was cut from $15.5 billion in 1986 to $14 billion in 1987.[58]

How long can a nation's producers and workers assume the burden of defending the free world? Can the United States, with its large budget deficits and Gramm-Rudman reduction goals, afford to maintain such a costly commitment? Is it wise for the U.S. government to continue borrowing from abroad to help pay for its ambitious peacekeeping role? Is the burden of being a political and military power possible without the undergirding of a strong economy?

Conversely, is Japan, as the world's emerging economic power, prepared to assume some political responsibility? Japan possesses the wealth, but does it have the political will to be a world leader? If the Japanese government steadfastly opposes increasing its defense spending beyond a meager one percent of its GNP, is the country likely to assert any kind of global economic or security leadership? Even if it does, are we prepared to allow Japan to revise its American-imposed peace constitution, which prevents it from sending troops or selling arms abroad? If Japanese leaders feel that the United States spends excessively on defense and exaggerates the Soviet threat throughout the world, will they be prepared to commit sufficient resources to the task?

Rebounding from the ruins of World War II, Japan has single-mindedly devoted its energies to building an economic power. Like the Venetians and Dutch in their heyday, Japan conceived a vision of economic dominance with limited political or military responsibilities; its brilliant execution of this vision only brightens its economic future. The Japanese have benefited from a nuclear arms race that has the superpowers investing valuable resources in weapons production. They are betting that, unlike seventeenth-century Holland, Japan will not suffer for its modest level of military preparedness.

The question is not only Japan's willingness to become a world-class leader but whether the world is ready to pass on the baton to the Japanese. Does anyone seriously believe Japan will follow through with a $30 billion commitment to helping today's struggling developing countries, as the United States did after World War II with the Marshall Plan in Europe and comparable aid to Japan? Since Japan has seven of the world's ten largest banks, is Tokyo prepared to share the debt burden of the less developed countries with the United States? Are Japan's Asian neighbors, some of them victims of Japanese imperialism in the past, ready for Japan to become powerful in the region once again? Is there confidence in Western capitals that Japan possesses the moral fortitude and the global vision to become a world-class power?

Maybe the cost of leadership is too great for a single nation to bear in the late twentieth century. Since World War II, Western nations have been coalescing on issues of mutual concern. NATO and the Coordinating Committee for Multilateral Export Controls are examples of multilateral efforts to protect the security interests of Europe, America, and Japan. The OECD, GATT, IMF, and World Bank are economic and financial institutions set up to deal with economic turbulence when it occurs on the world scene. The United Nations' many agencies are devoted to the more technical and humanitarian problems that beset much of today's world.

Since the advanced industrial economies of the West account for 80 percent of the world's GNP, all have a stake in maintaining their economic strength and political cohesion. But the same forces that make for the West's collective strength also threaten its unity. As a bloc, Western nations can agree on general principles, establish economic and security goals, collectively support institutions, participate in summit meetings, and chart the economic course into the twenty-first century.

But such visionary plans break down over bilateral trade problems, petty disputes, threats of protectionism, and calls for retaliation. Even the most economically integrated and politically compatible countries engage in heated exchanges over trade and financial issues. These fires could easily spread to an ugly trade war.

Throughout 1986, Canada and the United States angrily denounced each other's trade actions; the United States and the EC stood on the brink of an all-out trade war; Western countries openly discussed collective action against Japan; LDC debt countries caused U.S. and European officials many sleepless nights worrying about repayment schedules.

Paul McCracken, professor emeritus at the University of Michigan, writes that we may be headed toward world economic disintegration.

> When finance ministers, central bankers, presidents and prime ministers congregate this year, their major challenge (whatever the specific items on the agenda for economic policy) will be to

counter another one of modern history's major surges toward international economic and financial disintegration. The forces pushing toward fragmentation are coming close to being irresistibly strong.[59]

Never before has the world's economic fate been so dependent as it is today on the seven industrial leaders who attend the annual economic summit meetings. In recent years, these gatherings have been noted more for their side issues, photo opportunities, and glossing over possible trade conflicts than for squarely addressing the enormous economic problems at hand.

At the 1986 Tokyo summit, President Reagan and George Shultz seemed more preoccupied with getting Western countries to boycott Libya than trying to deal with balance-of-payments, growth differential, or exchange rate problems.

As world leaders assemble, they are often guided more by their interests back home than their responsibilities as world leaders. Decisive action to ensure greater equity among nations or, in the extreme, to avert an international economic calamity, may not be popular back home. As we move into a truly integrated economy, certain adjustments must be made. They frequently involve more imports and fewer domestic jobs, reduced trade barriers or an end to subsidies, and in some cases less prosperity or a lower standard of living.

This is not the kind of message national leaders want to give their constituents after a summit meeting, but it may be what is necessary to preserve the world's trading system. Rich countries, especially, need to commit to helping weaker nations, if for no other reason than to develop new markets in the long run.

During campaigns and shortly after elections, national leaders are generally parochial in their outlook. Short-term domestic political concerns tend to be in the ascendancy, making efforts to preserve the international economic order elusive.

In the mid nineteenth century, political institutions were

incapable of coping with the emerging world economy, and again during the Roaring Twenties, selfish national economic interests prevailed in a leaderless world trading system. The time of judgment has arrived for today's leaders. Their collective vision and actions will determine whether their nations can adjust to the challenge of maintaining a world trading system or whether they will resort to nationalistic policies that will undermine the international economic order.

America's trade crisis is really a world trade crisis. How the United States confronts its own trade and deficit problems and its unique leadership role in the Western world could well determine the economic fate of all nations well into the twenty-first century.

GLOSSARY
NOTES
SUGGESTED READINGS
INDEX

GLOSSARY

Ad valorem tariff: Tariff calculated as a percentage of the value of goods cleared through Customs, e.g., 15 percent ad valorem means 15 percent of the value.

African Development Bank (AFDB): Multilateral development bank established to promote African economic development and cooperation. Membership: 51 African and 19 non-African nations. Stock open to outside subscription but loans restricted to African members. The African Development Fund and Nigerian Trust Foundation are sources of concessionary loans within the AFDB.

Agency for International Development (AID): Administers assistance programs designed to advance the social and economic progress of the developing world.

Antidumping code: A code of conduct negotiated under the GATT during the Kennedy and Tokyo rounds providing for the imposition of antidumping duties on imports found to have been sold at less than fair value and to have caused or to be likely to cause material injury to a U.S. industry.

Antidumping duties: Special tariffs imposed to offset price advantages resulting from imports sold at below fair market value.

Association of Southeast Asian Nations (ASEAN): A multilateral development bank formed to foster economic growth and cooperation in Asia. Membership: 32 regional members receive concessional loans provided by the Asian Development Fund. Fifteen additional members (donor nations) provide the funds.

Balance of payments: A tabulation of a country's credit and debit transactions with other countries and international institutions. These transactions are divided into two broad groups: current account and capital account. The current account includes exports and imports of goods, services (including investment income), and unilateral transfers. The capital account includes financial flows related to international direct investment, investment in government and private securities, international bank transactions, and changes in official gold holdings and foreign exchange reserves.

Balance of trade: A component of the balance of payments, or the surplus or deficit that results from comparing a country's expenditures on merchandise imports and receipts derived from its merchandise exports.

Barter: Trade in which merchandise is exchanged directly for other merchandise without use of money. Barter is an important means of trade with countries using currency that is not readily convertible. *See* countertrade.

Bilateral trade agreement: Formal or informal agreement involving commerce between two countries. Such agreements sometimes list the quantities of special goods that may be exchanged between participating countries within a given period.

Bound rates: Most-favored-nation tariff rates resulting from GATT negotiations. May represent a reduced rate or a commitment not to raise an existing rate. A bound rate may not be increased without GATT concurrence or adequate compensation to affected trading partners.

Bounties or grants: Payments by governments to producers of goods, often to strengthen their competitive position.

Bretton Woods Conference: Meeting held at Bretton Woods, New Hampshire, in 1944 to set up a system for cooperation in international trade and payments and to devise an international monetary system. Sought the achievement of stable exchange rates and free convertibility of currencies. Established the IMF and World Bank.

Buffer stocks: Stockpiles of commodities maintained to moderate price fluctuations.

"Buy American" procurement policy: Discriminatory government purchase of goods and services from U.S. suppliers, despite their higher price or inferior quality, which functions as a non-tariff barrier to trade. Many other nations also require their government agencies to buy domestic goods even when imported goods are better and cheaper.

Caribbean basin initiative: Preferential system providing for duty-free treatment of goods produced in the Caribbean and Central American regions to promote regional growth and attract foreign investment.

Cartel: Arrangement among firms or governments that seeks to maintain an international monopoly on production of a specific good.

Central American Common Market (CACM): Organized to promote eventual free-trade area, Customs union, and liberalization of intraregional trade. Membership: Costa Rica, Guatemala, El Salvador, Nicaragua, and Honduras.

Chamber of Commerce: Association of businesspeople organized to promote local business interests.

Commodities: Goods exchanged in trade. Usually used in reference to raw materials and agricultural products.

Commodity agreement: International understanding regarding trade of a raw material. Usually intended to affect the price of the commodity.

Commodity Credit Corporation (CCC): Facility within the USDA created in 1948 to stabilize, support, and protect farm income and prices. Also seeks to assist in the maintenance of adequate supplies of agricultural commodities and facilitate their orderly distribution.

Common agricultural policy (CAP): Means by which members of the European Community seek to coordinate their individual agricultural policies and programs. Principal elements include the variable levy (an import duty equaling the difference between EC target farm prices and the lowest available market prices of agricultural imports) and export subsidies designed to promote exports of farm goods that cannot be sold within the EC at target prices.

Common line agreement: Understanding among the United States, France, Germany, and the United Kingdom regarding use of officially supported export credits in financing global trade in commercial aircraft.

Common market: Economic association in which there are no tariffs on intragroup trade; members share a common external tariff and free mobility of capital and labor.

Comparative advantage: Central concept in modern trade theory, developed by David Ricardo in the nineteenth century, that suggests a nation will export those goods it can produce relatively more efficiently than other goods.

Contracting party: Country that has signed the GATT and accepted its obligations and procedures.

Coordinating Committee for Multilateral Export Controls: Free-standing organization that serves as the primary forum for coordinating restrictions on exports to the Soviet bloc. Membership: all NATO nations, except Iceland, and Japan.

Council for Mutual Economic Assistance (CMEA): Soviet-bloc trade organization that promotes socialist economic integration and development.

Trade between members makes up 60% of CMEA's foreign trade, all conducted through state monopolies. Membership: Bulgaria, Czechoslovakia, East Germany, Hungary, Poland, Romania, the USSR, Mongolia, Cuba, and Vietnam. Long-term trade agreements exist with Yugoslavia.

Countertrade: Transactions in which the seller provides goods or services and, instead of receiving a cash payment, contractually agrees to purchase goods of equal value from the buyer. Also referred to as barter, offset, buy back, counterpurchase, and compensation trade. Has become prevalent in East-West trade and is increasingly important in trade with developing countries short of hard currency.

Countervailing duties: Additional levies imposed on imports to offset government subsidies, bounties, or grants by the exporting country. *See* export subsidies.

Customs: Authorities designated to collect duties levied by a country on imports and exports. "Customs" also refers to the procedures involved in such collection.

Devaluation: Lowering of the value of a national currency in terms of the currency of another nation. Devaluation tends to reduce domestic demand for imports in a country by raising its prices in terms of the devalued currency and to raise foreign demand for the country's exports by reducing its prices in terms of foreign currencies.

Dillon Round: Trade negotiations under GATT that took place in 1960 and 1961. Named for U.S. Undersecretary of State Douglas Dillon, who proposed the negotiations.

Domestic content: Requirement that a certain percentage of a product be domestically produced.

Dual pricing: Selling an identical product for different prices in different markets. Often related to export subsidies or dumping.

Dumping: Sale of a commodity in a foreign market at "less than fair value," i.e., less than the price at which the product is sold in the exporting country or to a third country. "Fair value" can also be the cost of production. Dumping is generally recognized to be an unfair trade practice. GATT permits the imposition of antidumping duties equal to the difference between the price sought in the importing country and the "normal" value of the product in the exporting country.

Duty: See tariff.

EC: See European Community.

Embargo: Restriction or prohibition on exports or imports with respect to either specific products or specific countries.

Escape clause: Trade law provisions designed to provide relief to domestic industries injured by increased import competition. Section 201 of the Trade Act of 1974 requires the ITC to investigate complaints filed by firms or workers claiming to be harmed or threatened with harm due to rising imports. Section 203 provides for relief action, if the complaint is valid, in the form of adjustment assistance or temporary import restrictions. Escape clause actions need not be based on proof of unfair trading practices.

ETC: See export trading company.

European Community (EC): Created in 1967 when the European Economic Community (EEC) merged with the European Coal and Steel Community and the European Atomic Energy Community. The EEC was formed in 1957 to establish a Customs union comprising France, the Federal Republic of Germany, Italy, the Netherlands, Belgium, and Luxembourg. It sought to eliminate Customs duties and other intraregional trade barriers, to erect a common external tariff against nonmember countries, to develop a common agricultural policy, and to ensure free movement of labor and capital. The United Kingdom, Denmark, Ireland, Greece, Spain, and Portugal have since joined the union.

Exchange rate: Price of one currency in terms of another, i.e., the number of units of one currency that may be exchanged for one unit of another currency.

Excise tax: Selective tax — sometimes called a consumption tax — on certain goods produced within or imported into a country.

Export Administration Act: Statutory authority for the President to restrict or suspend U.S. exports to protect the national security, protect short supplies, or further foreign policy objectives.

Export controls: Any restriction or regulation of exports, such as licensing requirements and embargoes.

Export credits: Direct credits or loans to facilitate exports.

Export-Import Bank (Eximbank): Promotes U.S. exports through the provision of direct loans, financial guarantees, export credit insurance, and discount loans. Originally established in 1934 to facilitate trade with the Soviet Union, the bank now concentrates its efforts on supporting U.S. exports to the Third World and helping U.S. firms in cases where government credit assistance is made available to foreign competitors. In effect, the bank subsidizes foreign purchasers of U.S. goods and services by offering foreign borrowers credit terms that are more favorable than those otherwise available in private capital markets. Most major industrial nations provide some degree of officially supported export credit assistance; the resulting competition among official export credit agencies plays an important role in the formulation of trade policy in the developed world.

Export management company: Private firm that serves as the export department for several manufacturers, soliciting and transacting export business on behalf of its clients in return for a commission, salary, or retainer plus commission.

Export quotas: Specific restrictions or limits on the value or volume of exports of specific goods imposed by an exporting country. Used to protect domestic industries and consumers from temporary shortages and moderate world prices of specific commodities. Also used in connection with orderly marketing agreements and voluntary restraint agreements.

Export subsidies: Direct government payments or other economic benefits granted domestic producers of goods to promote sales in foreign markets. *See* countervailing duties.

Export trading company (ETC): Special class of trading company established by the Export Trading Company Act of 1982. An ETC is a company principally engaged in exporting goods and services or in facilitating exports by unaffiliated persons. An ETC can also import, barter, and arrange sales between third countries. Properly certified ETCs are given limited immunity from antitrust actions and may be owned entirely or in part by bank holding companies.

External debt: Cumulative debt owed to foreign institutions.

Fair value: Standard against which U.S. purchase prices of imported goods are compared during an antidumping investigation. Generally expressed as the weighted average of the exporters' home market prices or prices to third countries during the period of investigation.

FAS: See Foreign Agricultural Service.

FCPA: See Foreign Corrupt Practices Act.

Foreign Agricultural Service (FAS): Export promotion arm of the USDA. Made up of a network of attachés and trade officers stationed overseas. Maintains worldwide reporting and intelligence system. Administers agricultural market development program. Works to reduce foreign trade barriers to agricultural exports. Manages the Commodity Credit Corporation (CCC).

Foreign Commercial Service (FCS): Overseas marketing arm of the U.S. Department of Commerce.

Foreign Corrupt Practices Act (FCPA): Statute outlawing bribes or other payments by U.S. corporations to foreign officials to procure business.

Foreign Credit Insurance Association (FCIA): Association of some 50 insurance companies that underwrites commercial credit risk for certain Eximbank programs.

Foreign trade zone: Area within a port or airport that is treated for Customs purposes as lying outside the Customs territory of the country. Foreign goods may enter the zone without payment of Customs duties pending eventual transshipment or re-exportation.

Free trade: Theoretical concept that assumes unhampered international trade, e.g., no tariffs, non-tariff barriers, etc.

Free-trade area (FTA): Arrangement between nations to eliminate trade barriers among themselves while maintaining national tariff schedules on trade with all other trading partners.

General Agreement on Tariffs and Trade (GATT): Multilateral organization whose members account for more than four fifths of world trade. Its primary objective is to liberalize trade and place it on a secure basis, thereby contributing to global economic growth and development. The principal international agreement delineating rules for international trade.

Generalized system of preferences (GSP): Extends duty-free treatment to certain goods entering the U.S. from eligible developing countries. The program sets "competitive need" limits on the importation of duty-free items—triggered by either a specific dollar amount or a percentage of total imports—and protects certain import-sensitive articles by denying duty-free treatment to goods in those categories. Eligibility is denied to Communist countries, unless they receive MFN treatment and are members of GATT and the IMF, and to the OPEC countries or other nations that control vital resources through cartels. Countries that have nationalized or expropriated U.S. property without adequate compensation are also ineligible. Under the GSP renewal, a part of the Trade and Tariff Act of 1984, countries reaching a per capita income of $8500 a year will be phased out, or graduated, over a two-year period. The 1984 extension also grants the President authority to limit GSP benefits for countries that have a poor track record on protection of workers' rights, open markets for U.S. goods and services, and protection of intellectual property rights. The program, administered by the Trade Representative, is scheduled to expire in 1988.

Gross domestic product (GDP): Total income earned within a country's boundaries.

Gross national product (GNP): The total value of goods and services produced in a nation during a specified period of time.

GSP: See generalized system of preferences.

Harmonization of tariffs: Tariff-cutting method designed to make tariffs on different items more nearly uniform within each country's tariff schedule. Usually involves formulas that will make large cuts in high tariffs and smaller cuts in lower tariffs. Different from the linear reduction formula, used in the Kennedy Round, which calls for identical percentage cuts in all tariffs to which it is applied. All tariff-cutting proposals during the Tokyo Round involved some degree of harmonization.

Harmonized system: A multipurpose international goods classification system designed to be used by manufacturers, exporters, importers, Customs, statisticians, and others in classifying goods moving in international trade under a single commodity code.

Import quota: Means of restricting imports by licensing importers and assigning each a limited import ceiling. Such licenses also specify the country from which the importer must purchase the goods.

Import substitution: Attempt by a country to reduce imports (and hence foreign exchange expenditures) by encouraging the development of domestic industries.

Industrial policy: Encompasses traditional government policies intended to provide a favorable economic climate for the development of industry in general or specific industrial sectors. Instruments may include tax incentives to promote investments or exports, direct or indirect subsidies, special financing arrangements, protection against foreign competition, worker training programs, regional development programs, assistance for research and development, and measures to help small business firms.

Infant industry protection: Temporary protection on behalf of a fledgling industry that has the potential to be competitive in the world market.

Informatics: Broad term used to refer to Brazil's information processing, computer, and digital telecommunication industries, as well as all research in these areas.

Intellectual property: Ownership conferring the right to possess, use, or dispose of products created by human ingenuity, including patents, trademarks, and copyrights.

Inter-American Development Bank (IDB): Provides 10- to 25-year loans, repayable in the currency loaned. Concessional financing available through the Fund for Special Operations, which allows repayment, wholly or in part, in local currency. Membership: 44 countries.

International Bank for Reconstruction and Development (IBRD), also known as World Bank: UN organization founded in 1945 to assist postwar reconstruction in Europe, the bank is an important source of credit for developing countries. Makes loans to member nations when private capital is unavailable. Loans made directly to governments or to private enterprises with government guarantees. Membership contingent upon IMF membership. Subscriptions to the World Bank capital stock based on IMF quotas. Voting rights are related to share holdings. Membership: 150 countries.

International Development Association (IDA): Affiliate of the World Bank that provides capital to the poorer developing member nations on more flexible terms than those of the IBRD. Membership: 135 countries.

International Development Cooperation Agency (IDCA): Plans and coordinates U.S. policy on international economic issues affecting the developing world. Made up of the Agency for International Development, the Overseas Private Investment Corporation, and the Trade and Development Program.

International Finance Corporation (IFC): Member of the World Bank group. Created to encourage the flow of capital into private rather than public investment in developing countries. Makes loans at commercial interest rates, usually as a lender of last resort.

International Monetary Fund (IMF): Created to smooth fluctuations in the world trade cycle, promote international monetary cooperation, and expand world trade. Provides for free currency convertibility between participating nations as well as temporary assistance for members with short- or medium-term balance-of-payments problems. Loans are contingent upon the fund's determination that the debtor nation is working to correct its deficit and shore up its currency. Members contribute to the fund on a quota basis designed to reflect relative economic strength. Founded in 1945 as a result of the Bretton Woods Conference. Membership: 146 countries.

International Trade Administration (ITA): Division of the U.S. Department of Commerce with chief responsibility over trade matters within the department's purview.

International Trade Commission (ITC): See U.S. International Trade Commission.

Invisible trade: Items such as freight, insurance, and financial services that are included in a country's balance-of-payments accounts (in the "current" account), even though they are not recorded as physically visible exports and imports.

Jackson-Vanick: Provision in the Trade Act of 1974 making MFN status for Communist countries contingent on a demonstrated relaxation of immigration policy.

Kennedy Round: Popular name for the sixth round of trade negotiations under the aegis of GATT, conducted during 1963–1967. Named for President John F. Kennedy.

Less developed country (LDC): Generally applies to all countries other than members of the Organization for Economic Cooperation and Development and the socialist countries of Eastern Europe.

Liberal: With reference to trade policy, "liberal" usually means relatively free of import controls or restraints and/or a preference for reducing existing barriers to trade, often contrasted with the protectionist preference for retaining or raising selected barriers to imports.

Linear reduction of tariffs: Across-the-board percentage reduction in tariff rates. Early GATT rounds were conducted on this basis with provision made for specific "exceptions." Exceptions were usually confined to products deemed so sensitive that increased imports might cause severe political or economic difficulties.

Market access: Availability of a nation's markets to foreign producers. A reflection of a nation's willingness to permit imports to compete with similar domestically manufactured goods.

Market disruption: Situation existing when a surge of imports causes sales of domestically produced goods to decline to such an extent that the domestic producers suffer major economic reversals.

Material injury: According to the Trade Agreements Act of 1979, harm that is not inconsequential, immaterial, or unimportant and is a result of increased imports or unfair trade practices.

MFA: See Multi-Fiber Arrangement regarding international trade in textiles.

MFN: See most-favored-nation treatment.

Mixed credit: Controversial form of export financing that combines foreign aid with direct credits to finance exports to developing countries. Eximbank's 1983 revised charter authorized the creation of a U.S. mixed-credit facility to be operated by Eximbank in cooperation with U.S. AID. Also called tied aid.

Most-favored-nation treatment (MFN): Commitment by one country to apply its lowest tariff rates on all products imported from another country. Major principle of GATT. *See* General Agreement on Tariffs and Trade and the Trade Act of 1974.

Multi-Fiber Arrangement regarding international trade in textiles (MFA): International understanding that allows participants to apply quantitative restrictions on textile imports when an importing country considers them necessary to prevent market disruption. Such restrictions would ordinarily be contrary to GATT. Provides that such restrictions not reduce imports to levels below those of the previous year. Encourages importing nations to increase textile import quotas through individual bilateral agreements.

Multilateral development banks (MDBs): African Development Bank, Asian

Development Bank, Inter-American Development Bank, World Bank group.

Multilateral trade negotiations (MTN): General term applicable to any of the seven rounds of negotiations held under the auspices of GATT since 1947.

National Advisory Committee on international monetary and financial policies: Oversees government policy regarding multilateral development banks and the World Bank. It also reviews the lending activities of the Eximbank and oversees the mixed-credit facility operated by the bank with the Agency for International Development. Its members are the secretaries of Treasury (chairman), State, and Commerce, the chairman of the Federal Reserve System, the president of the Eximbank, and the administrator of AID.

Newly industrialized country (NIC): Descriptive of a developing nation that has gained a certain degree of economic development. Most often refers to such countries as Mexico, Brazil, Korea, Taiwan, and Singapore.

Non-market economy: System in which economic activity is regulated by central planning rather than market forces. Characteristic of the economic systems of the Soviet Union and most other Communist countries.

Non-tariff barriers (NTBs): Import quotas, foreign exchange controls, performance requirements, or other non-tariff measures designed to restrict or prevent the international exchange of goods and services.

OECD: See Organization for Economic Cooperation and Development.

Offset requirements: Imposed by governments on foreign producers as a condition for approval of major sales agreements to reduce the adverse balance of trade impact of a major sale or to gain specific industrial benefits for the importing country. The exporter may be required to buy a specified amount of locally produced goods or services from the importing country or to establish manufacturing facilities in the importing country.

Orderly marketing agreement: Agreement negotiated between two or more governments in which the exporting country undertakes to ensure that international trade in specified "sensitive" products will not disrupt or threaten industries in importing countries.

Organization for Economic Cooperation and Development (OECD): Primary forum for economic discussions among developed nations. Made up of various committees and working groups that conduct studies and negotiations. Coordinates policies of member nations: Australia, Austria, Belgium, Canada, Denmark, Finland, France, Greece, Iceland, Ireland, Italy, Japan, Luxembourg, the Netherlands, New Zealand, Norway, Portugal, Spain, Sweden, Switzerland, Turkey, the United Kingdom, the United States and West Germany. Yugoslavia has special status. Founded in 1960. Headquarters, Paris.

Organization of Petroleum Exporting Countries (OPEC): Petroleum cartel.

Overseas Private Investment Corporation (OPIC): Self-sustaining U.S. government agency that provides investment incentive services to U.S. businesses in the form of political risk insurance and finance services, encouraging private investment in developing nations. Authorized by Congress 1969, established 1971, OPIC has sponsored development projects in more than 100 countries.

Payment in kind (PIK): Form of payment, other than cash, to a person eligible to receive a cash payment from the Commodity Credit Corporation.

PL-480: Agricultural Trade and Assistance Act of 1954. Vehicle for developing export markets for U.S. agricultural products, meeting humanitarian food needs, and spurring economic and agricultural growth in the developing world.

Protectionism: Deliberate use or encouragement of restrictions on imports to enable relatively inefficient domestic producers to compete successfully with foreign producers.

Reciprocal Trade Agreements Act of 1934: Statute providing authority for the President to enter into bilateral agreements with other nations for reciprocal tariff reductions. Also provided the authority for U.S. participation in the first five GATT rounds. Superseded by Trade Expansion Act of 1962.

Reciprocity: Lowering of barriers on imports in return for equivalent concessions from other countries. An underlying principle of GATT negotiations implying an approximate equality of concessions accorded and benefits received.

Retaliation: Action taken by a country whose exports are adversely affected by the raising of tariffs or other trade restrictions by another country. GATT permits an adversely affected nation to impose limited restraints on imports from a country that has raised its trade barriers after consultations with countries whose trade might be affected.

Section 201: Statutory basis for escape clause action. *See* escape clause and Trade Act of 1974.

Section 232: Presidential authority to restrict imports that threaten the national security. *See* Trade Expansion Act of 1962.

Section 301: Presidential authority to retaliate against unfair trade practices. *See* unfair trade practices, Trade Act of 1974.

Section 303: Statutory basis for countervailing duty procedure for imports from countries that have not signed the GATT Subsidies Code. No injury test is required.

Section 701: Statutory basis for countervailing duty procedure for imports from GATT countries that have signed the Subsidies Code. Requires an injury test. *See* Tariff Act of 1930.

Section 731: Statutory basis for antidumping procedure. *See* Tariff Act of 1930.

Sensitive products: Goods whose costs of production are such that any reduction in tariff or non-tariff barriers to imports is deemed likely to threaten the viability of the domestic industry.

Small Business Administration (SBA): Government agency charged with promoting and assisting small-business interests in the U.S.

Smoot-Hawley Tariff Act of 1930: See Tariff Act of 1930.

Special drawing rights (SDRs): Established by the IMF to take the place of gold as a supplemental international monetary reserve asset. The unit value of an SDR reflects the daily exchange value of a "basket" of five major currencies.

Standards: Technical specifications that establish acceptable or mandatory characteristics of a product, such as levels of quality, safety, performance, or dimensions. The Agreement on Technical Barriers to Trade negotiated during the Tokyo Round is a standards code.

State trading nations: Nations that rely on government entities rather than private corporations to conduct trade with other countries. Examples: Soviet Union, People's Republic of China, and the countries of Eastern Europe.

Targeted Export Assistance (TEA): TEA, authorized by Congress in 1985, is administered by the U.S. Department of Agriculture. TEA provides financial support or CCC commodities to U.S. agricultural producers whose wares face unfair policies in competitor nations.

Tariff: A duty, or tax, levied on goods transported from one Customs area to another. Tariffs raise the prices of imported goods, making them less competitive within the market of the importing country. "Tariff" often refers to a comprehensive list or "schedule" of merchandise with the rate of duty to be paid to the government for importing products listed.

Tariff Act of 1930: U.S. protectionist legislation that raised tariff rates on most articles imported by the United States, triggering comparable tariff increases by U.S. trading partners. The Tariff Act of 1930 is also known as the Smoot-Hawley Tariff Act.

Tariff and Trade Act of 1984: Statute providing authority for the President to negotiate a free-trade area with Israel, renewing the GSP program, making "upstream subsidies" countervailable, and expanding the President's authority under Section 301 of the Trade Act with regard to trade in services and foreign direct investment. Also expands steel import program to require modernization and reinvestment.

Tariff quotas: The application of a higher tariff rate to imported goods after a specified quantity of the item has entered the country at the usual rate.

Tariff schedule: Comprehensive list of the goods a country may import and the import duties applicable to each product.

Tied loan: Loan made by a government agency that requires a foreign borrower to spend the proceeds in the lender's country.

Tokyo Round: GATT negotiations begun in 1973. Involved more participants than previous sessions, including many developing countries.

Trade Act of 1974: Statute granting the President broad authority to negotiate international agreements reducing trade barriers. *See* trade adjustment assistance, countervailing duties, dumping, generalized system of preferences, most-favored-nation treatment, and Tokyo Round.

Trade adjustment assistance: Financial and technical assistance to firms, workers, and communities to help them adjust to rising import competition. Authorized under the Trade Act of 1974.

Trade Agreements Act of 1979: Statute implementing the trade agreements negotiated by the United States under the Trade Act of 1974 during the Tokyo Round.

Trade and Development Program (TDP): Finances the planning of projects in developing countries that are potential export markets for U.S. goods and services.

Trade Expansion Act of 1962: Statute providing authority for U.S. participation in the Kennedy Round of trade negotiations. Also authorized the trade adjustment assistance program and Office of the Special Trade Representative. Superseded by the Trade Act of 1974.

Trade Policy Committee (TPC): Senior interagency trade committee. Chaired by the USTR, it involves secretary-level individuals.

TSUS: Tariff schedule of the United States. *See* tariff schedule.

UNCTAD: See United Nations Conference on Trade and Development.

Unfair trade practices: Any act, policy, or practice of a foreign government that violates an international agreement or is unjustifiable, unreasonable, or discriminatory and burdens or restricts U.S. commerce.

United Nations Conference on Trade and Development (UNCTAD): Organization associated with the United Nations system that focuses on the measures that might be taken by developed countries to accelerate the pace of economic growth in the developing world.

U.S. Court of International Trade: Court that handles judicial review of trade remedy findings, such as the existence of subsidy, dumping, or material injury.

U.S. Customs Service: Administers the Tariff Act of 1930, as amended, and other Customs laws governing the collection of revenues from imports.

Also assists other government agencies: for example, helps enforce export control laws in cooperation with the Department of Commerce. Customs also compiles certain trade statistics.

U.S. Department of Agriculture (USDA): Oversees the development of export markets and all matters involving international agricultural trade. Also ensures that all trade policy decisions take U.S. agricultural interests fully into account. The Foreign Agricultural Service operates as the USDA's export promotion agency through its network of counselors and officers abroad. FAS trade policy specialists also coordinate USDA responsibilities under international trade and commodity agreements and work to reduce trade barriers to U.S. farm exports. Also under FAS jurisdiction are the PL-480 program and Commodity Credit Corporation export credit sales program. PL-480 seeks to assist the developing world through concessional financing for U.S. farm exports and direct donations of U.S. farm goods for humanitarian purposes. The CCC program provides risk insurance for agricultural export financing to some countries.

U.S. Department of Commerce (DOC): Most of the Department of Commerce's international trade functions are carried out through its International Trade Administration, established in 1980. ITA handles issues concerning trade development, trade administration, and trade policy. The U.S. and Foreign Commercial Services and the Offices for International Economic Policy, Trade Development, and Trade Administration are all under ITA's jurisdiction. The U.S. and Foreign Commercial Services maintain offices in the United States and abroad to provide information and marketing assistance to U.S. companies. The International Economic Policy office analyzes international trade and investment policies and works to reduce foreign trade barriers. IEP works closely with the USTR office and other government agencies to develop U.S. negotiating positions on issues involving GATT, OECD, UNCTAD, etc. IEP also monitors foreign compliance with negotiated trade agreements. The Trade Development office oversees the department's involvement with trade fairs, trade missions, and other overseas promotion events. It is also responsible for monitoring trade and investment policies as they pertain to specific business sectors. The trade administration division is charged with implementing U.S. trade laws and regulations. It controls exports under the Export Administration Act, undertakes antidumping and countervailing duty investigations, and administers U.S. foreign trade zones. ITA also is responsible, under the trade adjustment assistance program, for providing financial assistance to firms that are injured by imports. Through its Bureau of Economic

Analysis and the Census Bureau, the Commerce Department is the agency primarily responsible for the collection of trade and balance-of-payments data.

U.S. Department of Defense (DOD): Involved in international trade as it pertains to national security, DOD participates in the formulation of U.S. trade policy as part of its mandate to maintain a viable defense industrial base, retain independence and strength in modern technology, control strategic East-West trade, ensure access to strategic materials, and further international security goals.

U.S. Department of Labor (DOL): Administers the portion of the trade adjustment assistance program that provides retraining and financial aid to workers who have lost their jobs because of imports. The Bureau of International Labor Affairs helps represent the United States in trade negotiations and in international organizations such as GATT, OECD, and the International Labor Organization.

U.S. Department of State: Through its Bureau of Economic and Business Affairs handles matters concerning trade policy, international monetary developments, assistance to U.S. business overseas, and international energy policy, as well as aviation, shipping, telecommunications, foreign investment, patents, trademarks, technology transfers, commodity issues, and other international economic interests. State is also concerned with all bilateral and multilateral agreements and with U.S. participation in international organizations such as GATT and UNCTAD, especially insofar as these relationships affect and are affected by U.S. foreign policy.

U.S. Department of the Treasury: Involved in U.S. trade policy decisions to ensure that the macroeconomic effects of such decisions are fully considered, especially potential impact on inflation or unemployment. Treasury has lead responsibility for international monetary matters and is particularly involved in such issues as the relationship of trade to international monetary policy. The office of the Assistant Secretary for International Affairs oversees U.S. participation in the multilateral development banks, facilitates monetary cooperation through the IMF and other channels, formulates policy and conducts negotiations with respect to trade financing, foreign investment in the United States and U.S. investment abroad, monitors foreign exchange markets, and conducts overall financial diplomacy. The secretary of the Treasury, as chief financial officer of the U.S. government, serves as chairman of the cabinet-level Economic Policy Group and National Advisory Council and as U.S. governor of the IMF, the World Bank, the Inter-American Development

Bank, the Asian Development Bank, and the African Development Bank.

U.S. International Trade Commission (USITC or ITC): Independent government fact-finding agency that provides information regarding tariffs and trade to the President, the Congress, and other federal agencies. The ITC advises the President on the probable economic effects resulting from tariff or other changes under proposed trade agreements. Advises the President on all articles considered for GSP eligibility and the effect duty-free entry may have on U.S. producers of such articles. The commission also makes injury determinations and recommends relief action for industries suffering harm through imports under Section 201 of the Trade Act of 1974. Allegations of injury owing to dumped or subsidized goods are investigated by the ITC under authority of the Tariff Act of 1930. The commission also monitors imports from non-market economies, maintains statistical data on imports and exports, and conducts numerous studies pursuant to requests for information from the President or the Congress or on its own instigation.

U.S. Trade Representative (USTR): The Office of the U.S. Trade Representative is responsible for setting and coordinating U.S. trade policy and administering the trade agreements program. The office is headed by the U.S. Trade Representative, a cabinet-level official with the rank of ambassador. The USTR, as the President's principal adviser on international trade policy, is charged with representing the United States in all GATT matters, all OECD and UNCTAD activities that are trade related, and all bilateral and multilateral negotiations when trade, commodities, or direct investment are the primary issues. The USTR also serves as chairman of the Trade Policy Committee, vice chairman of OPIC, a nonvoting member of Eximbank, and a member of the National Advisory Committee on International Monetary and Financial Policies. The USTR, with the advice of the TPC, is responsible for supervising all policy regarding U.S. export expansion; GATT; implementation of negotiated agreements; protection of U.S. rights under international trade and commodity agreements; unfair trade practices; and direct investment matters to the extent they are trade related. The USTR also has lead responsibility for the conduct of all trade negotiations, bilateral and multilateral, affecting tariff and non-tariff barriers; escape clause compensation; Section 301 action; and commodities trade.

Value-added tax (VAT): Indirect tax assessed on the incremental increase in a product's value at each stage of the production process up to final consumption. The net tax to each processor is levied on the amount by which he has increased the value of the item in question. In essence, the VAT is a sales tax on all transactions, not just the final purchase. The tax is generally rebated when a product is exported. Used in the EC.

Voluntary export restraint (VER): Policy that limits exports of a particular product to specific destinations to ease competitive pressures on foreign producers. VERs are generally applied to avoid the imposition of quotas or tariffs by importing countries.

Voluntary restraint agreement (VRA): See voluntary export restraint.

World Bank: See International Bank for Reconstruction and Development.

NOTES

2. Trade Crisis in America

1. U.S. Department of Commerce press release, "Advance Report on U.S. Merchandise Trade: December 1987," 12 February 1988.
2. Telephone conversation with Kevin Rogers, manager of government relations, Port of Seattle, 21 January 1988.
3. For more information on U.S. and international trends in auto and truck manufacturing, see *MVMA Motor Vehicle Facts and Figures '87* (Detroit, 1987, *Economic Indicators: The Motor Vehicle's Role in the U.S. Economy* [Washington, D.C., 1987]), or contact Motor Vehicles Manufacturers Association of the United States, Inc., Washington, D.C.
4. Personal communication, U.S. Department of Agriculture, 18 February 1988.
5. Telephone conversation with Dr. Steven Matthews, professor of agricultural law, University of Missouri, 27 January 1988.
6. Personal communication, U.S. Bureau of Labor Statistics, Washington, D.C., 20 January 1988. Based on unpublished, seasonally adjusted figures for September and October 1986.
7. William F. Finan, Perry D. Quick, and Karen M. Sandberg, *The U.S. Trade Position in High Technology: 1980–1986* (Washington, D.C.: Quick, Finan and Associates, October 1986), 2, 49.
8. Art Pine, "Policy Makers Worry That Global Recession May Be on the Horizon," *Wall Street Journal,* 10 April 1987, 1.

3. How America Is Losing the Trade War

1. U.S. Department of Commerce, *United States Trade: Performance in 1985 and Outlook* (Washington, D.C.: International Trade Administration, October 1986), 11.
2. U.S. Department of Commerce, *1986 U.S. Foreign Trade Highlights* (Washington, D.C.: Government Printing Office, March 1987), 10.
3. William F. Finan, Perry D. Quick, and Karen M. Sandberg, *The U.S. Trade Position in High Technology: 1980–1986* (Washington, D.C.: Quick, Finan and Associates, October 1986), 2, 49.
4. Central Intelligence Agency, *Handbook of Economic Statistics* (Washington, D.C.: GPO, September 1987), 22.
5. Irwin L. Kellner, "Why Our Trade Gap Persists," *Manufacturers Hanover Economic Report*, September 1986.
6. CIA, *Economic Statistics*, 22.
7. *Economic Report of the President, Transmitted to the Congress 1985* (Washington, D.C.: GPO, 1985), 6.
8. Hobart Rowen, "Further Drop in Dollar Seen," *Washington Post*, 6 August 1986.
9. CIA, *Economic Statistics*, 39.
10. Ibid., 82.
11. Congressional Research Service Review, *Trade* 8, 2 (February 1987): 1.
12. Secretary of the Treasury James Baker III, speech to U.S. Chamber of Commerce International Forum, Washington, D.C., 23 April 1986.
13. U.S. Department of Commerce, *1986 U.S. Foreign Trade Highlights* (Washington, D.C.: GPO, March 1987), 82.
14. House Committee on Banking, Finance and Urban Affairs, Subcommittee on Economic Stabilization, testimony of Stuart K. Tucker, 99th Cong., 1st sess., 25 July 1985, Committee Print 99-34.
15. Department of Commerce, *1985 Foreign Trade Highlights*, (Washington, D.C.: GPO, March 1986), 27–28.
16. Morgan Guaranty Trust Company bulletin, "World Financial Markets" (New York, September 1986).
17. U.S. Department of Commerce, *United States Trade: Performance in 1985 and Outlook* (Washington, D.C.: International Trade Administration, October 1986), 61.
18. Office of the U.S. Trade Representative, *National Trade Estimate: 1986 Report on Foreign Trade Barriers* (Washington, D.C.: GPO, November 1986).
19. Ibid.
20. Stephen Brooks, ed., *A Letter from Europe*, "Beware of Jobsdoggling"

(Washington, D.C.: Delegation of the Commission of the European Communities, 27 February 1987), 1–2.

21. This memo, distributed internally at Hitachi's U.S. subsidiary, was obtained by U.S. semiconductor industry representatives and brought to the attention of the U.S. Department of Commerce. For additional information, see *The Brief of the Semiconductor Industry Association to the USTR*, "Investigation of the Semiconductor Industry Under Section 301 of the Trade Act of 1974, as Amended," 22 October 1985, 70; E. S. Browning and Stephen Kreider Yoder, "Hitachi LTD's Pricing for Semiconductors Prompts Protest by American Officials," *Wall Street Journal*, 5 June 1985, 34; Susan Chira, "Japanese Chip Dumping Cited," *New York Times*, 5 June 1985, 34; Michael W. Miller, "Microchip Firms in U.S. Yielding a Major Market," *Wall Street Journal*, 5 June 1985, 34.

22. Ibid.

23. U.S. International Trade Commission, *Wood Shakes and Shingles: Report to the President on Investigation Number TA-201-56 Under Section 201 of the Trade Act of 1974* (Washington, D.C.: USITC, March 1986).

24. Michael R. Sesit, "Foreign Nations Offer Cheap Export Loans, Rile American Firms," *Wall Street Journal*, 19 September 1985.

25. Ibid.

26. Ibid.

27. Ibid.

28. Victor K. Kiam, president, Remington Products, Inc., testimony before the House Energy and Commerce Subcommittee on Oversight and Investigations, 26 July 1985.

29. National Academy of Sciences, *Balancing the National Interest: U.S. National Security Export Controls and Global Economic Competition* (Washington, D.C.: National Academy Press, 1987).

30. Frank E. Samuel Jr., "Ease Up on Export Controls," *Washington Post*, 17 November 1986.

31. American Electronics Association, "American Electronics . . . Making a World of Difference" (Washington, D.C., December 1987).

32. Finan, Quick, and Sandberg, *U.S. Trade Position in High Technology*, 2, 49.

33. "Global Competition the New Reality," *The Report of the President's Commission on Industrial Competitiveness*, vol. 2 (Washington, D.C.: GPO, January 1985), 197.

34. Based on a Commerce Department formula which says that for every $1 billion lost in export opportunities there are 25,000 lost jobs.

35. General Accounting Office, *Export Regulation Could Be Reduced Without Affecting National Security* (Washington, D.C.: GAO, May 1982), ii.

36. Richard C. Gross, "Pentagon: Trade Bill a 'Gorbachev-Khadafy Relief Bill,'" UPI wire story, 22 May 1986.
37. House Foreign Affairs Committee, *Report of a Staff Study Mission to the Organization for Economic Cooperation and Development,* 12–15 February 1984, 98th Cong., 2d sess.

4. The Politics of Trade

1. Michael Barone, "Democrat Protectionism: It Won't Win Elections or Help the Economy," *Washington Post,* 29 September 1985.
2. Steven V. Roberts, "Congress Chiefs Warn of Action to Curb Trade," *New York Times,* 5 September 1985.
3. Ibid.
4. Raymond A. Bauer, Ithiel de Sola Pool, and Lewis Anthony Dexter, *American Business and Public Policy: The Politics of Foreign Trade* (Chicago: Aldine-Atherton, 1972), 79.
5. I. M. Destler, *American Trade Politics: System Under Stress* (Washington, D.C.: Institute for International Economics, 1986), 29–30.
6. Lane Kirkland, "The Free-Trade Myth Is Ruining Us," *New York Times,* 26 September 1986.
7. Owen Bieber, president, United Auto Workers, speech at Conference on Labor Rights and Trade in Washington, D.C., 6 March 1986.
8. E. E. Schattschneider, *Politics, Pressures and the Tariff* (New York: Prentice-Hall, 1935).
9. Donald Bruce Johnson, *National Party Platforms,* vol. 1 (Chicago: University of Illinois Press, 1978), 392.
10. Ibid., 408.
11. Ibid., 454.
12. Donald Bruce Johnson, *National Party Platforms,* vol. 2 (Chicago: University of Illinois Press, 1978), 859.
13. Ibid., 967.
14. *Congressional Record,* 98th Cong., 2d sess., 5 September 1984, S10742-43.
15. President Ronald Reagan, speech to National Association of Manufacturers, 29 May 1986 (Washington, D.C.: *NAM Report,* 29 August 1986), 4–5.
16. *Economic Report of the President, Transmitted to the Congress 1982* (Washington, D.C.: Government Printing Office, 1982), 8.
17. *Economic Report of the President, Transmitted to the Congress 1983* (Washington, D.C.: GPO, 1983), 7.

18. *Economic Report of the President, Transmitted to the Congress 1984* (Washington, D.C.: GPO, 1984), 5.
19. *Economic Report of the President, Transmitted to the Congress 1985* (Washington, D.C.: GPO, 1985), 6.
20. *Economic Report of the President, Transmitted to the Congress 1986* (Washington, D.C.: GPO, 1986), 9.
21. *Economic Report of the President, Transmitted to the Congress 1987* (Washington, D.C.: GPO, 1987), 6.
22. *Economic Report of the President, Transmitted to the Congress 1988* (Washington, D.C.: GPO, 1988), 9–10.
23. Lee A. Iacocca, chairman, Chrysler Corporation, speech at Democratic Issues Conference in Greenbrier, West Virginia, 2 March 1985 (*Congressional Record*, 99th Cong., 1st sess., 4 April 1985), H1935–H1939.
24. *A Democratic Program for Trade* (Washington, D.C.: House Democratic Trade Task Force, 17 October 1985).
25. Oswald Johnston, "House Democrats Unveil Plan, Similar to Reagan's, to Cut Trade Deficit," *Los Angeles Times*, 8 October 1985, 5.
26. Reagan, NAM speech.
27. Johnson, *National Party Platforms*, vol. 1, 282.
28. Stuart Auerbach, "Business Won't Fight Trade Bill," *Washington Post*, 12 June 1986.
29. Editorial, "Trade-Bill Terpsichore," *Wall Street Journal*, 14 May 1986; Editorial, "Take That, Foreigners!" *New York Times*, 19 May 1986; Editorial, "A Shin-Kicker Bill," *Washington Post*, 14 May 1986.
30. Jane Seaberry, "Trade Bill Push Appears Dead for This Year," *Washington Post*, 26 September 1986.

5. Perils of Protectionism

1. M. Paul Holsinger, "For God and the American Home: The Attempt to Unseat Senator Reed Smoot, 1903–1907," *Pacific Northwest Quarterly*, 60, 3 (July 1969): 154–160.
2. P. T. Ellsworth, *The International Economy: Its Structure and Operation* (New York: Macmillan, 1950), 495.
3. E. Pendleton Herring, *Group Representatives Before Congress* (Baltimore: Johns Hopkins Press, 1929), 2–3.
4. Ibid.
5. F. W. Taussig, *The Tariff History of the United States* (New York: Augustus M. Kelley, 1967), 492.

6. I. G. Swisher, *An Introduction to the Study of the Tariff* (Washington, D.C.: National League of Women Voters, 1931), 35.
7. "1,028 Economists Ask Hoover to Veto Pending Tariff Bill," *New York Times,* 5 May 1930, 1, 4.
8. Taussig, *Tariff History,* 517.
9. Reed Smoot, "Our Tariff and the Depression," *Current History* (1931): 174.
10. Ellsworth, *International Economy,* 501.

6. Tensions with Trading Partners

1. Doug Bereuter, "Farm Trade: A U.S. Viewpoint," *Europe* (April 1986): 12, 14.
2. Personal communication, Office of the United States Trade Representative, Washington, D.C., 28 January 1988.
3. House Committee on Foreign Affairs, Subcommittees on Europe and the Middle East and International Economic Policy and Trade, testimony of Ambassador Alan Woods, deputy U.S. Trade Representative, 99th Cong., 2d sess., 24 July 1986.
4. House Foreign Affairs Committee, Subcommittee on Europe and the Middle East, testimony of Honorable Danie Amstutz, undersecretary for International Affairs, U.S. Department of Agriculture, 99th Cong., 2d sess., 24 July 1986.
5. "Statement by the Principal Deputy Press Secretary to the President," *Weekly Compilation of Presidential Documents* (Washington, D.C., 5 January 1987): 1677–1678.
6. *The Current Market Outlook, The Boeing Commercial Aircraft Company* (Seattle: Boeing Company, February 1987), 48.
7. Jean-Louis Santini, "Airbus Case Strains Trans-Atlantic Ties: European Consortium Rejects U.S. Charges of Unfair Subsidies," *Europe* (April 1987): 15.
8. House Committee on Foreign Affairs, Subcommittees on Europe and the Middle East and International Economic Policy and Trade, testimony of J. Robert Schaetzel, 99th Cong., 2d sess., 24 July 1986.
9. *Congressional Record,* 62nd Cong., 1st sess., 1911, 2520.
10. Paul Wonnacott, "The United States and Canada: The Quest for Free Trade: An Examination of Selected Issues," *Policy Analysis in International Economics* 16 (Washington, D.C.: Institute for International Economics, March 1987), 14.
11. "Declaration by the Prime Minister of Canada and the President of the

United States of America Regarding Trade in Goods and Services," *Weekly Compilation of Presidential Documents* (Washington, D.C.: Office of the Federal Register, General Services Administration, 25 March 1985), 325–327.

12. Wonnacott, "U.S. and Canada," 2.

13. "Refined U.S. and Canadian Softwood Employment Data," Office of Industries, U.S. International Trade Commission, January 1986, 2.

14. U.S. International Trade Commission, *Wood Shakes and Shingles: Report to the President on Investigation Number TA-201-56 Under Section 201 of the Trade Act of 1974* (Washington, D.C.: USITC, March 1986).

15. Wonnacott, "U.S. and Canada," 2.

16. John F. Burns, "Trade Pact Foes Rally in Canada," *New York Times,* 6 April 1987.

17. Ibid.; Michael Adams and Donna Dasko, "Free Trade Opposition Declining, Poll Shows," *The Globe and Mail,* 6 April 1987.

18. John Crispo, "Free Trade: A Canadian Imperative," paper presented at Trade Policy Conference of the Ontario Progressive Conservative Caucus, 10 April 1987, at the Ontario Science Centre, Toronto, Ontario, Canada.

19. Wonnacott, "U.S. and Canada," 2.

20. Stuart Auerbach, "U.S.-Canada Pact to Cut Trade Rules," *Washington Post,* 5 October 1987.

21. Ibid.

22. *U.S.-Canada Free Trade Agreement* is available in photocopy from Congressional Research Service, Library of Congress. As of this writing it has not been approved by either the House or the Senate and has no document numbers.

23. Joseph Fromm, "Pacific Rim: America's New Frontier," *U.S. News and World Report,* August 1984, 45–48.

24. U.S. Department of Commerce, *1986 U.S. Foreign Trade Highlights* (Washington, D.C.: Government Printing Office, March 1987), 13, 18, 19.

25. Congressional Research Service calculations based on the World Bank Development Report, 1985.

26. John P. Hardt and Robert Sutter, "Economic Changes in the Asian Pacific Rim Policy Prospectus" (Congressional Research Service, Economics Division, No. 86-923S, August 1986), 2.

27. Alfred L. Malabre, Jr., "U.S. Economy Grows Ever More Vulnerable to Foreign Influences," *Wall Street Journal,* 27 October 1986; "The Grab That Never Was," *The Economist,* 11 April 1987, 28–29.

28. Hardt and Sutter, "Economic Changes," 4–5.

29. U.S. Dept. of Commerce, *1986 U.S. Foreign Trade Highlights,* 13.

30. Senate Committee on Labor and Human Resources, Subcommittee on Employment and Productivity, testimony of Bruce Smart, 100th Cong., 1st sess., 30 March 1987, S. Hearing 100–165, 20–23.

31. Kenichi Ohmae, "Japan's Rice-Paddy: Protectionism Begins on the Farm, and the Farmers Have the Votes," *Washington Post*, 3 May 1987.

32. "Action, Please," *The Economist*, 2 May 1987, 13–14.

33. John Burgess and Fred Hiatt, "Toyota Finds Ways to Hold Down Prices," *Washington Post*, 16 February 1988, A1.

34. William Glasgall, "An Investor the U.S. Can't Afford to Lose," *Business Week*, 4 May 1987, 31.

35. Ibid., 32.

36. Karen Pennar, "Not Just a Trade Crisis—A Leadership Crisis," *Business Week*, 4 May 1987, 33.

37. House Committee on Foreign Affairs, Report of a Staff Study Mission to Korea, Taiwan, Hong Kong, China, Thailand, Singapore, and Indonesia, 30 November–27 December 1986, 100th Cong., 1st sess., February 1987, 7, 10, 13, 20.

38. Fromm, "Pacific Rim," 45.

39. *China: Economic Performance in 1985* (Washington, D.C.: Central Intelligence Agency, 17 March 1986).

40. Dori Jones Yang and Maria Shao, "China's Push for Exports Is Turning Into a Long March," *Business Week*, 15 September 1986, 66.

41. Ibid., 68.

42. Julian Baum, "Shades of Communism: Reform in China after Mao Tse-tung," *Christian Science Monitor*, 9 January 1986, 15.

43. Stanley Rosen, "China in 1986: A Year of Consolidation," *Asian Survey* 27 (January 1987): 45.

44. Ibid.

45. Jay Palmer, "The Debt-Bomb Threat," *Time*, 10 January 1983, 42.

46. *The World Bank, World Debt Tables: External Debt of Developing Countries, 1985–86 Edition* (Washington, D.C., 1986), 250.

47. Palmer, "Debt-Bomb Threat," 42.

48. Ibid., 48.

49. Patricia Wertman and William Cooper, "The Latin American Debt Crisis and U.S. Trade" (Congressional Research Service Report for Congress, no. 87-19E, 14 January 1987).

50. Congressional Research Service Review, *Trade*, 8, 2 (February 1987).

51. Wertman and Cooper, "Latin American Debt Crisis."

52. U.S. Department of Commerce, *1985 U.S. Foreign Trade Highlights* (Washington, D.C.: GPO, March 1986), 28.

7. The Elusive Goal of Competitiveness

1. Stephen S. Cohen and John Zysman, "The Myth of a Post-Industrial Economy," *Technology Review* (February–March 1987): 55–57.

2. U.S. Department of Education, "A Nation at Risk: The Imperative for Education Reform," report to the nation and the secretary of Education by the National Commission on Excellence in Education (Washington, D.C.: Government Printing Office, April 1983), 5.

3. *Cornerstone of Competition: The Report of the Southern Governors Association Advisory Council on International Education* (Richmond: Southern Governors Association, November 1986); Cynthia Hearn Dorfman, ed., *Japanese Education Today* (Washington, D.C.: GPO, January 1987); William B. Johnston and Arnold Packer, *Workforce 2000: Work and Workers for the Twenty-First Century* (Indianapolis: Hudson Institute, June 1987).

4. "An Action Agenda for American Competitiveness" (Washington, D.C.: Business–Higher Education Council, September 1986), 21.

5. Torsten Husen, ed., *International Study of Achievement in Mathematics: A Comparison of Twelve Countries*, vol. 2 (New York: John Wiley and Sons, 1967), 287–311; Ian D. Livingstone, *Second International Mathematics Study: Perceptions of the Intended and Implemented Mathematics Curriculum* (Washington, D.C.: Office of Educational Research and Improvement, U.S. Department of Education, 1986).

6. U.S. Congress, Office of Technology Assessment, *Technology and Structural Unemployment: Reemploying Displaced Adults* (Washington, D.C.: Office of Technology Assessment, February 1986), 21.

7. Public Law 87-794, approved 11 October 1962. See also, "Special Message to the Congress on Foreign Trade Policy, 25 January 1962," in *Public Papers of the Presidents of the United States, John F. Kennedy, 1962*, 76.

8. Steven Pressman, "Trade Relief Program Target of Revival Effort," *Congressional Quarterly*, 18 January 1986, 123.

9. "Action Agenda," 15.

10. Ibid., 17.

11. Executive Office of the President, *Special Analyses: Budget of the United States Government, Fiscal Year 1988* (Washington, D.C.: GPO, 1988).

12. "Global Competition the New Reality," *The Report of the President's Commission on Industrial Competitiveness*, vol. 2 (Washington, D.C.: GPO, January 1985), 67.

13. Gene Bylinsky, "The Higher Tech Race: Who's Ahead?" *Fortune*, 13 October 1986, 31.

14. Guy de Jonguières and Anatole Kaletsky, "Beware the Simple Solution," *Financial Times,* 18 May 1987, 14.
15. Gregg Easterbrook, "Have You Driven a Ford Lately?" *Washington Monthly,* October 1986, 23–34.
16. *Budget of U.S. Government 1988,* 6c–36.
17. Fred V. Guterl, "Star Wars Is Bad for Business," *Dun's Business Month,* September 1986, 57.
18. Ibid., 58.
19. House Committee on Education and Labor, *Trade and International Economic Policy Reform Act of 1987.* H. Report 100-40 to accompany H.R. 4800, 100th Cong., 1st sess., 6 April 1987, 81.
20. Ibid, 35–38.
21. Bylinsky, "Higher Tech Race," 40.
22. *Making America Work Again: Jobs, Small Business and the International Challenge* (Washington, D.C.: National Commission on Jobs and Small Business, 1987), 35.
23. *Congressional Record,* 98th Cong., 1st sess., 1983, S591.
24. "Proposals to Establish a Department of Trade," 98th Congress, 2d session (Washington, D.C.: American Institute for Public Policy Research, 1984), 12.
25. Senate Committee on Governmental Affairs, hearings on S.121, a bill to establish as an executive department of the government of the United States a Department of Trade, and for other purposes, 17 March, 26 April, 11, 12 May, 24, 29 June, 14, 15 September 1983, 98th Cong., 1st sess., S. Hearing 98-474.
26. U.S. House of Representatives, H.R. 4432, A Proposal to Establish a Department of Trade, 98th Cong., 1st sess., introduced 16 November 1983.
27. House Committee on Foreign Affairs, Subcommittee on International Economic Policy and Trade, testimony of Charls Walker, 99th Cong., 1st sess., 8 October 1985, Committee Print L-12, 31–32.
28. Lindley H. Clark Jr., "Productivity's Cost Manufacturers Grow Much More Efficient, But Employment Lags," *Wall Street Journal,* 4 December 1986.
29. Karen Pennar, "Why Manufacturing Will Revive," *Business Week,* 12 January 1987, 66.
30. Kenneth Dreyfack, "Even American Knowhow Is Headed Abroad," *Business Week,* 3 March 1986, 61.
31. Norman Jonas, "The Hollow Corporation," *Business Week,* 3 March 1986, 57.

32. Tom Peters, speech at the Democratic Issues Conference in Greenbrier, West Virginia, 1 February 1986.

33. Norman Jones, "A Strategy for Revitalizing Industry," *Business Week*, 3 March 1986, 84.

34. Ibid., 57.

35. Editorial, "Is American Business Being Managed to Death?" *The Economist*, 13 December 1986, 71–72.

36. Ibid., 71.

37. Ibid., 72.

38. Peters, speech at Democratic Issues Conference.

39. Ibid.

40. Benjamin M. Friedman, Charles L. Schultze, Barry Bluestone, et al., "Do We Need an Industrial Policy?" *Harper's*, February 1985, 46.

41. Lester C. Thurow, "A World-Class Economy: Getting Back into the Ring," *Technology Review* 88 (August–September 1985): 27–31, 34–37.

42. Friedman, Schultze, Bluestone, et al., "Do We Need Policy?" 42.

43. Peter Behr, "Coalition Growing to Boost Level of U.S. Competitiveness," *Washington Post*, 5 October 1986, F1.

44. Ibid., F5.

8. Exporting in a Cutthroat Global Economy

1. U.S. Department of Commerce, *Competitor Nations Report*, November 1986.

2. Ibid.

3. Ibid.

4. Roger Lippman, "Stop Discouraging Exporters," *Journal of Commerce*, 10 December 1987.

5. *Employment and Payrolls in Washington State by County and Industry: Fourth Quarter, 1984* (Olympia: Washington State Department of Employment Security, January 1986), 3.

6. Unpublished report, "Foreign Agricultural Service" (Washington, D.C.: U.S. Department of Agriculture, February 1988).

7. *Conference Report: Inter-American Housing Conference* (Washington, D.C.: Columbia Institute for Political Research, 1984), 4–5.

8. Robert Busel, unpublished report, "Cost Comparison of 10 U.S. Style 80 Square Meter Homes versus Traditional Chilean Masonry Construction" (Santiago: Busel Construction, 1987).

9. Ibid.

10. *American Plywood Association Management Report* (Seattle: APA, 30 September 1985).
11. Booz-Allen and Hamilton, Inc., "Pacific Basin Telecommunications Equipment Trade Mission and Conference: Special Presentation to Congressman Don Bonker" (Bethesda, Md.: Booz-Allen and Hamilton, 28 February 1985). (Contact 301-951-2200).
12. *The 1987 India/Indonesia U.S. Congressional Trade Mission for Advanced Technologies* (Washington, D.C.: Columbia Institute for Political Research, 1987).
13. House Committee on Foreign Affairs, "Trade and Economic Policy Reform Act of 1987," H. Report 100-40, part 3, 6 April 1987, 108.
14. House Committee on Foreign Affairs, Subcommittee on International Economic Policy and Trade, testimony of Craig Nalen, president and chief executive officer, Overseas Private Investment Corporation, 99th Cong., 1st sess., 18, 20, 25 June, 17, 23 July, 19 September 1985, 77.
15. Department of Commerce, *Competitor Nations Report.*
16. Ibid.
17. Unpublished memorandum, American Plywood Association, 1986.

9. Updating the World Trading System

1. *Congressional Record,* "Debate on H.R. 4800, Omnibus Trade Act of 1986," 21 May 1986, H. 3083.
2. Paul A. Samuelson and William D. Nordhaus, *Economics,* 12th ed. (New York: McGraw-Hill, 1985), 880.
3. Ibid., 884–885.
4. Ibid., 888.
5. House Committee on Ways and Means, Subcommittee on Trade, testimony of U.S. Trade Representative Clayton Yeutter, 99th Cong., 2d sess., 25 September 1986, Committee Print 99–96.
6. Nicholas Bayne, "Making Sense of Western Economic Policies: The Role of the OECD," *The World Today* 43 (February 1987): 30.
7. Editorial, "Stop the Economic Summit Charade," *New York Times,* 6 June 1987, 26.

10. Trouble Ahead for the World Economy

1. Editorial, "The Show Can't Go On," *The Economist,* 21 November 1987, 13.

2. House Committee on Banking, Finance, and Urban Affairs, Subcommittee on Economic Stabilization, testimony of C. Fred Bergsten, director, Institute for International Economics, 99th Cong., 1st sess., 20 July 1985.
3. Lester Thurow, "America's Plunge into the Debt Abyss," *New York Times*, 3 September 1985.
4. *Economic Indicators* (March 1988), p. 35. Prepared monthly by the Joint Economic Committee of the U.S. Congress for the Council of Economic Advisers (Washington, D.C.: GPO, March 1988).
5. Blanca Riemer, "The Risks of a Free-Fall," *Business Week*, 2 February 1987, 28–29.
6. C. Fred Bergsten, *Resolving the Global Economic Crisis: After Wall Street* (Washington, D.C.: Institute for International Economics, December 1987), 3.
7. Joan Berger, "America's $250 Billion IOU Will Be Hell to Pay," *Business Week*, 27 October 1986, 70.
8. Ibid.
9. Ibid.
10. Ibid., 72.
11. Ibid.
12. Lindley H. Clark Jr. and Alfred L. Malabre Jr., "Debt Keeps Growing, With the Major Risk in the Private Sector," *Wall Street Journal*, 2 February 1987.
13. John M. Berry, "Economists Debate Growing Debt," *Washington Post*, 14 September 1986.
14. Ibid.
15. Clark and Malabre, "Debt Keeps Growing."
16. Ibid.
17. Mark Potts, "Corporate Debt Raises Controversy: Analysts Disagree About Impact on Big Business," *Washington Post*, 11 January 1987.
18. Clark and Malabre, "Debt Keeps Growing."
19. John Kenneth Galbraith, "The 1929 Parallel," *Atlantic Monthly*, January 1987, 65.
20. Gerald O. Barney, ed., *Global 2000 Report to the President: Entering the Twenty-first Century* (Washington, D.C.: GPO, 1980), 13–21.
21. *World Economic Outlook: A Survey by the Staff of the International Monetary Fund* (Washington, D.C.: The Fund, 1986).
22. Overseas Development Council, *Reforming U.S. Agricultural Trade Policy*, June 1987.
23. Ward Sinclair, "The World Doesn't Need Our Farmers," *Washington Post*, 29 December 1985.
24. Ibid.

25. Bureau of North American International Affairs (BNA), *Trade Reporter* 3 (1 January 1986): 7–9.
26. Ibid.
27. Editorial, *Christian Science Monitor,* 9 July 1987.
28. Anandarup Ray, *World Development Report 1986* (New York: Oxford University Press, 1986).
29. Robert J. Samuelson, "We Must Find a Way to End the Global Grain Wars," *American Banker,* 24 September 1986, 4.
30. BNA, *Trade Reporter,* 862.
31. P. T. Ellsworth, *The International Economy: Its Structure and Operation* (New York: Macmillan, 1950), 495.
32. Bruce Stokes, "Coping with Glut," *National Journal,* 1 November 1986, 2608.
33. Jean Jacques Servan-Schreiber, *The American Challenge* (New York: Atheneum, 1969).
34. Peter F. Drucker, "The Changed World Economy," *Foreign Affairs* 64 (Spring 1986): 768–791.
35. Congressional delegation trip to the Far East, visit to an aircraft factory in Bandung, Indonesia, and conversations with its president and director, Mr. Soeharto, 14 January 1987.
36. "Asia's New Bidders for Western Plants," *Business Week,* 17 March 1980.
37. Stuart Auerbach, "South Korea: New Trade Threat," *Washington Post,* 9 February 1986.
38. Joseph A. Boyd, former chairman, Harris Corporation, speech at Competing in a Global Economy Conference hosted by Congressman Bill Nelson, Melbourne, Florida, 11 December 1986.
39. Norman Jonas, "The Hollow Corporation," *Business Week,* 3 March 1986, 57.
40. Kenneth Dreyfack, "Even American Knowhow Is Headed Abroad," *Business Week,* 3 March 1986, 60–61.
41. Public Law 99-591, approved 30 October 1986. See also House Committee on Energy and Commerce, Subcommittee on Commerce, Transportation and Tourism, hearings on Expo-Maquita, 99th Cong., 2d sess., 10 December 1986.
42. Brian O'Reilly, "Business Makes a Run for the Border," *Fortune,* 18 August 1986, 70–76; Jeff Stansbury, "Mexico's Golden Mills," *Solidarity,* 1 September 1986, 6–8.
43. Jonas, "Hollow Corporation," 84.
44. Personal communication, Pat Choate, director of policy analysis, TRW Inc., 30 September 1987.

45. Martin Tolchin, "Influx of Foreign Capital Mutes Debate on Trade," *New York Times,* 8 February 1987, 13.

46. Martin and Susan Tolchin, *Buying into America: How Foreign Money Is Changing the Face of Our Nation* (New York: Times Books, 1988).

47. M. Tolchin, "Influx of Foreign Capital," 13.

48. Peter F. Drucker, *The Frontiers of Management: Where Tomorrow's Decisions Are Being Shaped Today* (New York: Harper and Row, 1986), 32–33.

49. Barry Bluestone and Bennett Harrison, *The Great American Job Machine: The Proliferation of Low Wage Employment in the U.S. Economy* (Washington, D.C.: Joint Economic Committee of the U.S. Congress, December 1986), 5.

50. Ibid., 6.

51. Ibid., 3.

52. "American Dream: Redefined for the 1980s," *The Economist,* 14 February 1987, 27–28.

53. Aaron Bernstein, "Warning: The Standard of Living Is Slipping," *Business Week,* 20 April 1987.

54. "American Dream," 27–28.

55. Robert Kuttner, "The U.S. Can't Compete Without a Top-Notch Work Force," *Business Week,* 16 February 1987, 20.

56. Hobart Rowen, "Japan's Clout Tied to Capital," *Washington Post,* 2 November 1986, 1.

57. The Honorable Charles A. Vanik, speech before U.S. Business and Industrial Council, Washington, D.C., 27 January 1987.

58. Central Intelligence Agency, *Handbook of Economic Statistics* (Washington, D.C.: Government Printing Office, September 1987).

59. Paul McCracken, "Toward World Economic Disintegration," *Wall Street Journal,* 9 February 1987.

SUGGESTED READINGS

2. Trade Crisis in America

Editorial. "Protectionist Politics Played to the Hilt." *Seattle Times,* 23 May 1986.

Editorial. "A Shin-Kicker Bill." *Washington Post,* 14 May 1986.

Lawrence, Richard. "Zeroing in on the 'Kamikaze' Bill." *Journal of Commerce,* 12 June 1986.

Roberts, Steven V. "House Democrats Offer a Bill to Spur Exports." *New York Times,* 14 May 1986.

Ryskind, Allan H., ed. "Zschau Pushes Red Trade Bill." *Human Events* (24 May 1986): 440.

Yeutter, Clayton. "It's So Bad, the Sponsors Must Want It Vetoed." *Washington Post,* 19 May 1986.

3. How America Is Losing the Trade War

Auerbach, Stuart. "Yeutter: Dollar May Have to Fall More." *Washington Post,* 4 September 1986.

"The Baker Initiative: The Perspective of the Banks." *World Financial Markets* (February 1986): 1–9.

Barcelo, John J., III. "Subsidies and Countervailing Duties — Analysis and a Proposal." *Law and Policy in International Business* 9 (1977): 779–853.

Berry, John M. "Volcker Advises Halt to Slide of Dollar." *Washington Post,* 8 April 1987.

Brown, Marshall L. "Soviet Reaction to the U.S. Pipeline Embargo: The Impact on Future Soviet Economic Relations with the West." *Maryland Journal of International Law and Trade* 8 (Spring–Summer 1984): 144–155.

Cohen, Richard A. "The Trade Agreements Act of 1979: Executive Agreements, Subsidies, and Countervailing Duties." *Texas International Law Journal* 15 (1980): 96–115.

Cooper, Richard N. "U.S. Policies and Practices on Subsidies in International Trade." In *International Trade and Industrial Policies,* ed. Steven J. Warnecke. New York: Holmes & Meier, 1980.

Dullforce, William. "Alternative Proposed to Baker Debt Plan [the Bradley Plan]." *Financial Times,* 30 June 1986, 18.

Grant, Lloyd. "ITC Injury Determination in Countervailing Duty Investigations." *Law & Policy in International Business* 8 (1983): 987–1008.

Guenther, Gary L. "Performance and International Competitiveness of the U.S. Semiconductor Industry, 1975–1988." Congressional Research Service of the Library of Congress Report No. 85-1064E (6 December 1985).

Guttentag, Jack M., and Richard J. Herring. *The Current Crisis in International Lending.* Washington, D.C.: Brookings Institution, 1985.

Johnson, Christopher. "Fleshing Out the Baker Plan for Third World Debt." *Banker* 135 (December 1985).

Kellner, Irwin L. "Why Our Trade Gap Persists." *Manufacturers Hanover Economic Report,* September 1986.

Kilborn, Peter T. "Officials Say U.S. Seeks Bigger Drop for Weak Dollar." *New York Times,* 14 January 1987.

Klein, P. A. "Reagan's Economic Policies: An Institutionalist Assessment." *Journal of Economic Issues* 17 (June 1983): 463–474.

Knoll, Michael S. "United States Antidumping Law: The Case for Reconsideration." *Texas International Law Journal* 22 (Spring 1987): 265–290.

Kuttner, Robert. "Jim Baker Remakes the World." *New Republic,* 21 April 1986, 14–18.

Loomis, Carol J. "Why Baker's Debt Plan Won't Work." *Fortune,* 23 December 1985, 98–102.

McLoughlin, Glenn J., and Nancy R. Miller. "Semiconductor Manufacturing Technology Proposal: SEMATECH." Congressional Research Service of the Library of Congress Issue Brief (regularly updated).

Marcuss, Stanley J. "Understanding Direct and Indirect Subsidies: Are the Problems Negotiable or Incurable?" In *Interface Three,* ed. Don Wallace Jr., Frank J. Loftus, and Van Z. Krikorian. Washington, D.C.: International Law Institute, 1984.

Mulford, David. "Banks, the Baker Plan and Strengthening the Global Economy." *World of Banking* 5 (May–June 1986): 6–9.

"The New Economic Realities." *Harvard Magazine* 89 (March–April 1987): 39–46.

Palmer, Jay. "The Debt Bomb Threat." *Time,* 10 January 1983.

Pennar, Karen. "Don't Expect the Trade Gap to Narrow Very Soon." *Business Week,* 15 September 1986, 159.

Ravenal, Earl C. "Does Poland Matter?" *Inquiry* 5 (August 1982): 24–28.

Reich, Robert B., and Felix G. Rohatyn. "Coping with Reagan's Economic Legacy." *World Policy Journal* 2 (Fall 1985): 1–32.

Riemer, Blanca, and William Glasgall. "Third World Debt: Bill Bradley May Have a Better Idea." *Business Week,* 28 July 1986, 26.

Rowen, Hobart. "Bradley Challenges Baker on Third World Debt." *Washington Post,* 6 July 1986.

———. "Conable Favors Baker Initiative over Bradley Plan." *Washington Post,* 22 July 1986.

———. "The Dollar and the Trade Deficit." *Washington Post,* 29 October 1985.

———. "Further Drop in Dollar Seen." *Washington Post,* 6 August 1986.

Russell, George. "A Game of Chicken." *Time,* 3 January 1987, 44–46.

U.S. Congress. Conference Committees. *Conference on Foreign Corrupt Practices Act.* 95th Cong., 1st sess. 1977. H. Rep. 95-831.

U.S. Congress. House. Committee on Banking, Finance and Urban Affairs. Subcommittee on International Finance, Trade and Monetary Policy. *A Bill to Eliminate Unfair and Predacious Export Financing Practices,* H.R. 3667. 99th Cong., 1st sess., 1985.

U.S. Congress. House. Committee on Energy and Commerce. Subcommittee on Oversight and Investigations. Subcommittee Staff Report on Unfair Foreign Trade Practices: *Selected Problems in Five Far East Countries.* Washington, D.C.: GPO, 1986. Committee Print 99-CC.

U.S. Congress. House. Committee on Foreign Affairs. *Hearings on the Global Debt Crisis: An Overview.* 18 June and 30 July 1986. 99th Cong., 2d sess., 1986.

U.S. Congress. House. Committee on Foreign Affairs. *Report to Accompany H.R. 3667.* 99th Cong., 2d sess., 1986. H. Rep. 99-457, part 2.

U.S. Congress. House. Committee on Foreign Affairs. Subcommittee on International Economic Policy and Trade. *Hearing on Economic Sanctions: Impact and Alternatives.* 99th Cong., 2d sess., 1986.

U.S. Congress. House. Committee on Foreign Affairs. Subcommittee on International Economic Policy and Trade. *Hearings and Markup on the*

Omnibus Trade Legislation. Vol. I, *Legislative Proposals on Mixed Credits,* H.R. 3296. 99th Cong., 1st sess., 1985.

U.S. Congress. House. Committee on Government Operations. Subcommittee on Commerce, Consumer, and Monetary Affairs. *Hearings on Federal Enforcement of Textile and Apparel Import Quotas.* 99th Cong., 1st sess. 1985, parts 1 and 2.

U.S. Congress. House. Committee on Interstate and Foreign Commerce. Subcommittee on Oversight and Investigations. *Hearings on Foreign Corrupt Practices Act.* 96th Cong., 1st sess., 1979.

U.S. Congress. House. Committee on Ways and Means. Subcommittee on Trade. *Testimony by C. Fred Bergsten.* 99th Cong., 2d sess., 1986.

U.S. Congress. House. Committee on Ways and Means. Subcommittee on Trade. *Requirements of the Manufacturing Clause of the Copyright Law.* 99th Cong., 2d sess., 1986. Committee Print 99-85.

U.S. Congress. House. *Export-Import Bank Act Amendments.* 99th Cong., 1st sess., 1985. Public Law 99-472.

U.S. Congress. Joint Economic Committee. *Hearings on the Impact of the Debt Crisis on the U.S. Economy.* 99th Cong., 1st sess., 1985. S. Hearing 99-501.

U.S. Congress. Joint Economic Committee. *Hearings on Managing the Debt Problem.* 99th Cong., 2d sess., 1986. S. Hearing 99-647.

U.S. Congress. Joint Economic Committee. *Hearings on Soviet Pipeline Sanctions: The European Perspective.* 97th Cong., 2d sess., 1982.

U.S. Congress. Senate. Committee on Banking, Housing and Urban Affairs. Subcommittee on International Finance and Monetary Policy. *Hearings on Fair Export Financing Act of 1985.* 99th Cong., 1st sess., 1986.

U.S. Congress. Senate. Committee on Banking, Housing and Urban Affairs. Subcommittee on International Finance. *U.S. Embargo of Food and Technology to the Soviet Union.* 96th Cong., 2d sess., 1980.

U.S. Congress. Senate. Committee on Finance. *Amending the Requirements of the Manufacturing Clause of the Copyright Law: Hearings on S. 1822.* 99th Cong., 2d sess., 1986. S. Hearing 99-767.

U.S. Congress. Senate. Committee on the Judiciary. Subcommittee on Technology and the Law. *Issues Confronting the Semiconductor Industry: Hearings on S. 442.* 100th Cong., 1st sess., 1987. S. Hearing 100-210.

U.S. Department of Agriculture. Economic Research Service. *Mathematical Modeling of World Grain Trade Restrictions,* 1987. Technical Bulletin No. 1735.

U.S. President, 1977–1981 (Carter). *Restrictions on Agricultural Commodity Exports of the U.S.S.R.;* communication for the President of the United

States transmitting a report on Soviet invasion of Afghanistan, pursuant to section 6(e) and 7(g)(3) of the Export Administration Act of 1979. 96th Cong., 2d sess., 1980. H. Doc. 96-252.

Wolff von Ameronsen, Otto. "Economic Sanctions as a Foreign Policy Tool?" *International Security* 5 (Fall 1980): 159–167.

4. The Politics of Trade

Bradley, Bill. *The Fair Tax.* New York: Pocket Books, 1984.

Congressional Record. Text of and debate on the Gephardt amendment to H.R. 3, the Trade and International Economic Policy Reform Act of 1987. 100th Cong., 1st sess., 29 April 1987.

Congressional Record. Debate on H.R. 4800, the Trade and International Economic Policy Reform Act of 1986. 99th Cong., 2d sess., 15–22 May 1986.

Destler, I. M. *American Trade Politics: System Under Stress.* Washington, D.C.: Institute for International Economics, 1986.

"Domestic Content Legislation: Is It in the Consumer Interest?" *At Home With Consumers* 4 (April 1983): 1–8.

Fraser, Douglas A. "Domestic Content of U.S. Automobile Imports: A UAW Proposal." *Columbia Journal of World Business* 16 (Winter 1981): 57–61.

Hufbauer, Gary Clyde, Diane T. Berliner, and Kimberly Ann Elliott. *Trade Protection in the United States: 31 Case Studies.* Washington, D.C.: Institute for International Economics, 1986.

Koplan, Stephen, and William Brock. *The MacNeil-Lehrer Report.* AFL-CIO representative Stephen Koplan and United States Trade Representative William Brock debate the effectiveness of a domestic content requirement for cars sold in the United States. New York: WNET/Thirteen, 1982.

Sek, Lenore. "The 'Gephardt Amendment' and the Senate 'Alternative': Proposals to Address Unfair Foreign Trade Practices Abroad." Congressional Research Service of the Library of Congress Issue Brief 87-719E, 19 August 1987.

U.S. Congressional Budget Office. *Domestic Content Legislation and the U.S. Automobile Industry: Analyses of H.R. 5133, the Fair Practices in Automotive Products Act.* Report prepared at the direction of the Subcommittee on Trade by the Congressional Budget Office, the Congressional Research Service of the Library of Congress, and the United States Trade Representative. Washington, D.C.: GPO. 97th Cong., 2d sess., 1982. Committee Print 97-33.

U.S. Congress. Democratic Study Group. *Domestic Content.* Washington, D.C.: Democratic Study Group Fact Sheet No. 98-19. 98th Cong., 1st sess., 1983.

"U.S. Foreign Trade Policy: Pro & Con." *Congressional Digest* 66 (June–July 1987): 161–192.

U.S. International Trade Commission. *The Effectiveness of Escape Clause Relief in Promoting Adjustment to Import Competition.* USITC publication 1229. Washington, D.C.: U.S. International Trade Commission, March 1982.

5. Perils of Protectionism

Berglund, Abraham. "The Tariff Act of 1930." *American Economic Review* (1930): 467–479.

Bidwell, Percy W. "The Smoot Hawley Tariff and Its Influence on America's Export Trade." *The Annalist,* 27 June 1930, 1355–1357.

Eichensreen, Barry. *The Political Economy of the Smoot-Hawley Tariff.* Cambridge, Mass.: National Bureau of Economic Research, 1986.

Ellsworth, P. T. *The International Economy: Its Structure and Operation.* New York: Macmillan, 1950.

Holsinger, M. Paul. "For God and the American Home: The Attempt to Unseat Senator Reed Smoot, 1903–1907." *Pacific Northwest Quarterly* 60 (July 1969): 154–160.

"Is Protectionism the Only Way Out?" *Institutional Investor* 19 (November 1985).

Jones, Joseph M. *Tariff Retaliation: Repercussion of the Hawley-Smoot Bill.* Philadelphia: University of Philadelphia, 1934.

Junker, Joel R. "U.S. Regulation of Imports: An Overview of Principal Statutes and Procedures." *Korean Journal of Comparative Law* 12 (July 1984): 109–150.

Marturano, Janice. "U.S. Legislative Import Relief Options: A Comparison of Procedures." *New York University Journal of International Law and Politics* 13 (Spring 1981): 1049–1073.

Morkre, Morris E., and David G. Tarr. *The Effects of Restrictions on United States Imports: Five Case Studies and Theory.* Washington, D.C.: GPO, 1980.

Schattschneider, E. E. *Politics, Pressures and the Tariff.* New York: Prentice-Hall, 1935.

Taussig, F. W. *The Tariff History of the United States.* New York: Augustus M. Kelley, 1967.

Watson, James E. "An Analysis of the New Tariff Bill." *Protectionist* 42 (1930): 121–126.

6. Tensions with Trading Partners

Chan, Steve. "The Mouse That Roared: Taiwan's Management of Trade Relations With the United States." *Comparative Political Studies* 20 (October 1987): 251–292.

Coalition for Fair Lumber Imports. *Lumber Fact Book: The Facts, Issues, and Policies Behind the Canada/U.S. Lumber Trade Problems.* Washington, D.C.: Coalition for Fair Lumber Imports, June 1986.

Curtis, Kenneth, and John Carroll. *Canadian-American Relations: The Promise and the Challenge.* Lexington, Mass.: Lexington Books, 1983.

Davey, Keith. *Canada Not for Sale: The Case Against Free Trade.* Toronto: General Paperbacks, 1987.

Donne, Michael. "The Challenger." *Europe* 235 (January–February 1983): 22–24.

Doran, Charles. *Forgotten Partnership: Canadian-U.S. Relations Today.* Baltimore: Johns Hopkins University Press, 1983.

Doran, Charles, and John Sigler, eds. *Canada and the United States: Enduring Friendship, Persistent Stress.* Englewood Cliffs, N.J.: Prentice-Hall, 1985.

Ferreira, Antonio da Silva. "The Economics of Enlargement: Trade Effects on the Applicant Countries." *Journal of Common Market Studies* 17 (December 1978): 120–142.

Holmes, John. *Life with Uncle: The Canadian-American Relationship.* Toronto: University of Toronto Press, 1981.

Kuzela, Lad. "More Entries in the Aerospace Race?" *Industry Week* 205 (14 April 1980).

LaPierre, Laurier. *If You Love This Country: Facts and Feelings on Free Trade.* Toronto: McClelland and Stewart, 1987.

McMullen, Neil. *The Newly Industrialized Countries: Adjusting to Success.* Washington, D.C.: National Planning Association, 1982.

McNaught, Kenneth. *The Pelican History of Canada.* New York: Penguin Books, 1982.

Richman, Louis S. "Airbus's Shaky Success." *Fortune,* 23 December 1985.

Russell, George. "Trade Face-Off: A Dangerous U.S.-Japan Confrontation." *Time,* 12 April 1987, 28–32, 35–36.

Santini, Jean-Louis. "Airbus Case Strains Trans-Atlantic Ties: European

Consortium Rejects U.S. Charges of Unfair Subsidies." *Europe* (April 1987): 14–15.

Scricciolo, Luigino. "Spain and Portugal on the Threshold of the EEC." *Spettatore Internazionale* 12 (July–September 1977): 215–238.

"Spain and Portugal in the EEC: The Mechanics of Accession." London: Agra Europe Special Report No. 26, 1985.

Tomlin, Brian, and Maureen Molot, eds. *Canada Among Nations.* Toronto: James Corimer and Company, 1987.

U.S. Congress. House. Committee on Foreign Affairs. *Report of the Twenty-eighth Meeting of the Canada–United States Interparliamentary Group.* 100th Cong., 1st sess., 1987.

U.S. Congress. House. Committee on Foreign Affairs. *The Expanding Role of the European Community in International Security Issues.* Report of the twenty-eighth meeting of members of Congress and of the European Parliament. 100th Cong., 1st sess., 1987.

U.S. Congress. House. Committee on Foreign Affairs. *U.S. Trade Relations with Asia.* Report of a staff study mission to Korea, Taiwan, Hong Kong, China, Thailand, Singapore, and Indonesia. 100th Cong., 1st sess., 1987.

U.S. Congress. House. Committee on Foreign Affairs. Subcommittees on Asian and Pacific Affairs and International Economic Policy and Trade. *Hearings on United States–Japan Trade Relations.* 99th Cong., 1st sess., 1985.

U.S. Congress. House. Committee on Foreign Affairs. Subcommittees on Asian and Pacific Affairs and International Economic Policy and Trade. *Hearing on Asian Trade Problems: Their Effects and Proposed Solutions.* 99th Cong., 1st sess., 1985.

U.S. Congress. House. Committee on Foreign Affairs. Subcommittees on International Economic Policy and Trade and Western Hemisphere Affairs. *Hearing on U.S.-Canada Trade Relations.* 99th Cong., 2d sess., 1986.

U.S. Congress. House. Committee on Ways and Means. *Written Comments on United States–Canada Free Trade Negotiations.* 99th Cong., 2d sess., 1986. Committee Print 99-16.

U.S. Congress. House. Committee on Ways and Means. Subcommittee on Trade. *Hearings on U.S. Trade with Pacific Rim Countries.* 99th Cong., 1st sess., 1985. Committee Print 99-25.

U.S. International Trade Commission. *Wood Shakes and Shingles: Report to the President on Investigation No. TA-201-56 Under Section 201 of the Trade Act of 1974.* Washington, D.C.: U.S. International Trade Commission, March 1986. USITC Publication 1826.

296 SUGGESTED READINGS

U.S. International Trade Commission. *Conditions Relating to the Importation of Softwood Lumber into the United States: Report to the President on Investigation No. 332-210 Under Section 332 of the Trade Act of 1930.* Washington, D.C.: U.S. International Trade Commission, October 1985.

U.S. Congress. Joint Economic Committee. Subcommittee on Trade, Productivity, and Economic Growth. *Cracking the Japanese Market.* 99th Cong., 2d sess., 1987. S. Hearing 99-1018.

Wonnacott, Paul. "The United States and Canada: The Quest for Free Trade: An Examination of Selected Issues" *Policy Analysis in International Economics,* 16. Washington, D.C.: Institute for International Economics, March 1987.

7. The Elusive Goal of Competitiveness

Business–Higher Education Forum. *An Action Agenda for American Competitiveness.* Washington, D.C.: Business–Higher Education Forum, 1986.

"Competitiveness: 23 Leaders Speak Out." *Harvard Business Review* 4 (July–August 1987): 106–123.

Finan, William F., Perry D. Quick, and Karen M. Sandberg. *The U.S. Trade Position in High Technology: 1980–1986.* Washington, D.C.: Quick, Finan & Associates, October 1986.

Friedman, Benjamin M., Charles L. Schultze, Barry Bluestone, Robert Z. Lawrence, and Bennett Harrison. "Do We Need an Industrial Policy?" *Harper's,* February 1985, 35–48.

Reich, Robert B. "Enterprise and Double Cross." *The Washington Monthly,* January 1987, 13–19.

Thurow, Lester C. "A World-Class Economy: Getting Back into the Ring." *Technology Review* 88 (August–September 1985): 27–31, 34–37.

Young, John A. *Global Competition: The New Reality.* Vols. 1 and 2. *The Report of the President's Commission on Industrial Competitiveness.* Washington, D.C.: GPO, 1985.

8. Exporting in a Cutthroat Economy

Bethel, James S., ed., *World Trade in Forest Products.* Seattle: University of Washington Press, 1983.

Cole, Jack E., and Richard J. O'Rorke, Jr. *Telecommunications Policies in Ten Countries: Prospects for Future Competitive Access.* Washington, D.C.: GPO, March 1985.

History of Wood Technology. Pullman: Washington State University, Department of Materials Science and Engineering, College of Engineering, April 1985.

India: The Subcontinent and American Wood: Report of an NFPA Trade Mission, 9–21 June 1986. Washington, D.C.: National Forest Products Association, 1986.

Price Waterhouse. *The Export Trading Company Guidebook.* Washington, D.C.: GPO, March 1984.

A Report on Pacific Basin Forestry Products and Services Exports. Washington, D.C.: Price Waterhouse, 1984.

U.S. Department of Commerce. *Issues in Domestic Telecommunications: Directions for National Policy.* Washington, D.C.: National Telecommunications and Information Administration, July 1985.

Viosky, R. P. *Pacific Rim Market Profile: Forest Products Trade by Country 6.* Seattle: College of Forest Resources, 1985.

The Wood Housing Market in Selected Pacific Basin Countries. Washington, D.C.: Columbia Institute for Political Research, 1986.

9. Updating the World Trading System

Acheson, A. L. K., ed. *Bretton Woods Revisited: Evaluations of the International Monetary Fund and the International Bank for Reconstruction and Development.* Papers delivered at a conference at Queen's University, Kingston, Canada. Toronto: University of Toronto Press, 1972.

Cooper, Mary H. "Bretton Woods Forty Years Later." *Congressional Quarterly Editorial Research Reports* 1, No. 23 (1984): 451–466.

Dormael, Armand van. *Bretton Woods: Birth of a Monetary System.* New York: Holmes & Meier, 1978.

Morrison, Ann V. "GATT's Seven Rounds of Trade Talks Span More Than Thirty Years." *Business America* (7 July 1986): 8–10.

U.S. Congress. House. Committee on Ways and Means. Subcommittee on Trade. *Hearing on the Results of the GATT Ministerial Meeting Held in Punta del Este, Uruguay.* 99th Cong., 2d sess., 1986. Committee Print 99-96.

U.S. Congress. Senate. Committee on Foreign Relations. *The Bretton Woods Agreements Act: Hearings on S. 2271.* 96th Cong., 2d sess., 1980.

U.S. Department of State. "An Agenda for the New GATT Round." *Department of State Bulletin* 86 (November 1986): 43–39.

10. Trouble Ahead for the World Economy

Batra, Ravi. *The Great Depression of 1990.* New York: Simon and Schuster, 1987.

Choate, Pat, and J. K. Linger. *The High-Flex Society.* New York: Alfred A. Knopf, 1986.

Gilmore, Richard. *A Poor Harvest: The Clash of Policies and Interests in the Grain Trade.* New York: Longmans, 1982.

INDEX

on Canadian timber pricing system,
33
complaints directed against USTR
and, 149–51
and export trading companies, 184
International Trade Administration
at, 151
and Japanese dumping, 32
on jobs displaced by imports, 53
and outsourcing, 238
and stock market crash, 15
Common Agricultural Policy, 92
Common Market, 202, 226
See also European Community (EC)
Communist Party, in Japan, 109
Competitiveness, 245–46
complexity of issue of, 167–68
definition of, 154
and education, 132–34
effect of hollow corporations on,
158–63, 238
of export financing, 185–87
and free-market theory, 163
and industrial policy, 163–67
and need for trade reorganization,
146–53
notion of, 129–32
and research and development,
138–46
road to, 76
and taxation, 153–58
and training, 134–38
Young Commission report on,
168
Constitution, U.S., 146, 147
Consultative Group on International
Agricultural Research, 222
Continental Bank (Illinois), 190
Coolidge, Calvin, 50, 70
Coordinating Committee for Multilateral Export Controls, 250
Corestale's Financial Corporation, 214
Corporations
debt of, 215–16
hollow, effect on competitiveness of,
158–63, 238
takeovers of, 160–61
Crane amendment, 188, 189
Cultural Revolution (China), 118
Customs Service, 87

Debt, U.S.
corporate, 215–16
foreign, 210–13
private, 214–15
public, 213–14
reduction of, 216–19
DeClercq, Willy, 94
Defense, Department of (DOD), 45, 164
Defense Science Board, 44
Democratic National Committee, 3
Democratic Party, 48–50
and competitiveness, 76, 129
and Job Training Partnership Act,
138
move toward protectionism of, 52,
55–56, 57
platform of, 52, 83
and road from free trade, 50–57,
76
trade as issue for, 67
and trade reorganization, 152–53
Democratic Program for Trade, A,
67
Deng Xiaoping, 118
Denman, Sir Roy, 30–31
Destler, I. M., 52
Dole, Robert, 49, 86
Dollar
comparative value of yen and,
109–10
and floating exchange rate system,
193
high value of, 194
trade deficit and overvalued U.S.,
18–23, 64
Domestic International Sales Corporation, 157
Dominican Republic, 226
housing for, 175
Drucker, Peter F., 234
Frontiers of Management, 241
Dual-use technology, 119
Dukakis, Michael, 56
Dumping, import, 32–33, 110, 112
Dun's Business Month, 143, 144
du Pont (E. I.) de Nemours, 70

Eastman Kodak, 238
Economic Development Administration,
167